The Intelligent Woman's Guide to Man-Hunting

Books and Monographs by Albert Ellis

AN INTRODUCTION TO THE PRINCIPLES OF SCIENTIFIC PSYCHO-ANALYSIS (*Journal Press*, 1950)

THE FOLKLORE OF SEX (*Charles Boni*, 1951; rev. ed., *Grove Press*, 1961)

SEX, SOCIETY AND THE INDIVIDUAL (with A. P. Pillay) (*International Journal of Sexology Press*, 1953)

SEX LIFE OF THE AMERICAN WOMAN AND THE KINSEY REPORT (*Greenberg*, 1954)

THE AMERICAN SEXUAL TRAGEDY (*Twayne*, 1954; rev. ed., *Lyle Stuart*, 1962; *Grove Press*, 1963)

NEW APPROACHES TO PSYCHOTHERAPY TECHNIQUES (*Journal of Clinical Psychology Press*, 1955)

THE PSYCHOLOGY OF SEX OFFENDERS (with Ralph Brancale) (*Charles C Thomas*, 1956)

HOW TO LIVE WITH A NEUROTIC (*Crown*, 1957)

SEX WITHOUT GUILT (*Lyle Stuart*, 1958; *Hillman*, 1959)

WHAT IS PSYCHOTHERAPY? (*American Academy of Psychotherapists*, 1959)

THE PLACE OF VALUES IN THE PRACTICE OF PSYCHOTHERAPY (*American Academy of Psychotherapists*, 1959)

THE ART AND SCIENCE OF LOVE (*Lyle Stuart*, 1960)

THE ENCYCLOPEDIA OF SEXUAL BEHAVIOR (with Albert Abarbanel) (*Hawthorn*, 1961)

CREATIVE MARRIAGE (with Robert A. Harper) (*Lyle Stuart*, 1961)

A GUIDE TO RATIONAL LIVING (with Robert A. Harper) (*Prentice-Hall*, 1961)

REASON AND EMOTION IN PSYCHOTHERAPY (*Lyle Stuart*, 1962)

THE INTELLIGENT WOMAN'S GUIDE TO MAN-HUNTING (*Lyle Stuart*, 1963)

IF THIS BE SEXUAL HERESY . . . (*Lyle Stuart*, 1963)

SEX AND THE SINGLE MAN (*Lyle Stuart*, 1963)

THE CASE FOR SEXUAL LIBERTY (*Seymour Press*, 1964)

NYMHPHOMANIA: A STUDY OF THE OVER-SEXED WOMAN (with Edward Sagarin) (*Julian Messner*, 1964)

THE THEORY AND PRACTICE OF RATIONAL-EMOTIVE PSYCHO-THERAPY (*Lyle Stuart*, 1964)

The Intelligent Woman's Guide to MAN-HUNTING

by

ALBERT ELLIS, Ph.D.

Lyle Stuart • New York

Fourth Printing

The Intelligent Woman's Guide to Man-Hunting

© 1963 by The Institute for Rational Living, Inc.

Library of Congress Catalog Card Number: 63-17347

Queries regarding rights and permissions
    should be addressed to
    Lyle Stuart,
    239 Park Avenue South,
    New York 3, N.Y.

Type set by The Polyglot Press, New York

Published by Lyle Stuart, Inc.

Manufactured in the United State of America

To Carol —
a most intelligent huntress

Contents

Contents

Introduction

Let's face it: practically all books and articles on HOW TO GET YOUR MAN AND LIVE HAPPILY WITH HIM FOREVER AFTER are full of hogwash. Why? Because almost all of them are written by women.

What would a woman in our society know about successful mantrapping? Even a clever woman? Almost nothing. Obviously, being a woman, she is not a man. Nor, in this respect, can we legitimately pull the old chestnut about *vive la différence*. A man, just because he is a man, knows perfectly well what it takes to make him like a woman. A woman, just because she is a woman, does not know what he wants. She may, of course, find out. But not, you may bet your engagement ring, from another woman.

Why? For several reasons.

First of all, most women in our society really don't *want* to know what pleases a man. They want to know, rather, where to find a male who is "naturally" pleased by what they prefer to give him. Which is quite a different thing!

Take, for example, a woman's making frank overtures toward a man. Practically all males love women to make frank, open, undisguised friendly overtures toward them: to pick them up on street corners, give them their telephone numbers, ask them for a date,

9

call them when they are lonely, and start taking off their own and the male's clothes when they are alone together. This is what the Walter Mittys of the world daydream about constantly, and what the less inhibited men imagine as the greatest—and rarest—of delights.

But will women deign to make such unvarnished overtures to the males they prefer? No, a thousand and one times no. Because they like to believe—as a result of their *own* fear of failure and rejection—that the men don't want them to take the initiative, but would rather show what red-blooded, assertive, rootin-tootin males they are.

The hell they would! The very last thing the poor male things want to risk is failure or rejection. And the very best way for a woman to make sure that they are gratefully, undyingly hers is for her to insure that her male friends can't possibly fail—because she herself sticks her neck out and takes all the risks that they, theoretically, should take. But will women ever, to themselves or their sisters, admit this? Naturally not. For if they did, they'd have to get off their sleek or plump derrières and do what *they're* most afraid of doing: heterosexually taking risks, making firm commitments and being honest about showing their feelings.

Secondly, most women are much too conventional to admit to themselves or to learn from each other the gory details of the real art of manhunting. For, in most modern societies, the female is not *supposed* to unzipper her foundation garments and fully and freely *give* of herself to every prospective husband that she meets. But, as almost any village idiot will quickly tell you, this is usually the easiest, and often positively the only, way that she is likely to impress her (no pun intended)

10

womanly virtues on almost any sane and intelligent man she encounters.

Consequently, in the vast majority of cases, the modern American woman bows to convention—and bows out of another possible prenuptial affair. Worse, she pigheadedly and wrongheadedly then rationalizes her stupidity by maintaining that no respectable man would marry her if she did surrender her chastity to him. And she has no trouble in convincing herself—and her equally other-directed (i.e., other-*women*-directed) sisters that her palpably false views are true.

In the third place, American women almost invariably set up the ground rules of their manhunting activities so that these rules are beautifully designed *not* to net them an intelligent, sane, and cultured husband but to bag a boorish dunce, a male supremacist, or what H. L. Mencken aptly termed, a typical member of the booboisie.

Millions of contemporary males do insist that women are *never* to take the initiative in a sex encounter and that the gal who wins her mate by giving away free premarital samples of her bedworthiness is, mister, no real lady. And every one of these millions of "real men" is, clearly, ignorant or stupid or seriously emotionally disturbed. Practically none of them, moreover, is likely to make anything but a narrow-minded, woman-downing, double-standard-bearing mate who will have about as much real respect for his wife as a human being and a person in her own right as he will have for Marcel Proust or Leonardo da Vinci or Albert Einstein.

Well? Well, *this* is the type of average man whom our females allow to play the tune and call the turn for setting the rules of their man-snaring game. And, with

11

all due poetic justice, this is the kind of man, at best, on whom the trap door before the altar generally swings shut. With consequent misery to both husband and wife, naturally, until divorce (if it can be mercifully arranged) does them part.

In other words: if, inspired by our woman-promulgated manhunting codes, a modern miss is highly "successful" in getting her man—and, as the vital statistics show every year, she much more often than not eventually is—she is almost guaranteed to wed an undemocratic, woman-downing satrap while leaving the few truly woman-accepting males of her acquaintance fall to her unsqueamish, "cheap" sisters—or to the everlasting joys of bachelorhood. The more she follows the rules of the usual female-endorsed man-baiting manual, the more likely is she to end up with the same kind of authoritarian-minded cad who married Mom and Grandmom. And the less likely she is to be, before, during, and after marriage, herself.

Women, then, know as much about locating, fascinating, stimulating, and maritally animating men as they do about the gentle art of mustache-tweezing. They usually insist on playing the tunes of twentieth century courtship with a medieval psaltery. And when, as is generally the case, they marry a sad sack of a husband (or, worse yet, are sadly sacked by prospective husbands), they frequently bewail their not following—instead, forsooth, their rigidly swallowing—the conventional rules of the mating game. And they run for still another hardcovered or paperbacked batch of hen's ems on HOW TO BE CHASTE BUT CHASED.

Enough! *One* book one day had to be written plainly telling the female of the species, in unsaccharined language, how to meet, greet, and treat the man—and I really mean *man*—of the tribe. This, ladies, is it. Much of what you are about to read, you probably won't like. Some of what follows, you will positively abhor. Tough. Strong medicines rarely tickle the palate. But they often, if taken regularly, settle the stomach. Or strengthen the guts.

Let us, too, get this straight at the start: the present book, *The Intelligent Woman's Guide to Manhunting*, is *not* cavalierly titled. This volume is *not* designed for the average feminine dunderhead. It assumes that its readers are intelligent: women who can, want to, and do read. And think. And read some more. And think some more. And think still more.

It also assumes that these intelligent, reading women primarily want to land a similarly intelligent, and probably also reading, man. Not that they might not enjoy Rock Hudson's looks. Or Dempsey's strength. Or Casanova's love-making ability. Doubtless, they would. But these intelligent, reading women, it is assumed, mainly want a long-lasting, well-wearing mate and companion. Not a dependent slob; or a woman-dominating autocrat; or a nose-to-the-grindstone business tycoon; or an ears-glued-to-the-TV-sportcast-fanatic. But a bright, cultured, firm but kindly *person*: a *mensch*.

These, then, are the main questions that this book will attempt to answer: Where can the intelligent woman find a suitably intelligent, truly strong, not too emotionally disturbed man? How, when she finds him, should she behave in relation to him? What, specifically, can she do to help herself win and keep him?

Now that hundreds of women magazine writers and scores of authoresses of books have had their say in giving what are mostly the wrong answers to these questions, what are, from a frankly *man's* point of view, some of the right ones? We shall, in the following pages, see!

The Intelligent Woman's Guide to Man-Hunting

Chapter 1

What Women *Think* a Man Wants in Women

What women *think* a man wants in women, and what most intelligent, sane men actually do want are as different—well, as masculinity and femininity. Women are generally, in this respect, the worst possible victims of projection. They essentially, if unconsciously, ask themselves: "What would *I* and my sainted mother (not to mention my cousins and my sisters and my aunts) want in a person, especially in a close woman friend?" Then they project this peculiarly feminine set of preferences onto the males they know, and rashly assume that *they* must want the same things in a woman, too.

Nothing could be more misleading. Certainly, there are *some* men who look for, in a female, exactly what females look for in another woman. Mama's boys, for example. And serious neurotics. And homosexuals. And other assorted kinds of kooks. But how many such men exist among the kind of prospective husband you, as a woman, are likely to be looking for? And who the devil wants them?

Take Jonathan, for example. Jonathan was a very well brought up boy, whose mother made a kind of substitute lover of him from the age of eight, when she kicked his father out of her bedroom and encouraged him to go fly his kite elsewhere (which, with his secre-

17

tary and a series of maids, he promptly did). Mama took Jonathan with her everywhere: including even women's rest rooms, when she could possibly sneak him in.

Naturally, he grew up to be a real, fine boy: courteous, pleasant, and quite devoted to women. And naturally, he always wanted a girl just like the girl who married dear old Dad—that is, a girl just as super-refined, pluperfect, and sexless as Mama.

When he finally married Marilyn—who had been chased around so many living rooms by one-track-minded males that she was delighted to find one of the brute breed who was perfectly content with a good-night peck—he asked nothing more of her than he would ever have thought of asking of his own mother. Namely: that she look like a well-groomed doll twenty-four hours a day; that she never use an expletive stronger than "Oh fudge!"; that she keep her sneaky little hands off him while he laboriously waded through the *New York Times* and the *Wall Street Journal* every evening from seven till eleven; and that she stop that terribly disgusting heavy breathing and panting whenever, every other Saturday evening, they had the kind of relations by which, alas, it was necessary that they procreate a Jonathan, Jr.

So much (as Marilyn finally said to herself and her lawyer) for Jonathan. Certainly such "men" exist. And certainly their ideals of womanhood are remarkably close to those of Queen Victoria. But that's *their* problem; and the intelligent woman of today who would make it hers had better hie herself, fast, to a competent psychotherapist.

Fortunately, such males as Jonathan are among the

small minority. The majority of educated and cultured young men are batty enough, and usually have amply more than their fair share of unassertiveness, withdrawal, and impotence. Or (as a mask for these very traits) have varying nauseating degrees of false confidence, demandingness, and male domination. Too bad; and I really sympathize with the girls of our society who have to keep putting up with this kind of rot.

The fact remains, however, that most American males definitely do *not* want the kind of females that most American women seem to think that they want. And the brighter and saner they are, the less does their notion of the ideal woman approximate that of their mothers and sisters. Let us, by way of illustration, run down the list of some of the main traits which men are supposed to crave in their Dream Girl, and let us see to what extent they actually do.

Respectability

Perhaps the main thing that the average girl *thinks* a man wants in a would-be spouse is respectability. His prospective wife should be—she feels—the kind of girl who, like Caesar's wife, is above suspicion; whom no one would even think of saying a nasty word about; who is as pure as the unpollinated flowers that bloom in the Spring, tra-la. What is more, she should come from a fine family; live in a most respectable neighborhood; have an expensively furnished and tastefully decorated apartment; be living with her family rather than by herself; etc.

Well?

Nonsense! The truly intelligent and mature contemporary male has about as much use for this kind of

19

respectability as he has for a shaving mug. This is not to say that he wants his potential wife to be so totally unrespectable that his friends and his boss will literally be shocked when she wears blue jeans to a cocktail party at the Waldorf Astoria or invites his buddies to share their bed as well as their board when they come to visit. After all, there are *some* limits to how disheveled, disorganized, and disreputable a man wants his mate to be.

Nonetheless: today's bright young man generally *wants* his girl to have had some sort of sex life before she met him, and to have her friends and his know perfectly well that she is not the Virgin Mary's maiden aunt. He frequently *prefers* that she not come from a fine, hoity-toity family that will forever after prove to be a royal pain in the backside to him, as they insist on a garish, expensive wedding, attendance at stuffy weekly dinners, and all kinds of other showy family rituals. He usually *prefers* his best girl to live entirely by herself, in a fairly inexpensive, doorman-denuded flat, where he and she and their friends can come and go as they please, without being subject to Gestapo-like prying neighbors or service people. He often does not give a hoot about the furnishings and the decor, as long as the chairs and the bed are comfortable.

Sue came around to her group psychotherapy sessions for weeks, bitterly complaining almost every single time that she couldn't make out well with any of the men she kept meeting because she didn't dare take them up to her sleazy apartment-hotel room, and therefore was only able to kiss them good night in the taxi and cut their evenings abortively short. At first, most of the girls in the group agreed with her, since she did live in a pretty crummy hotel, and the furniture in her room was, to use her term, quite ghastly. But the males in the group couldn't see this at all, and insisted that the appearance of a girl's place was the very last thing they concentrated on if and when they finally got in her door.

Finally, Sue's complaints became so repetitious that one of the other girls in the group, Maryann, got suspicious. "Look," she said to Sue with some degree of annoyance, "you keep blaming your poor social life on your stupid apartment or room or whatever you call it—"

"Room!" exclaimed Sue, almost in tears. "Let's face it: it's a really awful place. And I can't—"

"All right, all right!" Maryann interrupted. "So it's awful. Let's say it is. But how about your best girlfriend, Joan, that you keep telling us about so enviously. *She* makes out quite well with men, doesn't she?"

"She sure does! But she's not afraid to take men up to her place and let them stay, even all night if she wants them to. And now she's getting married in a few weeks. The luck I have!"

"Luck?" Maryann persisted. "It seems to me that your friend, Joan, *makes* her luck. Just like you make yours—only in reverse. And where, may I ask, has Joan been living all these last few months, when she's been doing so well with men, and now about to marry one?"

"Oh. Right down the hall from me."

"Oh! The same sleazy hotel? And what kind of a room does she have there, may I ask?"

"Well—I, I guess it's about the same—no, I even have to say a little smaller and worse—than mine."

"So! Even a little smaller and worse than yours."

21

"Oh. Oh, I see what you mean. Oh."

And Sue did see what Maryann meant. From that time on, she began to invite a few, selected male companions to her room, either before or after she went out with them. Her complaints to the group about her troubles with males considerably diminished.

The fact remains, then: while respectability and putting on the Ritz may be most appropriate for the girl who lives in a town like Stillwater, Iowa (perhaps 3,000 pop., most of them residing—but not exactly living—there since the days of the Indian wars), or for the girl who wants to marry a stuffed shirt with solid gold cuff links and a chinchilla bow tie, the girl who lives in any sizable modern city and wants to marry a real person rather than a bank account needs this kind of respectability like she needs a hole in her diaphragm.

Shyness and unassertiveness

Nineteenth century novelists wrote reams of eulogies to the unassuming modesty, the demure shyness (not to mention the shy demureness) of their ineffably beauteous, inexpressibly charming (and inestimably vacuous) young heroines. That, among other good reasons, is undoubtedly why the three-decker novel died a horrible, long-overdue death.

Many female (and, incredibly, a few male) journalists are still heaven-bent on ghoulishly exhuming this pre-twentieth century ideal of abashed young womanhood; and it is to be feared that only when most women's magazines find their way, with the dodo, to the Happy Hunting Ground for anachronistic publications will this inane image—of what the marriage-bent ingenue should ape—finally be annihilated.

There are several significant reasons why the shy and unassertive woman, especially when she has reached her mid-twenties, has as much chance of ensnaring a fine, alert, whippersnapper of a man as I have of becoming Pope Albert the First. To wit:

1. Her unshyer and eminently saner sisters have been gratuitously given, by her tight-lipped and tight-buttoned retreat, cards, spades, diamonds, and clubs in the game of love; while she has left herself with the facsimile on the outside of the card box.

2. Her tied tongue and locked legs are no longer attractive in a world where women commonly open up their heads and hearts to new acquaintances as well as would-be lovers.

3. The inhibiting shackles with which she binds herself may still be appropriate for the *hoi polloi* of the hinterlands; but they are sadly misapplied to the members of the urban smart set.

4. If, when she has reached the age of twenty-five, her pathological shyness has not helped—as we may well predict, statistically, that it will not help—her snare a mate, she will have by that time missed out on most of the easy matrimonial game. She then will be forced to try her trepidational ways on the remaining really difficult customers. *That* will give her something to be shy about!

5. Timidity and unassertiveness are just as healthy for the average young female as is a thrice-daily dose of cyanide. Being alive and kicking means, in the first and final analysis, *being* and *expressing* oneself. Self-

23

imposed inhibitions on self-expression are equivalent to suicide: only, in terms of extended suffering, much worse. The girl who sells her soul for a mess of pusillanimous pottage is, whether she mates or not, a big empty zero. And what man in his sound mind wants to marry and live with a cipher?

When Jane S. came for psychotherapy, because she felt depressed a great deal of the time and could find nothing worthwhile to live for, it became immediately apparent that a large part of her depression was closely linked with her pathological shyness. But when I quickly brought to her attention the fact that she was terribly shy, and that there was no reason why she *had* to be, she strongly resisted my suggestions and stoutly contended that she was *naturally* shy, and she sort of *felt* good to be that way.

"Perhaps so," said I, "but what does it *get* you to be this shy—or, to use a harsher-sounding (and truer) term, to be scared stiff of people?"

"*Get* me? Does it have to *get* me something?"

"No, it doesn't have to, in the sense of your deriving some special benefit from being shy. But it does have to get you something, in the sense of disadvantages."

"And they are?"

"They are what you've already indicated: lack of boyfriends—or, for that matter, girlfriends; a dull social and general existence; and, in the final analysis, depression, or the feeling that what's the use of going on if life is this dull and uninteresting."

"All those things stem from shyness?"

"Wouldn't they have to? Can you imagine anyone as shy as you who would *not* lack girlfriends, have a dull life, and finally feel depressed?"

24

"Hmm."

"Hmm, indeed! And let me go one step further. Not only should we ask, 'What does shyness *get* you?' but also, and perhaps more importantly, 'What does it get *you*?'"

"*Me*?"

"Yes: *you.* Your*self*, that is. Or maybe we should stress it differently: *your*self. For while you are shy, you are of course not being *you*."

"Who am I being, then, if not myself?"

"Obviously: the puppet of *others.* These others, you think—or, rather, you *un*thinkingly imagine—are going to be terribly critical of you if you *are* yourself, if you express your you-ness. Probably they won't be. Or they may even like you much better if you are you. Anyway, you're afraid they won't. So, to please *them*, you shyly, fearfully withdraw, and refuse to be you. You become what *they*, presumably, want you to be. Or, at least, you become so neutral, so hard to see, that they'll never notice that you are *not* what they assumedly want you to be. So you dance, in effect, to their pulling of *your* strings. Except, ironically, they aren't even pulling the strings. *You* are! You therefore make yourself into a do-it-yourself puppet, and absolutely refuse to be *you*."

"By trying to please them, then, I'm completely giving up on pleasing and being *me*?"

"Exactly. While if you tried, really tried, to keep being *you*, to do what *you* basically wanted to do, you in all probability would still win more of them over to your side than you're now doing; and, whether you did or not, at least you'd have your*self*."

Jane S. was a difficult patient; and it took me a good many more sessions before I finally convinced her that

25

she had everything to lose and nothing to gain by making herself behave shyly. When she started to see how *un*natural her "natural" timidity really was, and when I simultaneously got her to persist at her therapy homework assignments of meeting, by hook or crook, at least one new man every week, she not only lost most of her shyness but actually began to enjoy being self-assertive. Within six months she was engaged to be married, after accepting the third of the proposals she had received during this period. Her male acquaintances found her shyness to be as attractive as skunkweed. Once self-deodorized, and metamorphosized into an unblushing rose, she became much more marriageable.

Brainlessness

Numerous female-indited mating manuals warn the young woman never, oh *never*, to let her natural braininess show through to her suitors. Males, these manuals say, simply can't *stand* a girl who is as bright as are they; their poor, dear masculine egos are sorely offended by female wit and sagacity; and they must be continually led to believe that only they, of the heterosexual couple, have a well-nourished brain beneath their pointed heads.

Bosh!

Certainly there are many men, including highly intelligent men, who break out in hives when their girls display any degree of knowledge or wisdom, and who prefer to associate (euphemism for climb in the hay) with flibbertigibbety sexpots who haven't—or at least make sure that they don't express—a serious thought in

26

their heads. But how many of these truly bright males want to *marry* a thoughtless, harebrained woman? Damned few.

One of the most frequent complaints I hear, in fact, in the course of the many marriage counseling sessions I do every week, is that Mrs. Jones or Mrs. Smith or Mrs. Doe seemed to be such a bright, interesting young thing before the chiming of the wedding bells; but now that she's comfortably married, she doesn't read, discuss, or think at all; and she's consequently such a horrible bore that the sooner she runs off with the supermarket manager, the better!

Naturally, the girlfriend or wife who snottily uses her brain power to show her male up (particularly before others!), or who keeps ceaselessly proving to him (with facts, figures, and witnesses) that his stupid ideas are much inferior to her unexcelled gems of sagacity, is not going to endear herself greatly to him. But neither will the gal who deliberately acts like a dumb Dora whenever her male is around, just to show him what a gweat big bwight man he is. Sure he will think, under such circumstances, that he is God's intellectual gift to humanity—and that why the devil should he waste this gift on such a hopelessly stupid female?

If, moreover, a girl selects an otherwise keen male who actually does insist that she behave like an orangutan when she is in his presence, what does she need him for? If he is *that* emotionally insecure, she'd be better off to *use* her brain and eliminate him as a good marital prospect rather than scuttle her sense just to trap him into matrimony. Having an *affair* with such an egg may have a kind of fascination all its own. But living maritally and domestically under the same roof with this kind of character is quite another thing. Try it, if you dare, and see.

Stylishness

It has often been said that women in our society normally do not dress for men but for other women. Let me, with unabashed repetition, say this again. Certainly, some men insist that their girlfriends and wives adopt the very latest telstar-relayed Parisian mode. Which men? Well, homosexuals for example. And playboys. And weaklings who want their so-called egos raised by having a Dior-draped Miss America on their arm.

But the above-average, independent-thinking man? Never! As soon as he notes that his gal Saturday has closets full of expensive clothes, shelves full of makeup, and racks full of many-splendored shoes, he begins to ask himself some interesting questions. Such as: How much is all this stuff going to cost *me*, if we are married? How long am I going to have to wait, every time we go out, for her to put on her armor and war paint? What has she got to *hide* behind all that fancy camouflage? Has she any *other* thought in her pretty little head than clothes, clothes, clothes?

More important still: long before he even thinks of getting her anywhere near City Hall, the biologically normal male is far more interested in how a woman *un*dresses than in how she dresses. Her foundation garments may be just the thing, thinks she, to pull in her tummy and bulge out her breasts. But, thinks he: how the devil am I going to get beyond that coat of mail to see what delights are underneath? And her

28

fresh-from-Bonwit Teller cocktail dress may be wonderfully eye-catching, she tells herself, and bound to set his heart swiftly beating. But, he asks himself with his heart gently purring and his genitals roaring: how can I even *touch* her, with that horribly fragile, easily crushable gown between us?

The healthy, eager male, in other words, is primarily interested in one kind of feminine style: bed style. If the girl he dates is to wear anything at all, he prefers it to be a negligée. Or a bikini. Or any reasonable facsimile thereof. And noisy night clubs, crowded cocktail lounges, Sunday church services, and even a good Broadway or off-Broadway show, are at most of second-rate interest to him, especially at the beginning of a boy-girl relationship. He will take his date to a fashionable club or resort because *she* wants to go there; and, being interested in getting certain obvious ultimate rewards, he aims to please. But what *he* really wants is a private room—almost *any* old room—and clothes which are as casual and removable as possible.

Does this sound as if the male is terribly crass and insulting, with his little interest in style, flair, and finesse, and his one-track-minded absorption in getting to bed firstest with the mostest? On the contrary!—it is the ultra-modishly-minded female, if anything, who is the actual, if unintending, insulter. For the man is literally going for what every woman presumably eagerly wants him to go for: *her*. Her outer vestments, her falsies, her dyed hair, her artificial eyebrows, and her various other store-bought charms she can, to his way of thinking, keep.

He craves *her* body, *her* kisses and caresses, *her* conversation, *her* responses to his overtures. And how, prithee, is he to find *her* if she is hopelessly lost in all the expensive, armoring, look-but-don't-touch trappings of the *haut monde*? Does he insult her by his honest, lustful interest? Heavens, no! If denigration exists in their relationship, it is much more likely to be her *self*-deprecating insistence that she cannot possibly offer herself to him as she *is*, but must premaritally perfume her shortcomings because he obviously would not accept her if he knew what a twerp she *really* was.

Away, then, with the super-stylishness hokum! If you want to dress tastefully, individually, and even (if you can really afford it) expensively, go right ahead: be yourself. If you want to live in the finest neighborhood, be seen at the best places, go only to the hoity-toitiest resorts: fine. If that's your cup of tea, swig it to the dregs. But don't delude yourself that this kind of modish behavior has anything—except, probably, negatively—to do with your finding and keeping a real, yourself-loving man. Such a man will be interested in you, naked—and I mean naked—you, and not your fashionable, up-to-the-minute trimmings. Or, as Confucius could have said: To trap with trappings is to trap yourself.

Mothering

Every man, so the good (woman-authored) books say, wants to be mothered. Make him feel that you are always there, with his slippers at night and his rubbers (the kind you wear on rainy days, that is) in the morning, and he will become so unalterably attached to you that no other vixen can possibly erase your mark with her lurid lipstick.

What claptrap! Even little boys—yes, four-, six-, and eight-year-old little boys—frequently do not like to be mothered. The male, if he is biologically anything, is a pretty independence-seeking, why-the-deuce-don't-you-leave-me-alone kind of animal. That's why small boys play hookey, stay out late, at times even run away from home. That's why big boys often remain bachelors.

Do *some* presumably grown-up males dote on being mothered? Yes, ma'am; and if truly wise you were, you'd leave them to just that: their mothers. You'll probably never be able to drag such a man away from the Old Bag, anyway; and even after she (Allah be praised!) kicks the bucket, he'll still be with her, in spirit totally and in fact practically, in the coffin. Who needs it—*you*?

Come, now: let's face reality. A real mothering type of mother is almost always a real pain in the neck, as is any other form of strangulation. She worries too much—and thereby restricts her child's freedom. She plots, schemes, and plans—and prevents the kid from thinking for himself. She bans pleasant, exciting experiences; enforces the dullest and deadliest of routines; and generally kills with "kindness." Is *this* what you want to do to your dearly beloved man?

Besides, what boy above the age of eighteen really wants (except in the Freudian fairy tales, euphemistically termed case histories) to copulate with his mother? Elizabeth Taylor's step-son? Well, perhaps. But who else?

If you feel terribly motherly, beget and breed your own children. Or open a nursery school. Or marry—if you dare—a schizophrenic. But if, perchance, you happen to encounter a reasonably grown-up, moderately

31

mature man, for God's sake, lady, keep your cotton-pickin', mothering hands to yourself.

Be nice to this man, yes. Give him understanding and succoring *if and when* he asks for it. But don't spend your idiotic life *looking* ceaselessly for things to do for him, for ways to abdicate your selfhood by making life effortless for him. You may, in that way, win his attention and attachment as a lackey or an underling wins him. But not very much more than that. And, very likely, you won't even win that: since after awhile he may well find your services onerous and insidiously demanding. For a real man to want to stay with you and to love you deeply, you need his respect as well as his domestic involvement. And what spoiled brat actually respects his mother?

Do services rendered before marriage help yank a man out of bachelorhood and hogtie him to the marital hitching-post? Very definitely, in many instances. Take your boyfriend's suits to the dry-cleaners. Meet him at the airport when he is coming in from out of town. Help him on the research project he is doing. Show him, in many such ways as these, that you really care for him, are interested in his work, and will do anything you can to be of service—when he *asks* for it. Even volunteer certain acts that you know perfectly well he would like you to do but that he is too timid or too considerate to ask you for.

All this, however, is not mothering. Mothering is done by a woman who is convinced that she knows her (little or big) boy's needs and wants much better than he does, and that if he does things the way *she* thinks they should be done, he will be inordinately efficient and happy. Mothering is a *condescending*, holier-than-thou kind of behavior. It is also, perversely enough, mixed in with the credo that the mothering individual is no damned good *unless* she is of service to someone else: that her intrinsic worth as a human being *depends* on her telling another what to do, and sometimes doing it for him.

Although the mothering person's intentions are mostly good, she actually deprecates both herself and her succorant by her self-sacrificism. By managing to get both above *and* below her (often all-too-willing) victim, she makes it impossible for them both to achieve male-female complementarity and true equality.

So read, if you must, those blubbery, let's-make-John-happy-by-mothering-him articles in the women's magazines. Then do the opposite of what they say.

Romance-seeking

Everyone who sees Hollywood films knows, of course, that modern wedlock directly springs from romance, that the way to marry a man is to get him to fall violently in love with you, and that the only true method of keeping him from straying is to keep romance fiercely burning for every moment of your fifty-odd-year sent—er, marriage. How? Well, as everyone who reads Madison Avenue's best efforts knows, of course, by generously employing per year some six thousand, two hundred and eighty-three dollars and fifty-two cents worth of Alluring face cream, Come-hither cosmetics, Yougetmerightbelowthebelt perfume, and WhyshouldMmePompadourhaveanythingonme hair dye.

Everyone knows all this, obviously—except highly

intelligent, reasonably sane, cultured males. Such curious beings, normally enough, have more than average propensities for romance; and, given half a chance, they will violently commit themselves to heterosexual passions that, while not exactly putting poor old Abelard, Petrarch, and Dante in the shade, have a resplendent glory that is uniquely their own. High-level males, in other words, distinctly can love in a high-level romantic manner; and frequently they do.

But romantic love, to a man of this type, does not necessarily equal marriage: else, as I have noted in my book, *The American Sexual Tragedy*, most of us would obviously marry one of our first school teachers. Love is just not enough. And, as I keep repeating to my psychotherapy patients and marriage counseling clients, although it is usually foolish, these days, to marry anyone whom you *don't* love, it is even more foolish to marry everyone whom you *do*.

Nor, apparently, am I alone in noting this. Years ago, when I did a study of the love relationships of college women, I discovered that even these suggestible, highly romantic teenagers were hardly falling desperately in love with and becoming overly-determined to marry the first man whose physical attributes quickly set their febrile hearts pumping. Rather, they somehow managed to ask themselves, in most instances, such questions as "How bright, really, is he?" . . . "What are his chances of getting on well in life?" . . . "What kind of a father do I think he'd make?" . . . and "How much does he really think of *me*?"—all this before they let themselves "spontaneously" and "romantically" slide.

So, too, I later found, with most cognizing males. "Hooray!" they consciously or unconsciously shout to themselves, "for Sylvia's matchless (Pond-creamed) skin, flawless (Jergens-lotioned) hands, peerless (Revlon-tipped) lips!" But, a little more cautiously, they add: "*Who* is Sylvia? *What* is she?" And only after that *who* and *what* are, with more than a slight degree of practical evidence, reasonably answered do they allow themselves to "fall" in love and cart Sylvia off to the altar.

What is more, love is not all—not at least to the man who has most of his marbles. Sure, he can love Gloria because of her baby-blue eyes, Edith because she is so sweet, and Harriet because she puts a lady rabbit to shame. But he is also quite capable of remembering that Gloria doesn't shut up for a single minute, Edith falls apart when company is present, and Harriet hasn't cleaned her little apartment for the last seven and a half weeks. And who needs, thinks he to him, *that* kind of stuff?

If even erstwhile romance is not likely to charm the above-average bachelor into parting with a sizable chunk of his life savings for an engagement and marriage ring, his enthusiasm for romance in perpetuity is usually even more fragile. Sure he would like to feel ultra-impassioned about his wife and to devote oodles of time to keeping her romantically agog—*if* there were not endless bills to pay, housewares to be fixed, office work to be done, children to make arrangements for, etc., etc.

What's so damned romantic, anyway, he wants to know when courting a girl for several months, about looking into her eyes and softly holding her hand until three in the morning—when it's so late that she's too tired to do anything else, and he probably wouldn't

35

be very good at doing it even if she wanted to? Or about telling her sweet nothings for a couple of hours every time they meet, when he really wants to know what she thinks about birth control and how many children she's going to insist that they have if and when they get married? Or about listening to schmaltzy music in a crowded, uncomfortable cafe, when they could be having a fine intellectual discussion with some interesting friends?

The road to amative hell, in other words, is paved with unrealistic romantic expectations. Living steadily under the same roof with a man, or even seeing him two or three times weekly for months on end, ultimately becomes just about as romantic as living, after the first fortnight, in a new hotel or a boarding school. High romance is based largely on novelty, excitement, adventure; and *steady* dating or mating just cannot be *that* perpetually novel, exciting, or adventurous. The girl, therefore, who overemphasizes the romantic—as against, say, the intellectual, the companionable, the sexual, or the other—aspects of courtship is almost invariably going to be demanding the impossible from both her partner and herself. And probably the quickest and most effective way of irritating a boyfriend is to demand from him what he cannot possibly give (nor can anyone else).

Suggest if you will, then, an *occasional* walk in the wilds, or look at the sunset, or handholding at the top of a mountain. But, for cupid's sake! don't expect a *steady diet* of this kind of romantic frippery. Life largely consists of practical matters, small talk, amusement-seeking, intelligent discussion, physical pleasures, and half a hundred other quite down-to-earth, unethereal things. Use the brains beneath your hairdo to make *these* kinds of everyday contact with your boyfriend as vitally alive and non-boring as possible. And for the most part, leave the high-flown romanticizing exactly where it belongs—in Hollywood.

Chapter 2

What Men *Really* Want in Women

Assuming that highly intelligent, not too kooky males do not want in women what the lady journalists most often seem to want them to want, the obvious next question is: Well, what do they *really* crave in their female partners? A whale of a lot, actually. Including:

Assertiveness

The stupid man, be he honestly mousy or false-facedly gruff, frequently cannot bear an assertive woman who knows her own mind and tells it to anyone who asks. Needing to be in the spotlight himself (even though he may do nothing to get in it), he shies away from anyone, such as a girlfriend or wife, who is closely identified with him and who gets her own due share of public approval. Not always, of course: since lots of stupid men marry assertive gals and even seem to thrive on their mates' forwardness. But the weaker a man (consciously or unconsciously) feels himself, the more he seems to tend to be a male supremacist and to attempt to keep his woman from, to his own distorted way of thinking, "showing him up."

The moral of this? Patently: if you, as a woman, want to be yourself and speak your piece when the spirit moves you, stay away from weak and stupid men.

O.K. Now let us suppose you follow this sage precept and you set your cap for a male who is neither numbskull nor nut. Should you unassertively walk on eggs with him? Over his (and your own) dead body!

The bright man almost invariably *wants* a woman who, without being obnoxious or querulous, has a real mind of her own, and does not hesitate to use it. He wants her to be able to join him, when they are by themselves or with their friends, in a protracted, well thought-through discussion of the show they have just seen, the latest events in China, or the care and feeding of mothers-in-law. If she fortuitously happens to agree with him on these kinds of questions, and can articulately say why she agrees, fine: he is well pleased with her position. But he definitely does not want a yes-woman, who merely agrees because she knows she'd damned well better if she wants him to love her. *That* kind of woman he can easily find in a brothel; and even then she bores him after a surprisingly short time.

Assertiveness, as we shall show in more detail in a later chapter, is not equivalent to aggressiveness. To be assertive is to know what you want to say and to say it, or to know what you want to do and to do it. To be aggressive is (especially as usually applied to a woman in our society) to be determined, at all costs, to get what you want, and to fight like a vixen, in a most hostile manner, to get it. Men rarely like aggressive or so-called castrating females (though at times they may masochistically be subservient to them). They do, however, want a woman who is vibrant, alive and self-assertive.

Even when an intelligent man is rolling in the hay with his inamorata there is likely to be, especially over some period of time, as much talking and discussing as rocking and rolling. If, during the periods of palaver, she is all saccharine agreement and no firm dissent, he might just as well answer his own questions and have a one-man soliloquy. Moreover, as the months and years go by, what have a man and woman to give to each other, more than their own inimitable *selves?* This means, of course, their *own* views on life, literature, love, and what have you. To *grow* with another person essentially means to *learn* with that person; and how is a man to learn from his wife or sweetheart if she isn't able to open her big mouth and say boo?

Assert, then, your own real being. Think what you think and say what you think. When your man violently differs with your views, politely but firmly differ with his. Don't be browbeaten into nonentityness. If you can't respect yourself sufficiently to stand up for your own opinions, how long will it be, do you think, until you lose your man's admiration and respect? The male you keep by forcing yourself to be a mouse will be a mouse-lover—not a you-lover. Is that the best you can *really* do?

Guts

Being assertive and having guts are in some respects the same, but in other respects quite different. Many people who assert themselves freely, in that they tell you what their views are and try to get what they want out of life, nonetheless balk whenever their views or desires seriously buck up against social convention.

Females, in particular, in our society, will often be quite forward about speaking in public, meeting strangers at a cocktail party, or something along that order; but when it comes to clearly unconventional acts, such as asking a man to go to bed with them, they will be just as shy and gutless in this respect as they are gutsy and forward in the more traditional social pathways.

The vast majority of American women, in fact, are almost totally sexually ungutsy, and even the bravest among them use, as rationale for their sexual inhibition, the idea that men abhor sexual directness in women, and immediately conclude that any girl who is anything but indirectly suggestive is a whore.

Is this idea correct? The hell it is!

Uneducated, stupid, inept, and fascistic-minded men usually feel that a woman who has sexual (or almost any other kind of) guts is a low-down tramp. But who, we must keep ceaselessly asking throughout this book, wants *them*? Let them stew in their own goldarn fascistic juices—with, for poetic justice, the pusillanimous, sex-shy types of females who normally become their mates.

The brighter and bigger boys, however, are in quite a different class when it comes to labeling the girl with the guts as one of the sluts. Nothing pleases them more, in most instances, than the lass (be it her first or fifty-first date with them) who frankly and clearly indicates that the lovely dinner and that fine show are only the preliminary parts of the evening, and that the real show goes on at home, after midnight.

Take, by way of illustration, the case of Rhonda G. Rhonda came to me for premarital counseling because, although she was twenty-nine, unusually attractive, well-educated, and very socially adept, the men she was most interested in never seemed to stay around long enough for any attachment to grow up between them. The creeps she met, to be sure, adored her, and would keep calling and dating her, if she let them, forever. But the really good guys, whom she would meet once every few months or so, would show her a grand time for one date, possibly two, occasionally three— and that was it.

"What kind of people are these 'good guys' that you keep talking about?" I asked her.

"Oh, rather unusual, I'd say," was her reply. "Frankly, I think I know a good thing when I see one. And the good guys I'm talking about are sort of the cream of the crop."

"Meaning—what?"

"Well, they're not too young, since I don't particularly like young men. In their early forties, say. Usually doing exceptionally well in business or some profession. Single, of course, since I don't fool around with married men. Definitely on the highly intelligent side. And— I might as well admit it, since I have a weakness for good-looking men—almost always tall, well-built, and almost any woman's idea of an attractive guy."

"You really do pick them!" I smilingly said.

"Yes. But, naturally, they don't sell them at the supermarket, so I have to wait a reasonable length of time before the next one comes around to take my mind off the last one—who unfortunately scooted out on me several months before."

"O.K. So let's say that the men you choose are, by normal standards, pretty desirable. Now, what exactly do you do with them, when you see them on first and second dates?"

"Do? What, I guess, everyone else does. Dinner,

usually. Then maybe a show. Then back to my place for coffee and a long conversation. Sometimes, like the one I saw a few weeks ago, and who still hasn't called back, and who I might as well admit is a lost cause by now, all-night conversation."

"*Only* conversation?"

"Sure. At first, that is. Not that I wouldn't do anything *later*, you know. I'm really not *that* pure, and I have had my real affairs with men, and thoroughly enjoyed the sex. But these are *first* dates, mostly, that I'm talking about. And *that's* different!"

"Perhaps so," I said. "But couldn't we also say that these may be *first* men, too, with whom you're having these dates; and that maybe, well, *that's* different, too?"

"What do you mean by *first* men?"

"Simply that the type of men you seem to be having these dates with—the ones, that is to say, you're concerned about not later losing—are, from your own description, la crème de la crème—right?"

"Yes, I guess you could call them that. They're certainly outstanding compared to most of the other creeps who keep calling."

"And they're not only outstanding to you, but most probably would be, also, to other young, eligible, good-looking women in New York City. True?"

"Oh, definitely. I hardly delude myself that I'm the only one who would find them attractive—or the only one whom they might want to take out."

"Yes—or to take *in*. The type of man you describe is obviously a good catch for other girls besides you; and by the time he's reached the age you're selecting from and has got a few financial or professional successes in life, he knows perfectly well that he *is* a good catch and that lots of girls will want to catch him in bed long before they insist on catching him in church."

"In other words: my competition is keen."

"Right: damned keen. And while you're making your subtle distinctions between first, second, and umpteenth dates, and just how far, sexually, you can go on which date in the series, these other girls, or at least some of them, are quickly surrendering their 'all' without any internal or external debate. And to whom, if you were in *his* position, would you choose to return?"

"Oh, but that's not fair! How does he know that, if he just is a little patient with me, I won't be far better in bed than any of those other chippies who flop into the sack with him immediately? And I probably will, you know, I really will!"

"Yes, you probably will. But that's just the point: how *does* he know. From what he can see, you may put him off for weeks, or may never go to bed with him at all, or may, when you finally do break down and welcome him sexually, be entirely frigid. All the evidence that he has at his disposal—namely, that you play a great game of *talking* all night—hardly encourages him to conclude that you are the greatest thing worth waiting for since Cleopatra."

"Do you really think that he might get the idea, from my first or second date behavior, that I am actually *frigid?*"

"Why not? Or puritanical. Or determined to sell your sexual responsiveness at a price so high that it would hardly be worth paying for. Or—don't forget—he might think none of these things, might even believe that you are a pretty hot number when once the bedspreads are down—but also believe that you are not especially interested in *him* that way. Why not? Why shouldn't he think such things."

"Yes, I see now. Why shouldn't he? And me, fool that I've been, I've been thinking all the time that if I did let him have me the first or second date he'd surely think that I was promiscuous, was interested in anything in pants, was not really worth having, and so on. Evidently the male and female mind work quite differently!"

"Evidently they do. The thoughts that you have been putting into your dates' heads could certainly be held by *some* men. But honestly, now, do you think that the specific ones that you have been seeing—or, worse luck! *not* seeing after your initial encounters— were very likely to have had such thoughts?"

"No, I guess not. *I* had the thoughts. But I guess very few of them did. As you say, they probably mostly thought that I was a prude, frigid, or not interested in them. Christ! have I been stupid!"

"Probably so. But let's not have you beating yourself over the head, now, for your stupidity. So you made mistakes. So we all do. The point is: blaming ourselves for these mistakes will help us not a whit to eradicate them. On the contrary, it will probably help us—no-goodniks that all of us feel that we are for making the mistakes!—to make still more of them. So none of that crappy self-blaming, now! The only sane question is: What are you going to do *next* time? That's the thing you should almost exclusively be concentrating on."

"Yes. What am I going to do *next* time? No worse, I think I can promise you. And maybe a lot better!"

Next time, somewhat to my surprise, came with amazing rapidity. "You won't believe it," my young patient exclaimed when she came to see me the following week, "but I'm actually engaged! Or will be officially, at least, as soon as I decide which ring I want Judson to get me."

"Judson?" I asked. "Isn't he the boy you thought you lost out on a few weeks ago? Did he actually get in touch with you again, in spite of the fiasco of a first date you thought you had with him?"

"Get in touch with me, hell! And he never was going to again, from what he told me."

"Then—?" I asked with a puzzled look.

"Oh, yes. You mean, how could he tell me he never was going to see me again without actually seeing me to tell me. Well, he just wasn't—until I, right after I saw you last week, called him. What the devil, I figured: 'You have nothing to lose, kiddo. You've already loused up the deal, but good. So find some damned excuse to call him, and see if it's not possible to stir up a few embers again.' So I did. I called him that very night.

" 'Look,' I said, 'you'll never guess why I'm calling.' 'You're right,' he said, 'I guess I never will.' 'Well,' I grimly plodded on—oh, I was determined, really determined about that *next* time we had spoken about that afternoon—'I don't think you ever will either. I—' and I hesitated just a split-second, but then I muttered to myself 'Screw it! Nothing at all to lose!' and plunged: 'I was so goddam hot, when you left at seven in the morning that last time we met, and I was so damned mad at myself for letting you go—when that was the last thing I really wanted, myself, that, well, I've been kicking myself around the block every day ever since. And I'm still hot—mad at myself, that is, and in the other way, too.'

47

"There was a dead silence on the phone for several seconds. 'O.K.,' I said, 'you can put your teeth back in now. And how soon can you come over?' 'In about twelve and a half minutes,' he said. And he did. And *we* did. Ever since. And along about the sixth, or was it the seventh, time we did it that following morning—coincidentally, I think, about seven a.m. again—we decided that this sort of thing was too good to be wasted on single people, and that maybe we should apply for some kind of monopoly, a marital monopoly, on it. Which, on second thought, third thought, and fourteenth thought, we're still very much thinking of doing. So there! Next time, perhaps, there won't have to be any next times. Not, at least, while I'm still single!"

So gutsiness came to Rhonda G. As it has also come to many of the other females I have worked with in counseling and psychotherapy sessions. Not, by any means, always so rapidly; nor with such fortunate results. But almost always the American miss, in spite of her atrocious, ego-destroying upbringing, can be helped, or can even help herself, to face the facts of life realistically and to be just about as direct, straightforward, and risk-taking about sex-love chances as she expects (and rightly so, I believe) a strong man to be.

In so doing, she is very likely to scandalize her sainted mother, her best girlfriend, and almost any other convention-bound females in whom she chooses to confide. But her chances of similarly shocking the real men whom she would like to become seriously involved with are slim, and her chances of winning out with these men, over her more tradition-following competition, are excellent. For what self-respecting male, given the choice of a scintillating conversation

48

or a fully enacted bedtime story with an attractive young woman, would be likely to choose the former? And who would want him if he did?

Competence

The girl who gets the strong, hard man is often supposed to be an inept, fragile little thing who can't even put her garter belt on straight, and who has to run for masculine aid every time she has a light bulb to be changed. Such exemplary feminine weakness, we are variously told, will cement male-female relationships so solidly that Samson himself (were he interested) could never rend those dependency-succoring bonds asunder.

True? Certainly: in a few cases. The average above-average man, however, is about as thrilled with catering to the flaunted incompetence of a potential inamorata as he would be to running a two-man relay race with his partner on his back.

Lovely lady, remember this: The outstanding man in our society is almost always *busy*. No goofer or playboy, he; but usually an incredibly alive-and-kicking student, scientist, entrepreneur, sportsman, or other variety of activity-bent person. And consequently, when he thinks seriously about marrying some keen Young Thing, he is rarely notably encouraged by her lying abed until noon each day; taking four and three-quarter hours to be ready, at nine o'clock, for a seven o'clock appointment; or insisting that he rearrange the living room furniture that he moved for her yesterday because, oh dear, she forgot, yes, you know how it is, just plain forgot that the pattern of the living room rug, that really, yes, she was really so sure that it ran this way, actually does run, yes, now that you look closely at it in the broad daylight, my god yes!— actually runs *that* way.

To the contrary! The truly active, going-places man ordinarily wants a woman who, even if she is not the greatest helpmate in the world, at least does not *impede* his progress. Preferably, the better hostess, housewife, efficient mother, wall painter, rug cleaner, etc. she is, the better he likes it. For, however he might want to be there with her, pitching in on all the partying and housecleaning chores that just have to be done with nauseating regularity, even by single folk, he just hasn't the *time,* in many instances, to do even his own full share of the work—let alone hers!

The girl, similarly, who simply can't handle her own emotional problems, and is continually calling up her boyfriend to ask his advice, cry on his shoulder, and get him to come right over and comfort her—*maybe* she'll find a more than willing do-gooder who likes nothing more than to rush around in her hour of need to prove what a big strong man he is. But, among the truly up-and-coming males of our generation, she probably won't.

Moreover, even when she finds that, early in the mating game, her broadshouldered lover is more than willing to listen to her every gripe and moan, she is likely to be sadly disillusioned when she discovers how short a way that same griping and moaning is going to get her. Nothing can be more boring than repeated complaints about oh, the horror of it all, and ah, the injustices of the world. And women who are so palpably incompetent that they not only cannot find suitable solutions to most of life's little inequities, but who also actually *create* considerable hassles where few actually exist, are as likely, eventually at least, to be about as popular with vitally absorbed, empire-building men as are fleas at a dog show.

The solution to the problem of your being competent enough to attract and keep a man who himself is in the highly competent class is not very neat or obvious. For I cannot very well tell you, nor you tell yourself: "All right, dear: go be competent." It's not quite as easy as that!

What you can do, though, is at least give up your noble efforts to be *in*competent. Rid yourself, and fast, of the idea that ineptitude and feminine weakness are the royal roads to romance and stop convincing yourself that even smart males like their women beautiful but dumb. Whatever brains you happen to have been born with, use; and don't hesitate to show your best male prospects that you can, rather than that you can't, do various things well.

More specifically: plan (with paper and pencil, if necessary) some of your Saturday night activities yourself; then (tactfully, tactfully!) get lover-boy to accept your plans. See that the tight-rimmed pickle jars are pried open *before* he comes to dinner. Figure out (with professional help) a sensible contraceptive methodology that you can easily handle yourself and that minimizes any blundering around in the dark he might otherwise have to do. Get the superintendent of your building to fix the wretched window that is most likely to stick when you try to open it while your not-overly-handy boyfriend is there. See that you have ample maid or butler service for the evening if you happen to give a big party. Talk to BF only briefly when you call him at the office, unless he absolutely insists that the conversation go on and on.

More hints along this line: Be, in general, well-organized, and let him see that you are. Organize your appearance and your home: don't be too sloppy; but don't go to the other extreme of being compulsively tidy and clean. If he comes to your apartment, try to see that the place is reasonably in order—no curlers, stockings, and tampons all over the place! Show your prospective mate that you know how to shop, to cook, to serve, to clean up after meals.

A preparer of gourmet menus by the dozen you do not necessarily have to be (though that may help in some cases!). But at the very least you should know *something* about domestic affairs, and indicate that if your boyfriend is thinking seriously of marrying you, he need have few worries about your needing two maids and a business manager to keep your household in order.

Competence about *you* doesn't hurt either, and may be distinctly helpful. Are you overweight? Do you take your vitamins daily? Do you drink like a fish and get in everybody's hair when you are looped? Is your posture reasonably good? Do you know what to do, and sensibly do it, when you are sick, or tired, or out of sorts? The more you show your chosen male that you can ably, fairly consistently handle yourself, and that you are not too likely to need *his* continual succoring, the more he is apt to conclude that you will not be too much of a burden on him, especially after marriage, and that he can spend most of his time enjoying rather than bolstering you.

This does not mean, now, that you must show your boyfriend that you can and must do *everything* for yourself, and that any help on his part is as welcome as a kick in the shins. It is far better to let him do *some* things to help you, from time to time—while you still, in the main, competently go about helping yourself in his presence and behind his back. As usual, attaining the mean between the two extremes of utter helplessness, on the one hand, and complete lack of need for *anyone* else, on the other, is generally the best course you can take. Perhaps almost every man would, in some part of his psyche, want to have a child-mistress; but it is highly questionable how many males truly enjoy a child-wife.

Get the idea, now? The things that you have to do in his presence, manage to plan in advance and do reasonably well. The things, especially the onerous and failure-inviting things, that he has to do in your presence, manage to eliminate, to reduce to a minimum, to assume some of the responsibility for, to ease, or to help him with. Give him, at least some way back in his mind, the impression that when he is with you, as well as when you are with yourself, life somehow goes pretty smoothly, and hassles are few and far between.

Let me repeat, don't try to be a thoroughly competent jill-of-all-trades who is so well oiled and in such good working condition that she seems to be entirely *un*feminine. But squelch the I'm-such-a-poor-helpless-creature-that-I-desperately-need-a-big-strong-man-like-you-to-take-endless-care-of-me line, too. There must be *some* kind of reasonable mean between these two undesirable extremes.

O.K.: get your thinking cap on, your paper and pencil out, and find it.

Permissiveness without ingratiation

Blaming, as I spend most of my life talking to my patients and writing about in articles and books, is the root of practically all evil. Showing an individual, be he child or adult, that he is wrong and self-defeating in what he is doing is usually one of the most helpful things you can do for another human—*if,* in the process, you do not blame him for being wrong and self-defeating.

Can the man of your dreams be wrong, dead wrong, without being to blame for his idiotic wrongheadedness? Not only *can* he be, but—if we want to be scientific about it—he's *got* to be. For no one—yes, that's right, I said *no one*—is ever to blame for anything he does.

"No one?" you hasten to ask (as you mentally note: "Uh-uh! I knew it would happen, sooner or later. Another psychologist gone off his rocker!"). "Not even a murderer? Not even, say, Adolf Hitler? Not even Bluebeard?"

"Yes," I firmly reply. *"No one.* Not even a murderer. Not even Hitler. Nor Bluebeard."

Why? For very obvious reasons, if you come (which almost no one in our society does) to think of them. Let us define, first, what blaming means.

What it does *not* simply mean is assessment of wrongdoing. For clearly, if John gratuitously kicks Jim in the teeth, and John is wrong (i.e., mistaken, erroneous, unethical) for so doing, then it is perfectly correct for me to say to him, "Look, John: you've done the wrong thing by kicking Jim in the teeth." In saying this, I have merely described John's behavior and have objectively (in terms, that is, of what almost all people in our society consider to be right and wrong) assessed it as being mistaken. But I have not, by my statement, as yet blamed John for doing wrong.

If, however, by either direct words, the tone of my voice, or gestures of various sorts, I indicate to John: "Look, you dirty So-and-so, you *shouldn't* have kicked Jim in the teeth! How *could* you have done that horrible deed?" I am then not only assessing John's act as wrong, but am blaming him for *being* wrong.

In other words, instead of objectively telling John: (a) "You are wrong for kicking Jim in the teeth," and (b) "I'm sure that, if you admit that you are wrong, and try to be less wrong next time, you can refrain from kicking him in the teeth again," I am moralistically, blamefully telling him: (a) "You are wrong for kicking Jim in the teeth," and (b) "You're a perfectly lousy bastard for being wrong, since no decent human being would do a thing like that, and your chances of ever rehabilitating yourself and becoming fit for a respectable person to talk to are virtually nil."

Blaming, then, not only means that the blamed individual is wrong—but that he is *hopelessly* wrong: was born a skunk, always has been one, and will indubitably continue to be one. And blaming strongly implies, of

55

course, that the wrong individual who is blamed should be retributively *punished* for his being the rat that he is: should be made to atone for his atrocious sin, not merely by making restitution to the person he has wronged, but by experiencing physical torture (hell) and mental anguish (remorse) for aeons to come, perhaps for eternity.

"Well," you may ask, "isn't it perfectly proper for the wrongdoer to be punished for his misdeeds—that he be made to suffer, just as he has needlessly made his victims suffer?"

No, I reply, why *is* it proper to punish or excoriate a wrongdoer? First of all, since when do two wrongs make a right? Secondly, are your hands so perfectly clean of all wrongdoing throughout your lifetime that *you* can justly levy and carry out his "proper" punishment? Thirdly, in the event that you do punish the wrongdoer, what makes you so certain that this will deter him—as, presumably, as a moralist you are aiming to deter him—from committing another future wrong?

This is only the hub rather than the nub of the matter. There are many good reasons why, although showing a person that he is responsible for his acts and that it would be far better for him to change these acts in the future, is to react perfectly reasonably to his mistakes, showing him that he is a worthless slob and a lout for committing these acts is not only unjustified but almost always harmful rather than helpful to him or yourself. Details of these reasons may be found in my book, *Reason and Emotion in Psychotherapy* (New York: Lyle Stuart, 1962), as well as in various of my other writings with my associate, Dr.

Robert A. Harper (Ellis and Harper, 1961a, 1961b).

Suffice it to say here that blaming humans *even* when they are clearly in the wrong practically never helps to change them for the better and almost always helps to change you for the worse—for they remain pretty much the way they are, while you wind up with a needless angry pain in your guts.

This particularly goes with your best-beloved male. Wrong he may decidedly be about his words and deeds relating to you, others, and the world at large. All right: so he is wrong! The real, and only relevant, question is: How are you going, for his sake and your own, to induce him to be less wrong. Yes, *less* wrong, not perfectly right, nor even plain darned right.

For as long as he is a human, rather than (as you might possibly like him to be) an angel or a god, he is going to be enormously, ineradicably *fallible;* and fallible people—even as you and I—are never, for any serious length of time, right: they are always, at best, less wrong. And that, as I noted at the beginning of this section, is essentially why no one is ever to blame for being wrong: for as long as he is alive, that is more or less what he is going, as a human being, to be. To blame a person for being wrong is equivalent to blaming him for being alive. When he is dead, he will make no mistakes whatever. But not till then.

Getting back to you and your would-be lover or husband: The only sane and wise thing you can do when he makes the latest of his normal large batch of mistakes is to accept him, without any blaming whatever, as a wrongdoer. Not *like* him for his bloopers. Not cheer him on to make more. But accept, calmly accept, the fact that he has made another error, and that it is too damned bad that he has, but there it is: he has. *How* can you accept the low-life bas—er, poor wrongdoer—when he has made that very same mistake, that you told him about eighty times previously, once again? Very simply: the same way that you accept the rainy day that you prayed would be sunny, or that you accept your mother's appendicitis attack just when she was going to help you move to another apartment. To accept something undesirable means not to like it, not to want it, but (when there is just no other choice) to gracefully lump it.

And, I insist again, there *is* no other choice, or at least intelligent choice, when your boyfriend is behaving like a real heel or nincompoop. For he is *not* (in spite of your very best attempts at fantasy) Jupiter, Thor, Zeus, or Jesus Christ. (Nor are you, remember, the Virgin Mary!) And he *will* make blunder after blunder, mistake after mistake, until death or your fits of anger do you part. So you *must* accept his often-to-be-repeated misbehavior. Or else!

Accepting another's mistake, however, must be clearly differentiated from being a doormat for his whims. If you want to look the other way from your lover's errors, and calmly try to help him eventually make fewer of them, that's one thing. But if you do this by being nauseatingly ingratiating, pretending that he is always right, and never in any way objectively showing him that you do not agree with all his behavior, and that you could well appreciate his changing some of it, that's another thing entirely.

Permissiveness will usually go a long way toward

winning the undying devotion of a boyfriend (or child, or patient, or employee, or almost anyone else with whom you are in a close relationship). But servility or obsequiousness will only go a long way toward winning (from another as well as yourself) contempt.

"But how," you may ask, "am I to remain permissive without simultaneously becoming spineless and ingratiating?" A good question. And the answer: define, in the most concrete sentences possible, the behavior of which (*a*) permissiveness and (*b*) obsequiousness consists; then make sure that you are saying to yourself and acting upon the first and not the second of these sentences.

Take, first, permissiveness. To be permissive toward someone who is acting unangelically toward you is to tell yourself and be thoroughly convinced of the following self-statements: "I don't like the way he's behaving, and I wish to hell he wouldn't behave that way. But he has a perfect right, as a human being, to behave any way *he* likes, even though *I* don't like it. Being fallible, he has a right to be wrong. Now, if I don't want him to behave the way he is acting, then I'd better calmly accept, temporarily, this way: objectively point out to him that I don't like it, even though I am temporarily accepting it; and try my best to induce him, by various means, to modify his way of behaving. If I can get him to change, fine. If I can't, tough. I *want* him to act better, but I don't *need* him to. And if, finally, he doesn't change enough to suit me, and I still don't like the way he is behaving, I can always leave him and look for some other person who normally behaves more to my way of liking."

Take, now, ingratiation. To be ingratiating to someone who is acting badly toward you is to tell yourself
and to be quite convinced of the following kinds of
self-sentences: "I don't like the way he's behaving,
and I wish to hell he wouldn't behave that way. But
I can't *stand* the thought of his not loving me or of
his leaving me. I *must* have his acceptance and approval. Therefore, no matter *what* he does, I simply
can't afford to tell him I dislike his behavior, and I
certainly can't try to get him to change it. Therefore,
I'd better bow low, lick his bottom, sacrifice myself in
every possible way, and thereby see that there is no
possibility whatever that he will ever leave crummy
little me, even if in the process I thoroughly lose his
and my own respect."

See the differences between these two sets of internalized sentences? The first set, leading to permissiveness, stresses the fact that you *want* your man's love
but you do not *need* it for your happiness or survival.
The second set, leading to ingratiation, insists that you
do need his approval, and that you are a total slob
without it. Or, stated differently, the first set of sentences states that you are primarily interested in being
true to *yourself*, and that therefore you will accept a
man in spite of his wrongdoings because *you* want to
have a good relationship with him and because *you*
have to gracefully lump reality if you are to live successfully in this world. The second set of sentences
declares that there essentially is no *you*—except insofar
as this you is a puny derivative of *him* and what *he*
thinks of you.

Permissiveness, then, springs from self-acceptance,

while ingratiation derives from self-hatred and utter dependency on others. And if you can manage to train yourself to be permissive toward an erring male, you not only will probably win him, but you will invariably win yourself, your own self-esteem. If you go to the other extreme and become obsequious, you probably will not win your man, even though he may choose to stay and lord it over you forever, and you will certainly lose your own soul. Permissiveness follows the pattern of firm kindness to others—which it is necessary to follow in the correct handling of children, neurotics, and fallible boyfriends. Ingratiation follows the pattern of *un*firm kindness—which almost invariably leads to poor results with the same kind of individuals. Unpermissiveness, or angry retaliation, follows the pattern of firm *un*kindness—which also produces, especially in a heterosexual love relationship, dismal consequences. (Compare, A. Ellis: *How to Live with a Neurotic.* New York: Crown, 1957). You put up your money and you takes your choice. Which is it to be?

Concern without worry

About half the males who come to see me to talk about problems with their sweethearts or wives complain that these women are not sufficiently concerned with their welfare, do not care if they work themselves to death, show no interest whatever in their business or professional affairs, and generally don't give a plugged pfennig for what they think or say or do. The other half complain that their female partners are much too concerned with their welfare, are always worrying about their working themselves to death, show too much interest in their business or professional affairs, and generally plague them with over-absorption in every little thing they think or say or do.

Does this prove that you just can't please those lousy hairy-chinned creatures, and that you might as well not try? Not necessarily. It often proves, instead, that women are supremely indifferent to some of the most vital concerns of the men they insist they madly love—or else that they are obsessively worried about every little thing their man does or does not, and keep plaguing him incessantly about this, that, and the kitchen sink.

There is, of course, a middle ground. It is possible for a girl to be duly concerned about her boyfriend's affairs without being unduly worried over every little step he takes. And men—especially, busy, bright men—do want their little women to be sincerely interested in their doings. They want to be able to talk about their work, from time to time, and not just relegate it to the "Oh, yes, that's the beastly sort of stuff that you unfortunately have to do for a living" class of thing. They want to have their mates ready and able to throw a fine dinner or cocktail party for their business associates, or put in a good word for them with the head of the laboratory, or help them talk out at home a problem that could well use ventilation before they worked it out at the office.

So standoffishness from your boyfriend's affairs won't exactly help. And it may well encourage him to seek, elsewhere, someone who is just as good in bed as you are—and more interested in his non-sexual doings as well. On the other hand, reminding your man, every few moments, that he really is in a terrible fix with his partner; or that he'd better sell that mining stock he has fast, before it goes down to next to nothing; or that if he gets drunk once more, yes, just once more, at Dean Smith's semiannual cocktail party for the faculty, he might just as well kiss his job, yes, kiss his job goodby and apply for a fine spot, and I mean a fine spot, on the Bowery right now, yes dammit right now; reminding your man of *this* kind of stuff is not likely to endear him too fondly to you, either.

As noted before in the case of permissiveness and ingratiation, the dividing line between sincere concern and avid anxiety can fairly easily be seen if you look at the kinds of internalized sentences that you are telling yourself to create both of these feelings. To be concerned about the man you love, you must be saying to yourself something along these lines:

"I wonder what kind of a day he's been having at the office today. I really would like to know, so that I can better appreciate his life and make myself a greater part of it. And maybe I might be able to help him with some of his problems, too—as I'd certainly like to do. Of course, he may not care to tell me, right now, how things actually have been going today. Maybe he's too tired; or just doesn't feel like talking about it; or has had enough of this kind of thing for one day and would just like to relax and talk about something else. O.K.: If so, I'll soon find out and switch to another topic. I don't *have* to talk to him about his work, even though I'd really like to. But why not try? What have I got to lose? If he's eager to talk, we'll both enjoy it; and if he's not, we can easily switch to another topic. Anyway, let's try it and see."

To be over-concerned, or worried sick, or naggingly anxious (and anxiously nagging!) in regard to the man you most care for, you have to be telling yourself sentences such as these: "God! he looks tired. I'll bet that he had a simply *terrible* day at the office. And he probably feels just *horrible* about it. Now, let's see what I can do to help him. I've *got* to help him. I can't *stand* his being so upset as he seems to be.

"And if I can't help him with his worst problems, then what good am I to him at all? And what's the purpose of my being married to him, or even going on in this dreadful life? Oh, I *must*, I just *must* help take that load off his back. I'm sure he must want me to. He *couldn't* not want me to. And if he doesn't talk to me about it, as he sometimes doesn't when he's all upset like this, I just won't be able to take it again. I just *won't*. That'll really be the end between us. One more rebuff, like the cruel one he gave me when I tried to be so helpful to him last week, and I'll just about *crack*. That'll be it. The end. I just won't be able to stand it!"

Obviously, if we examine these two sets of sentences, we can see the clear-cut differences between them. The concerned woman *wants* to help her man, but can find other fish to fry if he, for any reason, doesn't at the moment go along with her wanting. The worried woman *needs* to help her man, and can find no other fish, flesh, nor foul for her cooking pot in case he wants to solve his problems by himself.

The concerned woman really accepts herself, and

therefore, at any given time, does not *have* to be fully accepted and approved by her mate. The worried woman does not really like or respect herself and therefore *has* to devote herself to her mate's cause if she is to view herself as being in the least "worthwhile." Where the concerned girl is preferentially *motivated*, the worried one is compulsively *driven*. Not only, then, is the latter sick, but the chances are enormously high that she will, by her driven behavior, sicken the relationship she has with the man she wants most to be with in life.

The moral is as obvious here as it is in the various other points we have raised in this chapter. Want what you want, and even at times want what you want when you want it. But in your relations with yourself and the man of your dreams, don't make the sad mistake of unconsciously or consciously transmuting your wants into needs. Babies (who would of course die without external care and succoring) need; healthy adults *need* very little (except for food, clothing, and shelter, without which they might actually die) but have many legitimate wants or preferences.

Go after, then, what you want. Be assertive—express the things you want to say, do the things you want to do. Have guts—find out what your sex-love preferences really are (and not what your mother and your maiden aunts *think* they ought to be) and let your man frankly know what they are. Be competent—discover what *you* think is the efficient way of doing things and don't try to act as if you haven't got anything in your head but Hollywood scripts. Be permissive—try to get the results you *want* to get from your chosen male, but accept (at least temporarily) without tears the results that you could well live without. Be concerned—endeavor, if you can, to help your mate with his life problems, but do not think that you have to worry yourself sick if he refuses your help or if he fails in spite of it.

Will you, if you closely follow all the do's and don'ts which we have so far outlined in the first two chapters of this book, be absolutely sure of winning and keeping the kind of strong, sane, highly cerebral kind of man that you want? You know perfectly well you won't be. But you will be sur*er* of getting your heart's desire than if you follow the usual "ladylike" ways. And whatever the ultimate outcome, even if it be the relatively sorry state of eternal spinsterhood, *you* will be a much saner and happier person to live with. By, of, for, and with—if necessary—yourself.

Chapter 3

How to Prevent Yourself from Being in
Desperate Need of a Man

Probably the worst possible way to win the man of
your choice is to be in desperate need of having him—
or of having any man whatever. For as soon as you
are convinced that you *must* have someone, that your
life and well-being literally depend on your winning
the esteem of this person, you are most likely to do
all the wrong things to get him.

The desperate need to be loved—or to be married,
or to have children, or to have grandchildren—is a
subheading under the main topic of worthlessness.
For individuals who *need* love, instead of merely *wanting* it strongly, fairly obviously are saying to themselves something along these lines: "I not only want
to be accepted and approved by the man of my choice;
but if I am not, then life cannot possibly hold any joys
for me, since I am really a thoroughly worthless person, in my own right, and I can only acquire some
measure of worth *through* loving another person and
having him, in turn, recognize that I am lovable."

The need to be loved, in other words, is basically
a need to prove one's own worth; and is a function of
basic insecurity and anxiety. In order for you to prevent
yourself from being desperately in need of a man,

you must tackle this underlying insecurity. Let us see, in this chapter, some of the main methods by which this can be done.

What makes you anxious

The main difference between practically all so-called normal and neurotic behavior is (as we have been noting from the start of this book) the difference between wanting or preferring something and needing or demanding it. The more you *demand* from life, and thereby imagine that you cannot possibly live happily without, the more likely you are, of course, not to be able to achieve your demands. And not only will their non-achievement lead to enormous disappointment and disillusionment—frequently accompanied by horrible feelings of depression and inadequacy—but the mere thought that you *may* not get what you are utterly certain that you need will inevitably lead to hypertension and anxiety.

Most of the patients I see in psychotherapy are over-anxious, quite insecure individuals who feel that they simply must be loved and approved by others, particularly their boyfriends or their husbands, or else they might as well end it all. Miriam S. is a good case in point. Miriam kept coming around to her group therapy sessions every week and often complained about how unloved she was, and how she never had the energy to do practically anything she wanted to do in life, largely because she kept depressedly ruminating about how none of the boys she was interested in ever really liked her, and how even her girlfriends were not completely on her side.

One day Miriam came in more upset than usual. The night before, she had gone to a movie just to pass the time, and had seen a rather boring science-fiction film, in the course of which some dreadful technicolored monsters kept attacking the inhabitants of the earth. She was rather upset while watching the film, but became even more frightened when she started to notice after returning home that the same kind of monsters she had seen in the film—pink and green and purple and whatnot—seemed to be lurking in the dark corners of her room, under the bed, in the recesses of her closets, etc. To say the least, she quickly became panicked.

Hardly knowing what to do about this dreadful situation, Miriam did what she normally did when confronted with any serious difficulty: she immediately called the latest of her long line of boyfriends and begged him to come over to help her drive away the monsters. Normally, he would have been willing enough to come to her rescue, but it just happened that he was recovering from a severe cold that day and did not want to risk going out in the icy streets.

Besides (although he did not overly stress this point) Miriam *had* called him over to her place only a week previously, because she had heard some noises which she attributed to rats—and which later turned out to be the knocking of her radiator pipes. And he had probably got his bad cold by coming over to see her that time. So this time he flatly refused to budge. She could if she wished, he said, come over to stay at his place (which was a long subway ride away) until she became sufficiently unafraid to return to her own; but come to her apartment that night he definitely would not.

Miriam was crushed by his refusal. Immediately, she retaliated with accusations of his never having really loved her very much, and his certainly not giving a damn for her now, and what good was a guy to a girl, anyway, when he couldn't go a little out of his way in her dire hour of need? He still refused to budge from his warm bed. Whereupon Miriam told him that she never wanted to see him again, gulped down several sleeping pills, and soon blacked out the monsters in a sleep that was so deep and prolonged that she never got to work the next day.

That evening, when she came to group therapy, she was not only still upset about the monsters she had been seeing, but was even more disturbed about the way her boyfriend had treated her, and the angry manner in which she had told him off and broken up their relationship.

The group was not particularly sympathetic. "Look," said Sandra (who herself was so direly in need of the love of others that she could easily recognize it in Miriam), "let's suppose that your boyfriend, when you called him to come chase away your monsters, had actually come over. What could he have done for you?"

"Yes," asked Lionel (who had been going with his own girl for several years now, without being able to decide whether to marry her or leave her), "what *would* he have done for you if he had come over?"

"Oh," said Miriam. "He would have chased away those monsters."

"He would. . . ?"

"How would he. . . ?"

"What do you mean he would. . . ?"

Questions and exclamations came from all sides of the room: all of them skeptical, all of them indicating that Miriam was feeding herself nonsense.

"Well," said Miriam, somewhat abashed, "why wouldn't he? After all, he was able to help me in things like that before."

"Crap!" said Sandra.

"Yes, pure crap!" echoed Lionel, in an even more definite, almost angry tone.

"What do you mean?" asked Miriam, somewhat bewildered.

"Can't you see?" asked Claire (one of the saner and less love-needful members of the group). "Can't you see that your boyfriend, or anyone else for that matter, really can't do *anything* for you like you're asking?"

Miriam, still bewildered, obviously could not see.

"Let's put it this way," said Sandra. "You wanted your boyfriend to come over to chase away *your* monsters—right?"

"Yes," answered Miriam. "If he came over, he'd show that he loved me. And that sort of love would chase away my monsters."

"*It,* the love, *it* would chase away your monsters?" Sandra persisted. "But how could it? They're *your* monsters—and *you,* of course, made them up. How, then, can anything outside you, such as your boyfriend's love, do something to remove what's *in* you. Can't you see that because *you* made up the monsters,

71

you're the only one, really, who can do anything about them, who can possibly remove them?"

"You mean," said Miriam, who was really a bright girl, and who had some familiarity from previous group sessions with the ideas Sandra and the others were presenting, "that the monsters really aren't there? I made them up? And if *I* make them up, then *I'm* the only one who can remove them? And my boy-friend's love, or anything like that, can't really do anything for me? Is that what you mean?"

"Exactly!" said Claire. "That's what we all seem to be trying to tell you. Nothing that you make up, in your own head, can be changed except by something else that you do in that same head. What anyone else, such as your boyfriend, does, is completely irrelevant—except in so far as you *make* it relevant by, again, what goes on in your own head."

"Only *I* can control my monsters, then."

"Right!" I, as the therapist who was leading the group, finally joined in. "Just as the members of the group have been telling you, only *you* can make up monsters—and only *you* can make them vanish again. And the bitter irony here is that you, and millions of people like you, keep going to such ridiculous lengths both to make up and then to destroy, but unfortunately only very temporarily to destroy, the monsters of your own making."

"Do you mean," asked still another group member, Jack, who up to this time had been thoughtfully silent, "that Miriam, like so many of the rest of us in the group, keeps going to great lengths to make up one set of monsters, on the one hand, and then to make up still another set to sort of cancel out the first set? And that she then goes on that way practically forever?"

"That's precisely it," I replied. "Just to put it a little differently: you first go to the movies, Miriam, see a lovely set of ready-made monsters there, and decide—unconsciously, no doubt, but still quite definitely—to use them for your own nefarious purposes. So, later that night, you bring out these ready-made monsters and start to give yourself a real hard time with them. Then, because you are having a hard time of it, you think about a possible antidote, and you quickly and rather cleverly concoct an anti-monster, a sort of anti-missile missile.

"This anti-monster you call 'love' or 'acceptance' or 'help for my hour of need.' Normally, now, you find that this anti-monster works beautifully, at least temporarily, to chase away the horrible monsters. You needlessly upset yourself, that is; then you look for and find some love and approval, particularly from your current boyfriend; and lo and behold! you are, at least for the nonce, no longer upset.

"In fact, after awhile you come to derive such great satisfaction from unupsetting yourself when once you have knocked yourself off your own pins, that you even sometimes get in the habit of dreaming up the monsters deliberately, with the thought in the back of your mind that you then will have an excellent excuse to dream up and use, for that day at least, the great anti-monster, Love. That, is probably what happened to you last night. You had nothing to do, wanted to be with your boyfriend, for some reason decided not to try to see him—"

"—I had seen him until very late at his place the day before," Miriam interjected.

"All right: you had seen him until very late the day before, and felt that it wouldn't be right to go see him again; or maybe, knowing he had a cold and couldn't very well come to see you, you wanted to see him but didn't want to go to the trouble of taking a subway ride to his place. Anyway, for some reason you at first decided not to try to see him again. So, for lack of anything better to do, you went to see the movie.

"The movie, perhaps, scared you a little, since you do find such kind of things generally scary. But then, quite unconsciously, you probably thought to yourself: 'Ah, maybe I can use this scariness to some purpose. Maybe I can somehow employ it to get what I really want tonight—the presence of my boyfriend.' With this thought in mind, you managed to bring on the monsters, when you got home; and then, of course, it was most logical for you to call your boyfriend and to plead with him to come over. Usually, as I said before, this would have worked very well: and even though you paid a kind of penalty—scaring yourself by your own monsters —you would have got what you most want, nay demand, out of life: love, approval, acceptance."

"Yes, I think I even thought of that when I was calling my boyfriend," said Miriam. "I sort of knew that I could handle the monsters myself. But I didn't *want* to do so. I wanted *him* to come drive them away for me."

"Yes," I continued. "That's the way it often becomes —or, rather, the way we *make* it become. But the real irony is, of course, that there aren't any monsters *or* anti-monsters. We make up *both* of them. In your case,

74

as you perfectly well know—since you are not *that* crazy!—the original monsters you saw do not exist. *You* (with the help of the film-makers) dreamed them up. But what you do not see very clearly is that the anti-monsters do not exist either. You make *them* up, too. Not love and acceptance themselves—you don't create them, since they do exist in their own right. But the power that they have over you: that's what you make up. It's pleasant being loved and accepted, particularly when you are in trouble. But instead of just feeling pleasant when you are accepted, you feel positively, absolutely *great*—by which you really mean no longer worthless, but a genuinely worthwhile person."

"Oh, I do, I do!" interjected Miriam.

"Yes—unfortunately you do. From a louse of the lowest sort you lift yourself, when you feel accepted or loved, to temporary heights of power and worth. And *that* is your anti-monster: your *belief* that you cannot truly like yourself and enjoy life unless you are thoroughly approved by others who are important to you. That belief is what drives you to try to coax your boyfriend out of his sickbed, and that even, as I said before, unconsciously drives you to make up some of your monsters at the start."

"And it's all so unnecessary!" exclaimed Claire. "You dream up the monsters, in the first place, and then you concoct the anti-monsters, in the second place, to drive away your original bad dreams. Wouldn't it be much simpler, more efficient, and infinitely less nerve-wracking if you recognized that both the anti-monsters and the monsters are your *own* creations, and that you can live very well without *both* of them?"

"Yes," chimed in Lionel again. "Otherwise, you'll be

riding on the sick merry-go-round, like most of us do, all your life, imagining dreadful things, that really don't exist, and then imagining pleasant, love-filled things to chase away the imagined dreadful ones. What a waste! Don't you see that you can do without *both* these kinds of nonsense?"

"Yes," said Miriam, very thoughtfully, wrinkling her brow and curling up her nose in a serious effort to comprehend what the members of the group were driving at. "I think I'm beginning to see it, or at least a little of it, now."

"And what will you do to keep seeing it clearer?" asked Claire.

"I'll keep working at it," Miriam answered, with some real conviction.

"Fine!"

"Good!"

"Great!" several members of the group exclaimed.

And Miriam did continue to work on her problem of needing rather than just wanting to be loved and accepted, and kept making significant progress on it.

Miriam's problem is a common and crucial one for most people who want to be accepted by a member of the other sex. Instead of merely preferring the responsiveness of this or that partner, they convince themselves that they absolutely need it and will presumably die without it. This is because they artificially and arbitrarily connect their chosen one's approval with their own feelings of worth: because they *define* themselves as worthless if he does not truly, dearly, and eternally love them.

If, then, you find that you do not merely want a man in your life, but that you desperately, violently *need* one, this is what you are almost certainly doing: depreciating yourself as a person, insisting that in, of, for, and by yourself you are a piece of garbage, and demanding that you become attached to a fine, stalwart male who will deodorize your stench, camouflage your intrinsic ineptness, and make you (at least while you are in his presence and basking in his acceptance) worthwhile. In other words: you are creating, out of whole cloth, a horrible monster—*you*—and you are then dreaming up a beauteous anti-monster—*him*—to save you from your imagined fate worse than death.

The only good answer to this self-constructed dilemma is obvious to devise but difficult to effect. You must *re*define yourself as a person, persistently and vigorously *challenge* the idiotic notion that you are only good when you are accepted and approved, and see yourself as worthy of living and capable of enjoying yourself *whether or not* you are loved by some beloved, *whether or not* you achieve what you would most like to achieve in life, *whether or not* you are generally acknowledged to be a wondrous, superexcellent woman.

You must, in other words, accept yourself and define yourself as worthwhile simply because you're *alive*, because you *exist*—and because, as long as you're alive and existing, there must always be *some* way in which you can enjoy living, *some* kind of happiness that you can create for yourself. If, while being alive and while finding enjoyable interests for yourself, you can manage to be successful, achieving, approved, or loved, that is fine: for by such means you can often be happier than you would otherwise be.

However *desirable* achievement and approval may

be, you do not *need* them for a happy existence; and, especially, you definitely do not need any *specific* kind of achievement or the love of a *particular* person. If you *think* you need to excel in a certain way or be adored by a given individual, then you will tend to be desperately depressed when you fail to get what you "need." Not, of course, because you don't get it, but because you *think* that you must have it.

Realistically reduce or eliminate your "needs," then. Sanely re-transform them to the more legitimate wants out of which, with a vengeance, you unconstructively created them. So you *want* to get married, have children, live for fifty years with a strong and bright man of your choosing. Fine! But you don't *have* to, you don't *need* to.

If the worst comes to the worst, you may never marry. Or may marry the man who is *not* your first choice. Or may never have children when you do marry. Tough! You will then be not *as* happy as you would ideally like to be. But you will not necessarily, under such relatively regrettable circumstances, be utterly miserable either. Unless you *insist* on so being.

Overcoming fear of what people think

Most of the desperate need to be loved and married —which so ironically is the greatest saboteur of loving and marrying that exists in our society—stems from the terrible fear of what other people would think of you if you were not ideally doted upon and mated. What, for example, would your parents think if you never presented them with the right kind of husband and several perfect grandchildren? What would your girlfriends think if they knew that you spent most Saturday evenings alone? What would the world think if it knew that you were so shy and graceless that no outstanding man would ever dream of becoming deeply involved with you?

Let them think!

Life, as anyone who is objective can quickly see, surely has enough *real* hassles without our creating half a billion false ones that infinitely multiply and complicate the real ones. Making a living, for example, can be a downright nuisance; and keeping physically healthy; and finding, among all the men who may be attracted to you, a single one who, after a few weeks of intimacy, doesn't bore you to death.

Life also has some very difficult people in it whom you are going to have to please, in many instances, whether you care to or not. Like, for instance, your curmudgeon of a boss; or the alcoholic doorman who misdirects your guests; or the cop on the beat who suspects that a goodlooking girl like you, with so many prosperous-appearing men friends, must surely be a whore.

O.K.: so life is rough. And for many practical reasons you often *have* to be nice to people you wish would quickly drop dead. But precisely because this is true it seems thoroughly idiotic for you to kowtow endlessly to strangers and acquaintances to whom you *don't* have to be overly civil, and who actually have little or no effect on your life.

Take, by way of illustration, your neighbors. Suppose they *don't* like the fact that your boyfriend sometimes stays over in your apartment all night; and suppose they *do* think you're a hopeless jerk, seeing that

79

you're away past twenty-five and are still far from married. Probably, having their own (self-created!) problems, they don't even give you and your boyfriend or you and your spinsterhood a single thought more than once a year. But let us suppose the worst: let us suppose that they do (as, of course, grandiosely, you *think* they do) cogitate about you and your ways forty-four times each day, and that they always come up with the same negative evaluation: "My! what a horrible trollop (or bitch, or nincompoop, or ugly old hen) she is! How can anyone stand her? No wonder she's still unmarried."

Well? Suppose they *do*. Are they going, these neighbors, by their under-the-skull or overtly-outspoken estimations of you, literally to skin you alive? To rape you? To burn down your apartment? To kill you dead dead dead?

And your parents? And your relatives? And your girlfriends? And your associates at work? Are any of them, assuming that they watch your every move and criticize your every manhunting effort, going to beat you with a whip? Twist your arms out of their sockets? Fry you in the electric chair? Come, now: let's be honest. *Are* they?

"Well, no," you reply. "I know that they're not going to hurt me or kill me, at least not physically. But what about the *mental* anguish they cause me when they look at me and talk to me disapprovingly?"

Well, what about it? Or, more precisely: anguish that *they* cause you? *What* anguish?

"Oh, you know, the anguish I feel when I know that they think I'm wrong, and when I know that they're blaming me severely for being wrong."

Oh, *that!* That crap.

"Crap? What do you mean, crap? I certainly *feel* it!"

Yes, unfortunately you certainly do. And it is anguish, real, live anguish that you feel. But how do *they* make you feel it?

"Well, uh, by criticizing me. By telling me that I'm doing the wrong things, and am just no damned good for doing these things."

That's right. That's just what they tell you. You're doing what in their eyes is actually wrong; and you are a double-dyed, hopeless no-goodnik for doing it.

"Well, isn't *that* sufficient cause for me to feel anguish?"

No, not at all. That is only a sufficient cause for you to ask yourself: "Let me see, now. Maybe they're right. Maybe I am wrong. *Am I?*"

"And if I *am?*"

If you are, then you obviously should go about changing your ways and trying to be less wrong in the future. But that's not the point in regard to what we're talking about at the moment. We're talking about—remember —their thinking you wrong for letting your boyfriend stay all night, and their thinking you criminal for reaching the horribly late age of the mid-twenties and still being unmarried. Honestly, now: do *you* think you're wrong about those kinds of things?

"No. I'm sure I don't. I have a perfect right, the way I live, to let whomever I want to stay over all night. And I guess I have a perfect right, too, to be over twenty-five and unmarried. What am I even saying 'I guess' for? Of course I do!"

That's what I thought you were thinking. *When* you actually bother to think for yourself. Now back to our

81

main point: considering that you really don't think you're wrong about this behavior that your relatives, friends, and countrywomen are blaming you for, and considering that they are highly unlikely to attack you physically, to throw you out of a job, or to force you to starve to death because you are engaging in acts which they deplore, how can these people possibly cause you the anguish which you say they are creating by their disapproval? By what magic, may I ask, are you managing to connect *their* criticism with *your* feelings of anguish?

"Oh, I see now what you're getting at. You mean that if I don't take their negative words and gestures too seriously, and I don't *use* their disapproval to rack my own mind with, there is nothing they can actually do to hurt me. I am therefore really, by taking their barbs seriously, hurting myself."

Precisely! That's the way it always is. While sticks and stones, as the old nursery rhyme truly sayeth, can break your bones, names may only hurt you if you *let* them hurt: if you yourself sharpen them up, give them poisoned barbs, and stick them into your own breast. If you live your life according to what I call the A-B-C method of personality development, instead of the A-C method which you now employ, you need never get hurt—or, rather, hurt yourself—by being called names; and then you can calmly go about your business of manhunting, or anything else, with maximum security and effectiveness.

"What is the A-B-C method of personality development?"

Simply the acknowledgment of what the Roman philosopher, Epictetus, pointed out some two thousand

82

years ago: that it is never the event, A, which makes us mentally or emotionally upset at point C; rather, it is the nonsense, B, which we tell ourselves about A.

"You mean that it is not people criticizing me, at point A, which makes me miserable at C; but my telling myself, at B, 'Oh, my God! I can't stand their criticism,' or something like that, which really upsets me at C?"

Correct! Whenever you get hurt, depressed, anxious, angry, guilty, or otherwise emotionally disturbed at point C, it is not what someone else did to you at point A that caused you to be disturbed, but your idiotic, senseless, illogical *interpretation* of A that causes you your discomfort at C.

"But why do you call my interpretation 'idiotic, senseless, and illogical'?"

Because it *is*. Otherwise, if it were a sensible interpretation, you would never get emotionally upset at point C. For what you are essentially saying, at point B, when you hurt yourself at point C, is a groundless sentence like "I can't *stand* his criticism of me!" when you really mean that you don't *like* it but you definitely *can* stand it—if you stop telling yourself that you can't.

Or else you are saying to yourself, at point B, an irrational sentence like "He is horribly hurting me with his critical words!" when you really mean that he may be *trying* to hurt you verbally, but that he cannot possibly do so—unless *you*, by taking these words overseriously (by convincing yourself, that is, that you are a worthless slob if his criticisms of you happen to include some truth), destroy yourself with them. So on two major counts, your inner interpretations, or internalized sentences, at point B are nonsense: first, because they just do not make any logical sense, but are a string of non sequiturs; and second, because they cause you needless pain, where other sentences, said under the same circumstances, would leave you, at most, regretful and frustrated, but not horribly pained.

"Other sentences such as what?"

Such as: "He criticized me severely for what I did. I surely don't like his criticism, and wish he were not so hard on me. But it *is* only criticism; and therefore I can easily stand it." These sentences would result in regret or disappointment, but never severe pain, hurt, depression.

"And what kind of sentences could I tell myself that would result in simple frustration or annoyance rather than anguish and upset?"

Sentences such as these: "I wish I could win him, since he seems to be a valuable man to have. But, from his non-acceptance of me, it looks like I can't. Too bad! —yes, it's really too bad. But I'll live. And there will be others."

"So, according to your way of looking at things, I *never* have to feel terribly hurt—if I never take other people too seriously and don't think that their low estimation of me means that I have to deprecate myself?"

Right. You never have to feel terribly hurt, upset, shaken, despairing, or anxious. You never have to be in desperate need of any man you want. And thereby, in all probability, you will immensely raise your chances of winning one of those whom you do want.

"Sounds easy. When can I start to use your A-B-C system of personality development? I sure can use it fast!"

84

It sounds easy, but it isn't. It takes much work and practice: much *stopping and thinking,* instead of unthinkingly accepting the irrational premises that you now believe, at point C, and that you keep belaboring your life with. But it can be done. And you can start immediately. In fact, seeing the dire love straits you're usually in, you'd better!

Chapter 4

How to Become Assertive Without Being Aggressive

Assuming that you are not in desperate need of a man, and that you can settle back more leisurely to find one and to win him, one of your main steps (as we briefly mentioned in the first two chapters of this book) is to show him, and yourself, that you can be healthfully assertive without being angrily aggressive. We shall consider some techniques for managing this fortunate state of being.

Overcoming hostility

Anger is the root of almost all evil in love. "A soft word turneth away wrath," sayeth the Bible. And a harsh word turneth away love, sayeth the psychologist. Just keep being angry and carping with your beloved and, no matter how righteously-based your rage may be, it will soon shred your affectional relationship. But good!

Isn't anger often justified? Isn't righteous indignation perfectly proper? Isn't it sometimes appropriate to show how irate you are, in order to get things done well and to get what you want out of life?

No, never. N-e-v-e-r. Not, at least, with your beloved.

Even with children, servants, employees, and other underlings a show of red-hot anger is rarely justified.

Sure, it will often scare the living daylights out of them and get them to do things your way. But at what a cost! Children at whom you are angry will tend, while jumping to your verbal whip, to hate themselves forever. Servants will also jump—temporarily. They will then hate your guts and spend much of the rest of the time soldiering on the job. Employees likewise. And almost everyone else you can name.

When you do get the results you want to get from them by cursing your head off, you also invariably get other results that you very likely don't want at all: internalizing of your angry words, which makes the recipient feel utterly incompetent and worthless; or defensive externalizing of your angry words, so that their recipient somehow manages to feel that *you* were wrong in yelling at him, and that you're a no good skunk who doesn't deserve his cooperation or devotion.

With people with whom you are in love relationships, the situation is ten times worsened. Not only do they, like those with whom you are not so closely attached, hate you and/or themselves at the time when you are angry with them; but, far worse, your angry words keep taking a slow-burning, insidious effect far after your target person feels immediate self-denigration or after he returns hostility for you. For most kinds of enduring love are based primarily on trust. We keep loving another person not only because he is nice to us or because he has certain lovable traits, but because we unconsciously predict that he will *continue* to be nice to us, will *keep* having these traits.

Love, then, is most importantly *future*- as well as *present*-oriented. If, when you start falling in love with a man because he has beautiful features and a gorgeous build, you suddenly discover that he is a leper and that his physical beauty is shortly doomed, you will be surprised how quickly, in the great majority of instances, you will forget him as a serious love object.

So with anger and nagging. If you love a man for his sweet disposition and his unusually fine responsiveness to you, and then you begin noting that on many occasions he completely loses his temper, roundly excoriates you for the slightest mistakes you have made, and is at these times thoroughly incapable of sympathizing with you or understanding your side of things, how long do you think you are going to be able to maintain any high level of feeling for this man? Try as you may to forgive and forget, the cumulative effect of his steady nagging and backbiting is bound to sink in; and before you know it, you will find your love-filled thoughts turning in other directions, toward those who are less angry and more forgiving. Love begets love; and hate begets lovelessness.

What, then, is the answer? If hostility is the foe of amour, how are you going to stem the tides of your normal hatreds and preserve your loving relationship with the man you most want?

By, as we must keep repetitively advocating in this book, looking at, thinking about, challenging, and changing the internalized sentences of which your hostility essentially consists. For hostility, like all other sustained emotions, is not, as it at first blush seems to be, an instantaneous, automatic reaction to another's behavior; it is, rather, a swift reaction to your own philosophy *about* that behavior. It is not your boyfriend's *actions* which make you mad at him. No, it is your *beliefs* about his actions which really start you feeling that he is a cad and a numbskull, and treating him accordingly.

One of my patients, Marylou S., was a particularly good example of what in common parlance is called an angry bitch. And not without, in the eyes of her close friends and relatives, some reason. For her boyfriend, Robbie, with whom she had gone steadily for a year, was admittedly a difficult customer. He pedantically caught her up on every other sentence she uttered, and showed her that she was not as correct as she thought she was. He insisted that she subscribe to all the rules of his fundamentalist church group. And he himself, after exacting the highest possible standards of conduct from her, was hardly angelic. In fact, he regularly got drunk every other week or so, and raised the roof for a couple of days before he sobered up again.

Feeling so unjustly penned in by Robbie, Marylou took excellent advantage of his own lapses from sobriety and excoriated him unmercifully, both privately and publicly, whenever he lapsed from grace. "You!" she would scream at him. "You, who are so high and mighty about what I and what others should do. Look, just look, at what you did now! Totally wrecked the car, this time, so that it's only good for the junk heap. And hardly a half of it paid up, too! Oh, you big plaster saint! Telling other people what to do—hah!" And on and on like this she would go.

"Why bother to screech at him like that?" I would quietly ask Marylou, whenever she came for another session of violent complaining. "Why not, if he's as bad as you say he is, calmly leave him forever, and let it go at that?"

"What!" she would scream, almost as if *I* were Robbie and *I* had done her in again. "After all that time, a full year out of my life, that I've spent with that no-good louse? Why should I leave him? And how would *that* get me married, anyway?"

"It might not get you married," I replied. "But it would get you a little peace of mind. Wouldn't you rather be happy than married?"

Apparently she wouldn't. Or, more to the point, she was determined to be happy *and* married; and if that rat, Robbie, thought he was going to prevent her from achieving this blissful state, well he just had better get an entirely new thought. For he wasn't going to get away with this one!

I finally calmed Marylou down a bit—mainly by convincing her that just one more heated fight between her and Robbie would undoubtedly do the trick. Either he'd get drunk, after their fight, and really kill her or himself this time; or he'd just go off, perhaps even to another town, and never return again. Is *that* what she truly wanted, I rhetorically demanded: his or her sudden demise or Robbie's point-of-no-return leave-taking? No, she replied, she didn't; but what could she possibly do to *stop* haranguing and fighting with an impossible (though at times admittedly lovable) son-ofagun like that?

"Do you really want to stop being terribly angry toward Robbie?" I asked.

"Yes," said Marylou, "I think I finally do. I've been thinking over what you've been telling me during these last few weeks, and I have to admit you're right. Fighting with Robbie isn't going to change him a bit—except

91

for the worse. And it's got, as you predicted it would, so that it's doing me in, too. My insides have been bouncing around like a basketball for the last month and it's got so that I don't enjoy eating any more—me, who used to be the plate-licker of my entire family! I guess I've had it. Either I stop being angry all the time or I'm going to have a real breakdown. I think I see that now."

"Fine," I said. "Now let's see if we can get you to see just one more thing. And that is that you *can* stop being angry. No matter what Robbie or anyone else does—including all the wrong things in the world—*you* are in your own saddle seat, and *you* don't have to anger yourself."

"Sounds great. But *how?*"

"By giving up your grandiosity."

"My *grandiosity?* Oh, my God: that's rich! I thought, as even you have agreed, that Robbie was the one of us with the grandiosity, the see-how-great-I-am-ness. *He's* the one that thinks he's God, and that I'm sort of one of his minor prophets, who should do his every bidding. Why, do you remember that time he—"

"Uh-uh," I interjected. "Temper, temper! You're all set to go off again now. Cut the crap! Sure I remember the time when Robbie did this and Robbie did that. And sure I agree that he's one of the rip-raringest, most grandiose bastards that ever resided this side of heaven. But that's not the point. However omnipotent Robbie may be trying to be, it's *your* grandiloquence we're talking about right now. Let's, please, get back to that —and let the reformation of Robbie, if it occurs at all, be the subject for *his* therapeutic agenda, not yours."

92

"You're right. Let's get back to me. Now what is this grandiloquence of mine that you say I have?"

"It's your basic stock in trade. Grandiloquence means empty, bombastic talk. And that's exactly what you're saying to yourself—empty, bombastic talk—most of the time. Not only you, but every person who, like you, makes herself terribly angry at poor people like Robbie."

"I know what you're trying to get me to see," said Marylou, "but I'm afraid that it still escapes me. You say that I, with what you now call my grandiosity, keep making myself angry. But doesn't Robbie, or anyone else like him, have *something* to do with it. *Would* I become—make myself, as you say—angry if he did *not* act the way he does?"

"No, you probably wouldn't. If Robbie were a perfect angel, and never did anything to annoy you, you probably would not make yourself angry—at *him*. But just as soon as someone else came along who wasn't such a blasted angel, or as soon as Robbie temporarily fell off his heavenly perch, you would then revert to angering yourself just as much as, perhaps even more than, you do now. For your bombastic philosophy is: "If the world is going perfectly the way I want it to go, then I can be calm and happy. But just as soon as it goes a little, or especially a lot, worse than I demand that it go, then it's totally unfair to me, this world; it *shouldn't* be the way it is; and I can't *help* being unhappy in such a horribly unjust, anti-me universe."

"And that philosophy, assuming that I really have it, is what you call grandiose?"

"*Isn't* it? It puts you right in the dead-center of the entire cosmos, and assumes that, if things don't go

93

exactly the way you want them to go, this entire cosmos is unfair and unethical: that it *shouldn't* be the way it is."

"But why *should* it? If I want things to be in a certain way, why *shouldn't* they be that way?"

"Why *should* they? Besides you're not really expressing any wants; instead, you're making *demands.* For every time you tell yourself that things *shouldn't* be the way they are—when, of course, they *are* the way they are—you are tacitly demanding that they not be."

"But isn't it true that *some* things shouldn't be the way they are—like murder and theft, for example?"

"No. It's true that it would be lovely if murder and theft didn't exist. But that hardly proves that they *shouldn't*. All *shoulds, oughts,* and *musts* are absolutistic, perfectionistic demands on life and the universe. Behind them there is the assumption that because *I* don't want a thing so, it *shouldn't* be; and the whole cosmos, including any god that may exist in it, is centered around me, sees that what *I* think is right actually is right, and arranges things so that everyone else will agree that what I think is right and will set about acting in the manner that I want them to act."

"Yes, but don't many other people, besides myself, think that it is right to be honest and not to commit murders?"

"Sure, many of them do. But many others, also, don't. There is never one hundred per cent agreement on what is right and what is wrong; and even if there were, how long would it last? All *shoulds, oughts,* and *musts,* however, assume that there is such one hundred per cent agreement—and they assume, moreover, that the universe and its various gods all stand ready to back up that agreement."

"In other words, when I say that my boyfriend *shouldn't* behave the way he does, I am really saying, according to the way you put it, that every single person in the universe would agree with me that he shouldn't act that way, and that the universe itself, well, wouldn't *allow* him to act any differently, and would fall apart in, uh, complete disorder if he did do what I and it and everyone feels that he *shouldn't* do."

"You've put it unusually well. That's just what your —and everyone else's—*shouldn't* means: that anyone who disobeys that *shouldn't* is indubitably, *absolutely* wrong; and that he is disrupting the perfect, invariant order of the world and all the things in it by doing what he supposedly *shouldn't*. While, on the other hand, if you say that your boyfriend or anyone else whom you think is mistaken is doing what you and most other people consider to be wrong and that it would be better for you, these other people, and even for himself if he changed his behavior, then you are stating an opinion rather than an absolute dogma, and there is at least a good chance that your opinion is correct, and that you may be able to induce your boyfriend to follow it."

"Now I'm beginning to see. I show my grandiosity, whenever I become angry, because my anger really means that I am utterly convinced that the person I am angry toward *shouldn't* be the way he is, when what I really mean is that there is an excellent likelihood, for both his and my sake, that it would be better if he were otherwise. But, by being angry, I blow up

95

that likelihood into an absolute certainty, and there really *is* no such certainty in the world, and I am grandiose for believing, for foolishly convincing myself, that there is."

"You've hit it right on the nose again. All anger is basically a demand for certainty. It not only insists that the individual at whom you are angry *must* behave differently, for otherwise he puts an element of chance into a universe that cannot possibly tolerate such an element; but it also insists that you, who are angrily demanding this of him, cannot possibly thrive in a world where there is uncertainty and probability rather than absolute certitude. Anger, in other words, is a subtle confession of your own weakness and your own seeking for thorough assurance—which, of course, can never really exist."

"The angrier I get, the more bigoted I really am—for I refuse to let Robbie make the mistakes that he's certain to make anyway."

"Yes, as I pointed out several years ago, in my book *Sex Without Guilt,* anger—or blaming others for being the way they are—essentially is a form of fascism. For just as Hitler and Mussolini blamed people for having traits they personally abhorred—such as being Jewish or being Negro—the angry individual is blaming others for having traits that *he* personally does not like. And although it is perfectly proper to *dislike* others for various reasons, it is hardly proper to blame them, and think that they should be annihilated, for having the traits you dislike."

"My anger at Robbie, then, is grandiose because I am *demanding* that he be the way I would *like* him to be?"

"Correct. You are insisting that because you *want* him to change—which is quite legitimate—he *must* do so. Once you stop that grandiose insistence, then he may listen to you more open-mindedly; and there is a greater chance that he actually will change. But if he doesn't—tough! You still, for your own good and the sake of your own blood pressure, have to accept Robbie and the world the way they are—even when you don't *like* them that way."

"I see."

And Marylou did see. She almost immediately began to act more acceptingly with Robbie: to show him that she *wanted* him to change but that she didn't *need* him to do so. As it happened, he didn't change very much; so that, finally, concluding that he was too emotionally disturbed, she broke off with him. But she managed to do so without seriously hurting either him or herself; and, as she said to me a few weeks later: "Things haven't turned out the way I wanted them to be with Robbie, and I regret that they haven't. But this has still been the finest experience, I think, of my life: accepting him the way he is without giving him or myself a terribly hard time. And even though things didn't work out with him, I am sure that, next time, there's a much better chance that they will work out with someone else—and someone who is inherently better suited for me. So I really am grateful for the chance to go through these last several weeks of trying in vain to help Robbie change. It hasn't worked; but *I've* worked. And that's by far the most important thing."

A year later, after she had unfrantically got into a re-lationship with another man, Marylou did marry, and has since had no reason to regret her choice. Moreover, what she learned from calmly (and not hysterically or guilt-ily) failing with Robbie has helped her greatly in her pre- and post-marital relations with her present hus-band. Once her dire need to have her man act exactly the way she thought he should act started vanishing, she was able to ungrandiosely accept herself and others more lovingly and to find more of what she wanted in life.

Raising your level of frustration tolerance

One of the very best ways to sabotage your romantic life is to be a spoiled brat or a cry-baby—or to have what we psychologists frequently call low frustration tolerance. For a girl who is unable to bear frustration will normally not only demand that she have exactly what she wants, but demand it precisely when she wants it—meaning, right now, pronto, immediately! And her unreasonable demands will quickly be communi-cated to the men she wants to win—who, if they are even moderately sane, will soon conclude: "She's a very nice girl, bright enough, sufficiently beautiful, and all that sort of thing. But who needs her kind of childishness? Who wants to live with *that?*"

Low frustration tolerance, moreover, is one of the chief sources of goading aggressiveness, as distinguished from healthy self-assertion. The self-assertive woman asks herself: "What do I truly *want* in life, and how can I go about getting it?" The obnoxiously aggressive woman asks: "What must I, right this very second, absolutely have? And how, by hook or crook, no matter how many toes I may have to step upon, can I immediately get it?"

If the self-assertive woman is temporarily blocked from getting what she desires, she tells herself: "Too bad. I can't get what I want right now. Let's see what I can do to get it later. Or let's see, if this is going to be impossible, how I can get along very well in life without getting this thing I want." The psychopathically aggressive woman tells herself, when she cannot quickly get her heart's desire: "How awful! I simply can't stand this frustration! I'll fix those people who are blocking me! I'll show them! Now let see how I can hurt them as much as possible, so that they'll simply *have* to give me this thing that I need."

Low frustration tolerance, then, leads to anger at the world and the people in it—including, often, one's best beloved.

Alice R. was a charming, vivacious girl of twenty-seven, who had been married at the age of eighteen and divorced two years later, mainly because, as she put it, she couldn't stand her "goddam selfish sonofabitch" husband. For the last seven years, before I started to see her for psychotherapy, she had gone with innumerable men, most of them quite eligible as husbands, and several of them more than willing to marry her. But they, too, were almost always found to be "too goddam selfish" or "too wrapped up in their work" or something like that; so that she always ended up by rejecting them. But she did, however, very much want to marry and to give her eight-year-old daughter a strong, kindly father.

"What do you mean," I asked Alice during one of

the early therapy sessions, "that all the men you meet are, as you put it, 'too goddam selfish'?"

"Oh, you know. They only think of their own pleasures or their own work. Never think of what *I* really want to do. Won't go out of their way to help me when I need them. You know."

"How often do you generally need them?" I asked. "From what you have told me, you're a pretty competent person in your own right, and do very well at the office, without feeling that anyone around there has to help you in your hour of need."

"Oh, that's different. That's the office. And you just *can't* expect people to help you much there. But in my social life it's quite another thing. I *am* a woman, don't forget. And women should be waited on in many little ways, shouldn't they? Otherwise, we all might as well be one sex and stay away from each other!"

"You mean that whenever you want something, even if you can easily get it yourself, some man should be around to wait on you and get it for you?"

"Well, no. I'm not as bad as *that!* But—well, take what happened the other evening, when I was seeing John. I wanted to go to dinner early, since I hadn't eaten much all day and I was practically starving. And he wanted to go to dinner, too, but he said that he really ought to make some calls first, some business calls that he just had to get through that night, and that if he waited to make them later he probably wouldn't be able to get the people. So he asked if he could use my phone, make the calls, and then we'd go to eat. I didn't like the idea, but I naturally said yes. Then—would you believe it?—he spent the next damned forty-five minutes on my phone, calling god

100

knows who, and leaving me there to twiddle my thumbs and practically starve to death until he had finished. Now, don't you call that terribly selfish? Do you think I should even consider marrying someone like *that?*"

"But he *did* have to make the calls, didn't he?" I asked. "He wasn't going out of his way to make unnecessary ones, just to keep you waiting, was he?"

"Oh, no. I guess he did have to make them. But for forty-five minutes! And me just about starving!"

"Now, look," I said. "Let's stop the nonsense! You were hungry, yes. So, probably, was he. But forty-five minutes longer to get around to eating wasn't going to cause your demise. And, if it was, you could have got *something* to nibble on before you actually went out to dinner. Now how is it that you always convince yourself, in cases like this, that you're absolutely starving, and will perish any moment, when you really mean that it's somewhat inconvenient for you not to eat immediately, but that you could damned well stand the inconvenience?"

"Are you trying to say that most of my hunger was actually put on—that I didn't really have to eat that quickly?"

"I'm not trying to say this; I'm saying it. And you know perfectly well that I'm right in saying it. Most—not all, but most—of your hunger *was* put on. Suppose, for example, that your boyfriend, instead of having to make those telephone calls, had brought you a beautiful new dress that night, and wanted you to wear it to dinner. And suppose that putting on the dress and its accessories would have taken you forty-five minutes, and that you'd therefore have to keep *him* waiting

101

before you went to dinner with him. Would you *then* have been 'starving' so violently that you couldn't possibly wait?"

"Well—well, no, I guess not."

"You *could*, under those circumstances, have waited a bit more patiently and gracefully?"

"Yes, I suppose I could."

"Well? Isn't it obvious, then, that it wasn't your hunger that got you all upset and angry about waiting, but your *attitude*? Isn't it clear that it wasn't the internalized sentence, 'My! my stomach's growling, I simply must eat,' but, rather, the sentences, 'That selfish sonofabitch! How could he make those telephone calls when I'm so hungry?'—isn't it clear that *these* latter sentences were the real ones that were making you so frustrated—and even so hungry?"

"You're saying, then, that I wasn't even actually *that* hungry, as I made myself out to be, but that both my hunger and my frustration were highly exaggerated by the angry sentences I kept telling myself."

"Yes, that's exactly what I'm saying. Not that you weren't hungry at all—for it's most likely that you were. And you really would have *liked* to eat quite soon. But, unfortunately, you translated that liking into a *demand* to eat immediately. And when your demand was not acceded to, you *then* convinced yourself how hungry you were, how you absolutely could not stand being frustrated, and what a horrible sonofabitch he was for not feeding you immediately."

"My very demand to eat made me much hungrier than I really was?"

"Yes. Isn't that so? Think about it, now. Isn't that what happened?"

102

"Hmm. You may well be right. In fact, now that you make me think about it, I do remember something, something that kind of proves that you *are* right."

"Oh?"

"Yes. It was a little before six when he came to call for me to take me to dinner, and I really was hungry. But I remember thinking to myself, right after he came: 'Good! Now we can eat. Let's see: if we go to the restaurant next door, we will probably be waited upon right away, and that will be fine. But I'm rather sick of that place, and the food's not really that good there. Why don't I suggest that we go to Mario's instead. It will take us fifteen minutes or twenty minutes until we're seated and served. But it's a much better place, and I think it's worth the wait.' "

"Ah! See! So you weren't exactly starving! And you could, by your own decision, afford to wait awhile to eat—when there was some good incentive to do so. But his telephone calls weren't just that good enough incentive for you. So you *insisted* to yourself that you were starving, and that he was a sonofabitch for keeping you waiting. Just as I thought!"

"Yes, I'll have to admit you're right."

"O.K.: but the point is not that I'm right, but that you're wrong. And not merely this time, since this is unimportant. But so many of those other times you've told me about. You want something from your boyfriend, such as to take you to dinner promptly. Then he balks, for some reason, and doesn't get you precisely what you want at the split-second that you want it. Then you give *yourself* a real pain in the neck by insisting that you *must have* what you want.

"Then, finally, you beat him unmercifully over the

103

head, and blame him interminably for not getting you
what you, by this time, are utterly convinced that you
must immediately have. By this kind of childish lack
of frustration tolerance, therefore, you are not only
frustrating *yourself* much more than you are *being*
frustrated by outside events; but you are also winding
up with hostility toward your, whomever he may be,
current boyfriend. No wonder you feel that all of
these boyfriends, including your ex-husband, have been
'too goddam selfish'!"

"I see what you mean. I'm seeing these men as
much more selfish than they actually are—because I
am making myself much more frustrated than I actually
need be. And my low frustration tolerance is getting in
the way of my accepting men more tolerantly and seeing them in a truer and more kindly light."

"Exactly."

"But what can I do about this, if this is so? How
can I lower my frustration, or raise my tolerance of
frustration?"

"Isn't it obvious, from what we have been saying,
how you can do this? Think about it for a moment.
How do you suppose you could increase your frustration tolerance?"

"Hmm. By—by, I guess, showing myself that I
don't have to have everything I want the very moment
that I want it. By convincing myself that I won't starve
to death, or otherwise die, if I don't get what I want in
the next half-second."

"Right. By changing your sentence, 'I absolutely,
positively must have what I want right now, this second!' to 'I wish I could have what I want right away,

104

but I can, if necessary, wait awhile, and even if I never get everything I want, it won't kill me.' "

"How about the sentence, 'I must have what I want right away, and if he doesn't give it to me, he's no damned good, and I hate him!' Mustn't I change that one, too?"

"By all means! For even if he *can* give you what you want right away, and even if for some reason he does *not* do so, he is not a louse. He is simply a man who is not giving you what you want. And your problem is to get him to change his mind and to give it to you. But calling him a louse or a skunk will hardly, in most instances, help him change his mind or give you what you want."

"How right you are! After I got angry at John, and made such a fuss for his making those calls for forty-five minutes, he threatened to leave entirely, and let me have dinner by myself. I had a job calming him down. And I guess we wasted another forty-five minutes arguing!"

"See? That's what usually happens. The more you demand that you must have your piece of taffy *right now*, the less you tend to get it right then—and sometimes ever to get it. So isn't it worth working on your low frustration tolerance?"

"I guess it is. And I certainly have a lot of work to do in that connection!"

It would be nice to report that Alice immediately did begin to buckle down to work against her own low frustration tolerance and her consequent anger at her boyfriend, but unfortunately she didn't. She *saw* the problem clearly, but refused to do much about

105

solving it. She calmed herself down sufficiently to get along better with John, and soon after to marry him. But she quit psychotherapy long before she had actually worked through her underlying carping against frustration and she has not, to my knowledge, had a very smooth marital relationship. Too bad; but that is *her* problem.

Your problem, if your level of frustration tolerance is low, is to do the work that Alice mainly refused to do: namely, clearly to see that you are upsetting yourself when things go badly, and then to *work against* this kind of self-upsetment by persistently observing your own angry sentences and challenging and questioning them most vigorously until you begin to replace them with more reasonable (but still realistic) assessments of what is happening to you.

You must not try to *like* grim reality (for there is no reason why you should like it), but gracefully to lump it when there is little or nothing that you can do to change it. And you must not try to cheer when your male friends are inconsiderate, unreliable, or cold, but to refrain from thinking of them as utter bastards for being the unfortunate way that they are.

If you can work against—and continue, to some degree for the rest of your life working against—your own hostility and your own low frustration tolerance, as has been emphasized in this chapter, you again will have no absolute certainty that your marital Dream Boat will dock. Maybe it never will. But at least your *chances* of getting it into port will be distinctly enhanced. And your chances of being, yourself, a happier, less bitter and depressed human being will be infinitely better.

Chapter 5

What to Look for in a Man

Let's assume, now that you have been seriously chewing on this book for several chapters, and have begun to be more assertive, more permissive, less anxious, and less hostile in regard to the problem of meeting and winning a man, that you are faced with the concrete problem of having few or no males around with whom you would even care to get deeply involved. What kind of man should you then look for? And where should you go to look for him?

Let us consider the first of these questions before, in the next chapter, we go on to the second. The man you will probably want to have, especially if you are considering a long-term marital arrangement, would best be accoutered with the following kind of traits.

Emotional stability

Let's face it at the start: most men are kooks. Most women are, too; but that, unless you are an eagerly seeking lesbian, is probably not too much your problem. So let's, for the nonce, stick to the kookiness of men.

Like all nuts, an emotionally unstable man can be most stimulating and fascinating. His moods may be of

107

the never-a-dull-moment kind. His very inconsistencies may be charming. Because he is undisciplined (as nearly all kooks are), he may have more time to devote to you instead of to his work. And, best of all, he may be more interested in love—not sex, but real, honest-to-goodness love—than any other man you have ever met. For neurotics *need* love: violently, incessantly. And they are often obsessively-compulsively seeking it and plumbing its depths when even a bare smidgeon of it is around. So your half-crazy lover may be, in some respects, the most satisfactory man you ever had.

But don't be fooled! Screwballs are essentially, especially in the final analysis, bores. On a once-a-week or even a twice-a-week basis they may be most tolerable, even more than a bit exciting. But for heaven's sake, don't try to *live* with one! They are obsessive-compulsive, at bottom, only about themselves: and not even, in one sense, about that. For they are really worried almost all the time, about what others (including you) think of them, and not about what they would truly like to do to make themselves vibrant and happy.

Neurotics, in other words, are always striving for what Helmuth Kaiser called *fusion*. They are not really interested in talking *to* you but in fusing *with* you—that is, in getting your complete, undivided attention, and meriting your undying devotion no matter how badly they behave toward you. Consequently, they carry on two conversations at once: one, a fairly objective conversation, in which they are dispassionately responding to what you say, and appropriately discussing politics, the weather, your trip to Europe, or whatnot; the second, a most subjective conversation, which is essentially going on with *themselves,* in which they are ceaselessly debating: "Was that the correct thing I said? Will she like me any more, now that I've said it? Does she really care for me, or is it just my money she's after? I know that she's smiling, but I'm sure that she actually hates me, and thinks I'm a dunce for talking like this." Etcetera, etcetera!

Emotionally disturbed men, you'd better see and admit, may often *seem* to be keenly interested in you; but actually they are only interested in what you think of *them.* And they go on incessantly, interminably trying to get you to think well of them—and hating your guts when they even slightly imagine that you don't. What is more, the way in which they try to get you to love them is hardly a sane or sensible one— such as the technique of being so nice to you that you will just have to love them in return—but is usually a nastily testing, negative way: such as being unkind and inconsiderate to you, to *see* whether you then still accept and love them.

Because disturbed males (exactly like disturbed females) are self-centered (that is, centered on others loving them) instead of self-interested (that is, interested in what *they* really want to do in life), they actually do not give a fig for you in most ways; cannot see what your side of a story is; often cannot be reached, no matter how hard you try to communicate with them; and frequently dive into defensive shells of various sorts—such as over-sleeping, refusing to see anyone socially, being hostile at work and at home, gambling, drinking, etc. And, having one-track minds ("What, oh what, does So-and-So think of me?"), they

109

are generally bores to be with and are not truly interested in *living* in this infinitely variegated and absorbing world.

Neurotics, to make matters still worse, are usually unsatisfactory fathers, inadequate sex partners, poor providers or savers, inept at facing crises, and otherwise lacking in many traits which are exceptionally important in a good husband. They have so many self-sabotaging symptoms and defenses that, in another of my books it has taken me thirty-six pages to list them (*How to Live With a Neurotic*. New York: Crown Publishers, 1957). A neurotic is about as nice to live with as is a cobra—only not so easily caged.

Should you, therefore, swiftly eliminate every emotionally unstable member of the other sex whom you meet, and rigorously date and try to marry only those who are completely stable and sane? No: for there aren't any such animals, apparently, in our society. All of us are more or less kooky; and if you keep looking for a thoroughly non-neurotic mate, you will have to outdo Diogenes before you find one. Unless spinsterhood is your devotedly chosen lot, please be reasonable and make *some* compromises in this respect.

"But look here!" you may with some justification be saying by this time. "What the devil kind of a choice do you offer me? First you tell me not to marry a nut. Then you tell me that nothing but candidates for the looney-bin are actually available for mating. What kind of a box are you putting me in?"

Not as tight a box as you might think. In the first place, I have only been telling you not to *marry* a neurotic. But I didn't, remember, say that you couldn't love one, have an affair with one, or even live for awhile

110

with one. Go right ahead: enjoy yourself. Just don't delude yourself that screwballs are delightful in *marriage;* for they practically never are.

In the second place, there are nuts and nuts. Although just about everyone in our society (as well as, probably, in all other human societies) is *more or less* crazy, some are certainly craz*ier* than others. So you can, if you are sensible, look for a man who is not *too* looney— even while frankly admitting that he is not likely to be completely sane. You can often find, for example, someone who is compartmentally screwed up: who is, say, pretty daffy at work but not hard to get along with at home. Or you can find a man who is cracked in a limited and relatively unimportant kind of way: who is, for instance, a rabid butterfly collector, but who in other respects is reasonably on the ball. Or you can find a mate who is zany, all right, but who just happens to be zany in a similar manner to you: say, one who would rather play bridge than eat, and who is a great partner for a bridge fiend like you.

Better yet, perhaps (since it is not easy to find the particular kind of lunatic whom you would enjoy living with), you can look for a man who is just about as neurotic as everyone else is, but who at least *knows* and *fully admits* that he is. Living with a queer duck is bad enough; but staying with one who thinks that he is the sanest of the sane (and that perhaps you and everyone else is balmy) is impossible.

So you *can* consider an *admitted* neurotic—especially if he is working on his problem, perhaps going for psychotherapy, and is well on the way to eventually becoming *less* disturbed. In fact, you can frankly tell any potential husband, if you find him too kooky for your

111

domestic tastes, that just as soon as he does admit that he is somewhat off his rocker, and just as soon as he begins to *do* something about his emotional upsets, you will *then* be glad to consider him seriously as a mate.

Suppose that the love of your life either does not admit that he is batty or else admits that he is but refuses to do anything about it—should you then marry him and try to be a therapist to him? Yes and no. Yes, as we show in a later chapter of this book, there is often much that can be done to help a disturbed partner overcome some of his worst emotional difficulties. But no, it isn't too wise to literally marry him until you are pretty certain that you *will* be able to help him in his connection. How can you make pretty certain of this? By either living with him for a fair period of time before you marry him; or else seeing so much of him, even though you do not live with him, that you are able to work with him on his problems and actually *see* that he is making some considerable progress.

Suppose, though, nothing works in this respect. Your dream man is a real nut; he won't admit it or go for help; and none of your own efforts to get him saner are taking any effect. But you still love him, find him fascinating, and are most loath to leave him. What then?

Leave! Love him, if you will. But if you are at all interested in a permanent, marital affair with some one with whom you have at least a fair chance to live happily, love him from a distance. Every once in a while—say, about one in a thousand cases—a woman is satisfactorily married to a severe neurotic or a psychotic husband. Don't fool yourself that you are going to be the lucky (and infinitely hardworking!) exception. Insist that your disturbed lover be professionally treated. Accept nothing but real tries on his part to get over his disturbance: don't swallow any pious resolutions or promises about changing tomorrow. If he won't, even for the love of you, do anything to help himself change, what makes you think that he *ever* will do so? Stop kidding yourself, girlie. *Leave!*

Marriageability

Marriage is by no means the only legitimate or worthwhile sex-love relationship. Many individuals, especially those who have been married and have divorced or lost their mates, thrive on living alone for the rest of their lives—but also thrive on intermittent or even permanent love affairs along with their domestic privacy. Other individuals remain solidly married, at least legally, to one mate—but actually carry on one or a succession of romances with partners other than their mates. Still others follow different kinds of non-marital patterns and end up with surprisingly good love relations. So let us not assume that everyone *must* marry in order to enjoy love and sex; nor that *you* must be among the majority who do marry in our society.

If, however, you do want to marry the best man you can find—as the chances are high that you do—then you must be concerned with your chosen one's marriageability. By this, we do not mainly mean that you should ascertain at the start whether or not he is already married. For even if he is, that does not mean

113

that he must *continue* to be; and he of course *can* divorce his wife and marry you.

This, though, is definitely *not* to be counted upon. Innumerable married men go for long periods of time with women who *think* they are going to divorce their wives—and then the men just don't. Not that they necessarily love these wives with whom they stay; often, in fact, they loathe them. But there is many a slip between a man's having an affair with another woman and his literally leaving his wife for her. Money—yes, m-o-n-e-y—matters may easily keep him wedded to and even living with his first ball and chain. Or his relatives. Or his children. Or his job. Or his feelings of guilt. Or Lord knows what else.

Does that mean that you should never, under any circumstances, go with a married man if you yourself are intent on marrying? No, not never; but hardly ever. Or, at the very least, it means that you should never go with a married man *too long*. For a few months, yes: since he may well leave his wife at the end of that time. For a year or so, occasionally: since it still may take him some time to get up the guts, the money, the drive to leave her. At anything over a year, however: watch your step!

Certainly, there *may* be extenuating circumstances. In one case I know about, a married man went with his secretary for five years, until his children became old enough to go away to school. Then, just as he said he would, he divorced his wife and married the secretary. In another case, a married woman stayed with her husband for three years, until he got on his feet financially; and then she left him for the bachelor

114

with whom she had been having a clandestine affair during the entire period.

These, however, are the exceptions. Most of the time, if a man does not leave his wife for your board as well as your bed after you have been intimate with him for a year or more, he just is never going to do so. He may say he is, and may even think he is; but he probably isn't. And I have rarely seen women unhappier than several who have consulted with me after they stayed three, five, eight, and more than ten years in a sex-love relationship with a married man and *then*, finally, discovered that he definitely was not going to leave his wife and family for them. So beware of the relationship with a married man that goes on for any length of time. Unless, of course, you really *don't* want to marry him.

Most unmarriageable men are not in that state because they are already married to someone else, but are actually as technically single as any other bachelor is. But they just aren't—or at least believe that they aren't—marriageable. Some of them—in fact, a large number of them—would probably like to marry, but are terribly afraid of doing so. Some are afraid of women; some of sex failure; some of financial responsibilities; some of raising children; and so on.

These fearful men aren't necessarily hopelessly unmarriageable—since it is *possible* for them to overcome their fears, especially if they go for psychotherapeutic help—but they are certainly not the best marriage bets. Coaxing or trapping them into marrying, moreover, will only help overcome their fears in a certain percentage of cases; and in many instances, in fact, cajoling them

115

into marriage will only serve to enhance their fears, and only a divorce will calm them down.

Usually, the best tack for you to take with a man who is terribly fearful of marrying is flight. The quickest and farthest that you get away from him, the better. Let him live "happily" ever after with his mother. If he won't go for psychological help, you'd better seek it yourself: in order to help you get over him.

If fearful men are poor marriage bets, hostile men are even worse. The male who hates women; or who loathes people; or who abhors anyone who balks him in any way—this man you need like you need cancer. There seem to be, in general, two kinds of people: acceptors and malcontents. Acceptors graciously go along with reality, even when it is notably unpleasant; malcontents inwardly or outwardly seethe and rage at even the slightest of life's inconveniences. If the man you dearly love is a malcontent and is not willing to do anything about changing his unusually low level of frustration tolerance, marry him as readily as you would marry a rattlesnake.

Many other men, who are neither overly-fearful of marriage nor too hostile to be good husbands, are still essentially unmarriageable. Males, for instance, who are highly dedicated to some cause and who will therefore never have the time nor energy truly to be absorbed with a wife and children. Or men who have nomadic occupations (such as that of being a sailor or a big game hunter). Or men who are unhappy staying at home, and have to be out doing something literally every night of the week.

Many of these individuals might make good husbands—*if* they weren't so absorbed in various anti-

116

domestic pursuits. But since they are so absorbed, and most probably will not change in the next fifty years, you'd be far wiser to let them be what they most want to be, and to look elsewhere for someone who is really *interested* in the marital state.

In sum: in looking for a man to marry, focus not only on his advantageous qualities but his advantageous *marital* traits. Always remember the words of the English poet, George Wither, who (to paraphrase a little) said of any of his potential girlfriends, "What care I how fair she be, if she be not fair to me?" Wonderful and fine, indeed, may your would-be husband be; but how wonderful and fine, really, is he *to you?* And how long is he likely to remain so after the two of you legally pledge your troth and actually go to *live* together? Let me repeat again what I so often tell my patients in this connection: Don't, normally, marry any man you don't love; but don't, also, marry every man you *do*.

Permissiveness

Just as you yourself, as we noted in Chapter 2, should strive to be permissive with the man you want to win as your mate, so should you look for a husband who himself is reasonably permissive, and who doesn't equate wifehood with servility. Good-looking and strong your chosen male may be; bright as a whip, and with a substantial bank account. But if he is any substantial kind of bigot, moralist, or male supremacist, lady leave him be: poison is his name and Mrs. Dead Duck yours if you are crazy enough to marry him.

"Well suppose," you ask, "the next man I meet is

117

unusually fine in most respects, but he just happens to be conservatively or orthodoxly raised, thinks that women's place is in the home, and has several similar ideas. In most ways, he's great, but he just happens to be conventional in regard to women and marriage. What then?"

What do you mean, I counter, *he just happens to be?* Rubbish! People—except in naive Freudian and behavioristic thinking—just don't happen to be anything. They *make* themselves, for the most part, into what they are; or they fail to make themselves what they are not.

Granted that your unusually fine man was raised by tradition-bound parents, or reared as a Holy Roller or a Seventh Day Adventist. That's no excuse for his *maintaining* bigoted, anti-female sentiments. All of us, practically, are raised with all kinds of religious, socio-economic, political, and other bushwah. But those of us who are sufficiently sane and self-approving invariably *re-think* the nonsense with which we were inculcated, and discard at least a great deal of it before we reach our majority.

So ignorance is no excuse. Any man who is raised by some orthodox group which will not accept women as people and who *still*, by the time you meet him as a marital prospect, believes the hogwash with which he was reared, is distinctly suspect. The chances are at least nine out of ten that he really *wants* to believe the nonsense that he does—that he *prefers* to see women as second-class citizens and feels pretty good (because of his own deep-seated feelings of inadequacy) to think of them in this category.

If, then, the man of your choice is seriously authoritarian; if he obviously feels that men were born to master women; if he has a holier-than-thou attitude toward scores of people, including yourself; if he can only think in terms of severely hating and punishing all wrongdoers—if this is a reasonable facsimile of the man you love, then you'd better get hard at work at *un*-loving him, or at least at matrimonially disengaging yourself from him, as quickly as possible. For no matter how much he may swear that he cares for you and how sincere he may seem to be in his romantic allegations, he is really a liar: for he loves no one and nothing—except his crummy fascistic orthodoxy.

Above all, instead, look for a marital partner who is truly permissive: who will, without necessarily liking much of what you do, nonetheless give you gracious permission to do it; and who, when he disagrees violently with you, will firmly attempt to persuade rather than coerce you into seeing and doing things his way.

This does not mean that you should avidly seek out a man who is so meek and weak that he will gladly let you do anything you want, including walk all over him, because he doesn't think himself worthy of trying to get you to desist. Such a man is as spineless, in his own way, as the dogmatic fascist is in his. The mid-way male, who is firm enough to know what he wants and to go after it, but kind enough to allow you, too, to know what you want and to go after this, is the sort of male you should normally seek. Is such a male rare? Indeed, he is. Which is no reason why you shouldn't keep looking until you find him.

119

Communicativeness

Marriage is a *social* institution. If you really don't care for social discourse, and would rather go live in a modern version of a cave, by all means hop to it. *Everyone* shouldn't marry; and mayhap the mating game is just not your malted milk. If you do want to marry, however, it is to be assumed that you want some reasonable measure of companionship, of clearcut communication with your mate.

O.K.: look for just that—*before* you make a serious move toward the altar. The world, you might as well know from the start, is literally full of uncommunicative husbands. Some read the newspaper all night. Some dote on television. Some sit glumly quiet, doing nothing, just nothing. Some sleep practically all the time they're home. Some communicate beautifully—with neighbors, friends, relatives, children: in fact, with everyone except you. Some are always opening their big mouths—at the office, at the Elks Club, at cocktail parties; but almost never at home.

This is not quite so unusual as it may at first sound. For husbands and wives, after they have been married for a period of time, often simply *don't* have very much to say to each other; while, when strangers are present, things quickly become much more interesting and novel, and there is considerably more that can be said. Marriage—let us face it squarely and honestly—is *not* the most charming, exciting relationship between men and women that has ever been invented. It has its distinct limitations as a mate-inspiring or talk-inciting institution. So do not, please, unrealistically expect too

120

much from it in the way of constant verbal stimulation and interchange from your poor human, strictly limited and fallible partner.

Nonetheless!—there are extremes of uncommunicativeness in man-woman relationships; and if your would-be mate is at one of these extremes, you'd better put up the bright red danger signals to yourself before it is too late, and *do* something about his buttoned-lip tendency. Such as? Well, you might see if he has any distinct blocks to communication—e.g., his fear that you will put your foot in his mouth if he dares open it, or his fear that he will give himself (meaning, his underlying feelings of worthlessness) away if he talks too much. And if he has such blocks, you might try to help him remove them by taking the initial brunt of the talking on your own shoulders; by showing him that you will not pounce on him cruelly when he says the wrong things; by frankly discussing with him why he is verbally blocked; or by insisting that he get professional help in unblocking himself.

And if such techniques as these do not work? Run, girlie, run! Bright and handsome and rich indeed your man may be. But there *are* others equally endowed; and some of them *are* less tied up in uncommunicative knots. The main essence of marriage is talking and copulating. If you haven't got at least that to begin with, you might as well not start!

Sexual drive

Sex isn't everything. But a marriage completely without it usually isn't very much of anything. If your boyfriend does not like to play tennis, go to the movies, or go out socially with you, your relationship may possibly still survive on an amicable plane. But if he doesn't truly like to go to bed with you, your chances of having a good marriage are not merely low, they are almost nonexistent.

How can you tell, before marriage, whether or not your chosen man really cares for you sexually, and is likely to keep caring for you in that manner for years to come? Obviously, there is only one valid test: try sex with him and see. This does not mean, now, that you should merely try kissing him passionately goodnight, or pet with him in the car, or even go away for a single weekend in a hotel or motel before you seal the marital knot legally. Almost anyone can pass *that* namby-pamby kind of sex test, and the great majority of males usually do. Including, alas, those who later turn out to be the world's worst imaginable bedmates.

Should you, then, actually try to live with a man before marrying him: live, that is to say, under the same roof, and at night in the same bed, with him for a considerable period of time before you legally wed? You certainly should.

If I had my way, in fact—which it seems most unlikely, at the moment, that I am going to have—we would pass a special law in this country, unequivocally stating that no girl should be allowed to marry the man of her choice unless she proved that she had, prior to the wedding ceremony, lived domestically with him for at least a year.

Why so long? Because most couples can easily fool themselves and each other for a few weeks or a few months, and remain sufficiently in love during such a period of time to make themselves genuinely believe that they are well suited for each other for a lifetime. But very few couples can keep up such a pretense for a full year. Sooner or later, their real nasty little selves begin to show through, especially when they have to be with each other day and night, through sickness and through health, for 365 full days. And until they actually see the other's nasty little self, and see their own honest reaction to what the other truly is, they rarely have the foggiest idea of whether they would like to stay married forever.

Sex, in particular, is a tricky business in marriage. In our society, where almost everyone is pretty sex-starved before marriage, few couples have low sex drives during their courtship period. On the contrary, they tend to become sexually obsessed, to think that they want to spend all their time in bed together, and to adore almost every minute of their petting and their fornicating—even when (as more than infrequently happens) they are far from adoring many nonsexual aspects of each other.

Sex desire, as any expert in the field knows, thrives on novelty, newness, variety, and abstinence. In a few instances, as most of the prissy marriage manuals exaggeratedly emphasize, it gets better and better as the years go by. But this is usually because it was so horribly bad at the start, in some inhibited couples, that it couldn't possibly get any worse, and had to improve as their inhibitions finally decreased. Where, however, a man and a woman are not notably sexually repressed to begin with, their sex interest in each other

123

in most instances wanes rather than waxes as they go through weeks and years of steady monogamous congress.

If they are both sufficiently high-sexed creatures, they can greatly enjoy each other in bed in spite of the relative monotony of their persistent relations. Even then, they rarely get *maximum* satisfaction from this one-track diet. And if, as frequently occurs, one or both of them are moderately- or low-sexed, it is almost incredible how seldom, after a few years of marriage, they can actually have intercourse—and how little they can miss not having it with each other.

Does this picture of sex in American marriage seem unduly grim, and is it likely that you, personally, can do something to make it less grim in your own marriage? Yes. For the picture we have been drawing is that which is based on our *existing* methods of sex education for courtship and mating. And a more idiotic and happiness-destroying procedure of preparing husbands and wives for the joys of sexual mating was doubtless never invented. But it can, in various individual cases, be radically changed.

The average American female (as I show in detail in my book, *The American Sexual Tragedy*) is brought up to avoid masturbation, to be guilty about even relatively light kissing and petting before marriage, and to remain a technical virgin until the night after her wedding. She learns practically nothing, except very surreptitiously and from the least trustworthy sources, about how best to bring herself and her male partner to maximum pitches of arousal and fulfillment; and in her own blundering way, aided by the enormous re-

124

pressiveness of her society, she generally manages to bring both him and herself to high peaks of desire— and to leave either or both of them hanging there dangerously, often ending up with genital congestion and sexual indigestion.

In consequence, she frequently becomes relatively or absolutely frigid and finds it almost impossible to get a full orgasm except under unusual circumstances; while her date often becomes afflicted with premature ejaculation, erectile incapacity, over-delayed orgasm, or other varieties of impotence.

When, with this kind of sexual heritage, boy marries girl in our culture he and she are most likely to have a honeymoon that is maximally frustrating and minimally fulfilling. Or else they may have a honeymoon that is the one, and practically the only, highlight in their ensuing long marital history.

Even healthy individuals have a hard time making it sexually in monogamous marriage, since our biological urges are *not* particularly monogamous and they *are* varietistically trended. But unhealthy individuals, who because of their sexually repressive upbringing have never had steady sex satisfaction before marriage, and who are both over-eager and over-inhibited at one and the same time, have even less of a chance to reach their maximum fulfillment after the glamour of the wedding day has given way to the dull routines of everyday domesticity.

To return to our main theme: The more you get rid of your unhealthy sexual upbringing *before* you wed, the better you are likely to get along sexually within the confines of monogamic mating. Which means? Something, preferably, along the following lines:

125

1. Gather ye rosebuds while you may and start your sex life as early rather than as late as possible. Learn the ins and outs of your own genital apparatus when you are still in your teens, and don't hesitate, not for one guilty moment, to satisfy yourself sexually when no suitable partner is around. Females, in particular, often require certain special kinds of strokings, massagings, and manipulations of their clitoral and vulval areas if they are to achieve maximum orgasmic satisfaction; and unless you yourself discover, through your own straightforward experimentation, exactly what most satisfies you, it is unlikely that you are going to be able to show your male partners what is your own cup of erotic tea.

2. If, when you are young and vulnerable to watch and censure, you are terribly afraid of actual coitus, do not hesitate to pet—and to pet up to and including full climax. Petting that is prolonged and that does not lead to orgasm may possibly result in over-stimulation, genital engorgement, and consequent physical and psychological ills. Petting that invariably leads to climax is literally good, clean fun, and has virtually no disadvantages. Both you and your boyfriends can be satisfied indefinitely with this kind of sex relations; while complete or partial refraining from petting is likely to be quite disruptive and unenlightening.

3. If you have premarital coitus make sure that you are well aware of proper contraceptive methods, and that you use one or more of such methods every single time. Do not rely on the so-called "safe period," since it is not that safe. And don't leave responsibility for birth control up to the male, since he can be notoriously careless about those things and never quite has the

incentive that you do to avoid pregnancy. Consult with a reputable gynecologist, and strictly follow the procedures he outlines. If you have any super-romantic notions in this respect, get rid of them fast. Having intercourse under safe and secure conditions can be infinitely more romantic than having them "spontaneously" and carelessly.

4. Syphilis and gonorrhea among heterosexuals are prevalent, today, only among highly promiscuous individuals, and even then only among those who tend to be ignorant and to come from lower-class levels, where sexual carelessness is rife. If you restrict your sex relations to relatively mature, sensible, responsible males of middle-class or upper-class status, and to those whom you are reasonably certain are not also indulging in promiscuous homosexual affairs, it is most unlikely that you will ever become venereally diseased.

5. Forget, except for practical purposes, about your sexual reputation. If you live in a girl's dormitory at school, and may well be thrown out of the place if you come in late or are known to have had sex-relations with a boy, naturally you must seriously consider obeying the idiotic rules of your school, since the possible penalty for not doing so is hardly worth the sexual gain. But if all that is going to happen to you if you have premarital sex relations is that some of your acquaintances or friends are going to censure you or boycott you for being a "whore," then hurry, hurry, hurry to have such relations, in order thereby to rid yourself of the "friends" who are surely not very worthwhile knowing anyway.

Your main goal in life, remember, should not be that of liking yourself and feeling yourself to be perfectly respectable when other people happen to approve your behavior, but that of liking yourself *whether or not other people approve of you.* If you refrain from having a sex life because you are terribly afraid of what your friends and acquaintances will think, you not only give up harmless pleasure but (far worse!) sell your soul in the process. Better you should copulate and retain your integrity as a person than remain chaste and be a moral coward.

6. When you are having any kind of sex relations with boys be as honest and straightforward as you can possibly be about your own urges and what is needed to satisfy them. Don't shut your mouth and groan to yourself while your boyfriend clumsily tweaks you in the wrong spot or carelessly leaves you unfulfilled. Tell him—yes, in plain damned English tell him—what you want and how he can do what you want. Guide his hands and his body. Teach him how to kiss properly. Show him the positions you have previously discovered to be the best ones. If he thinks you are terrible for knowing so much, or feels that you are imposing on him by asking him to do what most satisfies you, good— you'll know better than to try sex again with him next time.

7. Try a reasonably large variety of sex partners before you settle down to one one-and-only. Don't be cowed by the term "promiscuity"—which, rightly defined, means indiscriminate sexual congress. Almost no girl, except a real prostitute who sells her favors to anyone who comes along, is truly promiscuous, since most girls get hundreds of sex offers from men every year, and even if they accepted a score or more of these offers they would be far from being indiscriminate in

128

their selection. So don't surrender to the promiscuity bugaboo.

Experimental variety—or what Rey Anthony has called selective promiscuity—is the cornerstone of sane sexual choice. For one man, you will find, has a touch like none of the others you have ever known. Another can prolong intercourse for an hour or more. Still another can show you things you never dreamed existed and make you enjoy manipulations you never thought you could possibly like. And how would you *know* which one of these lovers was good—or, for that matter, bad—if you had never, never tried?

Even having poor sex relations can be most instructive. The calm, unromantic, good technician that you can rely on having a good time in bed with may, after awhile, seem rather boring and uninteresting to you. But when you have had, interspersed in between his biweekly visits, a couple of romantic cats who declaim the most high-flown love spiels imaginable, but whose manual dexterity equals that of a lumbering polar bear, you may decide that the technician's skills were more than you first cracked them up to be, and that love is not by any means entirely verbalization.

The main point is that you and your sex partners are always distinct individualists; and all the good intentions and best training in the world will not make a concert virtuoso out of a tone-deaf boy. Unless you try at least several sex partners before you settle down to an exclusive sex-love contract, you will never, in all probability, fully know either what you do or you do not want when the chips are down and the bed clothes are flying.

Moreover, unless you often discover with A, B, and

C what really sends you in the hay, you are not too easily going to be able to induce D, with whom you may want to end up for the rest of your days, to do the special things that split your guts and make your goose pimples swirl. Would you, if you were aiming to become a first-class gourmet, rely on a single cook or a narrow batch of recipes? Why, then, should you limit your sexual gourmetism to a commonplace partner or two who is most unlikely to have been specially born for the total assuagement of your own inimitable libido?

8. Don't spend any considerable amount of time trying to reconvert homosexuals, fetichists, impotent males, and other kinds of sexual queer ducks. If any man keeps taking you out steadily but never makes any serious passes, don't assume that it's his great love or consideration for you that holds him strongly in check. Assume, rather, that he has some kind of sexual problem; and, if possible, try to get him to talk about it openly.

If he seems to be only moderately inhibited—as in the case of a male virgin who just hasn't the courage to try to break the ice—help him along as much as you can, and do not hesitate to practically rape him. But if his sexual aberration or evasiveness persists, don't start seeing yourself as the Florence Nightingale of the boudoir, who is absolutely determined to help this poor soul achieve a virility that surpasses all understanding. After several unsuccessful tries that leave you still totally frustrated and him as lilywhite as when first you met, insist that he go for professional aid—or else!

It's hard enough, in this world, to mate quite successfully with even the most physically healthy of lovers—since, Beelzebub knows, he's likely to have as many *nonsexual* peculiarities as a queer has heterosexual inhibitions. So don't add the extra handicap, to your potential relation with a man, of his being a real sexual screwball and refusing to do anything psychotherapeutically about it. If he won't see a therapist, you go for your own kind of sex therapy—with someone who knows a swinging chick when he sees one, and is more than willing to look.

Basic compatibility

Almost any two highly intelligent and fairly sensible human beings can have a pretty good marital relationship if they really want to adjust to each other. But an excellent question that is too little asked about most men and women who are contemplating marriage is: Why the devil should they *want* to?

You can, in other words, dote on a man who loves to stay at home while you love to go out a great deal; who wants to have sex relations every day when you want them once a week; who is wholly absorbed with music and science while you only care for art and literature. You can love such a man, remain married to him for forty years, and somehow manage to make innumerable adjustments to his likes and dislikes, so that neither of you is too miserable staying together. Of course you can, if you work very hard at it, achieve and maintain this kind of adjusted marriage. But why on earth *should* you—when in all probability you could fairly easily find another lovable man who dovetails much more closely with you in regard to staying at home, having sex relations, and being absorbed in art and literature?

Are, then, all truly compatible marriages made in heaven? Must one be *born* to get along easily with one's mate, instead of having to have enormous difficulty, all one's marital life, adjusting endlessly to the whims and traits of this mate?

Largely, frankly, yes. For although, as we said above, almost any two highly intelligent people of the other sex *can* make it in marriage, they are in nine cases out of ten idiotic if they do. All of us have so many highly individualistic styles of living—such as our sleeping and eating habits, our biological rhythms, our energy levels, our exercise patterns, our physical handicaps and health deficiencies—that we can quite *easily* live under the same roof and get along well with one member of the other sex while only with the very greatest difficulty and with oodles of painful adjustments can we get along even moderately comfortably with another member of this same sex.

Obviously, therefore, when it comes to marrying—though not necessarily to loving or going to bed with —a man, you'd better damned well try to find one who rather *naturally* goes along with many of your ways of doing things and who *innately* seems to be attuned to many of your own basic likes and dislikes.

This particularly applies to what may be termed your vital or main interests. In one of my favorite books, *Creative Marriage* (which just happens, coincidentally enough, to be written by myself and Robert A. Harper), the authors point out:

"Every marital relationship . . . has to be something of a compromise, has to include some sacrifices of interest. If many of your minor interests—such as eating Chinese food or looking at the late late show on television—have to go by the board because your mate won't share them and objects to your participating in them very often, that may be too bad, but your marriage will probably survive. If, however, even a single one of your most vital interests must be sacrificed to marriage, beware! If, for example, you do not merely enjoy Chinese food, but are an outstanding authority on it, and are compiling a massive tome on Chinese cooking; or if your one main enjoyment in life is viewing the late late television show—then you really have a serious problem if your spouse objects to these pursuits."

The moral seems clear: Consider, long before you actually marry, what your own and your would-be partner's vital interests are. If these beautifully mesh, or at least are not in serious conflict, fine!—continue to consider the possibilities of marrying this person; and, as we noted previously, think seriously of living under the same roof with him for many months at a time, to see if the meshing of major interests that seems to exist is as much a truth as a pious hope.

If it becomes obvious that, in spite of the fact that you love each other madly, you have several important incompatibilities, then consider establishing every kind of sex-love relationship that you might possibly share together—except marriage. For the chances are then ninety-nine out of a hundred that *that* particular kind of monogamous, domestic, two-for-all-and-all-for-two relationship is just not going to work.

Chapter 6

Where and How to Look for a Man

Assume that you are emotionally ready to look for a suitable man and that you pretty well know what to look for. How, now, do you actually go about looking? If there is a gentle art of manhunting, of what does it consist?

It consists, by and large, of the same kind of art as that involved in writing, swimming, painting, collecting stamps, or doing almost anything else that you might really want to do. I am fond, in this connection, of quoting Sinclair Lewis's famous definition of the art of writing. "What," he was asked one day by an aspiring young writer, "have you found, in all your experience as a novelist, the art of writing to be?" "The art of writing," Lewis is reputed to have said, "is very simple. It consists of putting the seat of the pants to the seat of the chair—and writing!"

So with the art of looking for a man. It largely consists of putting the balls of your eyes to the front of your head—and looking! *Where* should you look? Anywhere, naturally, that you happen to be: in the office, on the street, at a party, on a bus, at a museum or art gallery, in a classroom, on the beach, at a dance, around your own neighborhood, on a trip, at a picnic, at a meeting, etc. As long as you keep actively, assertively looking, you are almost certain to find several good prospects within a reasonably short period of time. But you must, honest and truly, *keep looking*.

This, apparently, isn't as easy as it sounds. For millions of women, clearly, don't really look at all for the man they want. Or look very half-heartedly. Or look in theory—with their eyes, at a distance—but not in practice—with their whole being, at close range. Or look in the places where it is quite obvious that their chances of finding the kind of man that they, personally, want are exceptionally small.

Let us suppose, for example, that you have decided to take up painting, or to collect antiques, or to take some courses at a nearby university. Normally, in order to carry out your intent, you will do quite a bit of research. Thus, in regard to painting, you will read some material on the subject, look in the classified directory for art schools or private teachers, send away for catalogues of the schools you find, discuss with your friends what experiences they may have had with painting teachers, have an interview with an art school or teacher, perhaps sit in on a few trial classes, check your progress when you are taking a class to see if you are doing well enough in this particular class, and do a score of other things to investigate which teacher or group is best for you.

You will carry on this variety of activities in regard to picking an art school or getting involved in some hobby because, in most instances, you will be thoroughly unashamed—in fact, even quite proud—of what you are doing and because you will have a desire to do it as promptly and efficiently as possible.

Not so, alas, with the gentle art of manhunting! For

136

some of the most idiotic reasons imaginable, we have encased this art, in our society, in an aura of hesitation and shame, and we have particularly brought up our females so that they are unusually reticent about looking for what may well be the most important thing in their whole lives—a suitable husband—while at the same time we have raised them to be quite bold and shameless about seeking many far less important things—such as a hobby, a sport, or a new dress.

Why have we done this? Largely, historically speaking, because males have always been socio-economically supreme in our culture, and have preëmpted for themselves most of the advantages of taking the sexual initiative. Thus, in the old days, our girls would not think of going alone to work, to a theater, to a dance, or to various other social functions; and they would—of course!—never consider calling a male on the phone, asking him to dance at a party, or proposing marriage to him.

Today, we are somewhat more liberal about a female's taking the initiative in various aspects of life, and especially in boy-girl relations. But we are far from being truly equalitarian in this respect, and intimations of shame still overhang most actions where the girl unhesitatingly goes after what she wants and tries her very best to get it.

This anti-feminist, male-supremacist attitude is what you have to fight . . . and fight! . . . and fight! For if in any way you willingly go along with it, you will almost certainly reduce your chances of finding the kind of man you want and winning him for your very own—just as you would reduce your chances of finding the

137

kind of job you really want if you shyly stayed in the first job you happened to get and let the males in your office, but never yourself, take the initiative in pushing forward on this job or looking for more suitable and better-paying work elsewhere.

Before, then, we make any attempt to give you specific directions on where and how to look for the man of your choice, let us spend a little time trying to get you over some of the emotional blocking that you almost certainly must have in this connection if you are a normal female who has been raised in this highly abnormal society.

Overcoming emotional blocks against manhunting

Linda Q. was an attractive, bright girl of twenty-six, who had graduated with honors from college and had worked for six years, first as an assistant, then an associate, and recently as a full buyer for one of New York's largest department stores. She did exceptionally well on her job, was liked by her bosses and her co-workers, and got along swimmingly, at least in a superficial sort of way, in her social relations. Girlfriends she had galore—except that, in recent years, almost all of them began marrying and having children, while Linda, who at first blush seemed to be the real princess of them all, never seemed to get anywhere with her numerous dates, and didn't even get close to an engagement. Both her girl friends and her parents kept wondering about this, and finally induced her to come for psychotherapeutic aid.

"Where do you look for suitable male companions?" I asked Linda the first time I saw her.

"Oh, the usual places. I go to dances all the time. And weekends at resorts. And cocktail parties, when I can get to them. But I never seem to find what I want at any of these places. I'm sure that the kind of fellow I would like just rarely goes to these kinds of affairs—though Lord knows I meet many men all the time, and even have difficulty getting rid of some of them who just aren't my type."

"Well, what do you think *is* your type? Is there something special in a man that you are looking for, and that you are not likely to meet in the places in which you have been looking?"

"Well, I guess there kind of sort of is. You'd probably never think it of me, since I'm not exactly the shy, retiring type myself; but that's what I kind of want in a man. A—well, a very sensitive person; not in the least brash, nor with a lot of gall, like my father has, and like I've always hated him for having; and definitely not cruel or cold or well-armored and insensitive, again like my father is. Someone, I guess—yes, I guess that's it, like my mother, whom I've always been very close to, and who is soft and buttery."

"Did you ever actually meet a man, like the one you describe? Do you think one actually exists?"

"Oh, yes; I know he does. I had one just like this, five years ago. He was almost just like my mother, and he got along beautifully with her, incidentally—would have made the perfect son-in-law. I think, in fact, he almost liked her more than he did me. Not that we didn't get along well, the two of us, for we did, and had a lovely relationship. I've never known anything like it before or since."

"And—what happened? Why didn't you marry him?"

139

"He was a foreigner—an Indian. Over here on a diplomatic mission for the U.N. And he had to go back to his own country. Besides, it just couldn't have worked out, there were such great cultural differences between us. He was Mohammedan, and though I don't think he really believed in it, his religion was tied to his political career. He couldn't give it up without ruining himself politically. And I could never have become a Mohammedan, or anything like that. So we had to break up the relationship, before it became too involved. But he was so *sweet*. Yes, that's what I really want: a *sweet* man. And there are so few in this country—or anywhere!"

"But there must be *some*. In a metropolitan area like New York, where there are some tens of thousands of men to choose from, surely there must be a *few* of the kind of men you'd like."

"Oh, there are. I'm sure there are. Every once in awhile I meet one, when I'm waiting for a bus, or sitting in a restaurant. And I'm sure, just by looking at him, that he's the type I would like. But what can I do—go up to him and say, 'Look: you seem to be such a sweet man, just like Armandi was. Don't you think we could, well, get together?' You certainly couldn't expect me to do a thing like that, could you?"

"Why not? If that really is the only way you could meet such a man, and you are not likely to find one at the usual dances and cocktail parties you go to—"

"—Oh, I'm not! I assure you. I just *never* do!"

"All right, then: what's *wrong* with accosting one in the street, if necessary, and telling him that he looks just like the lost Armandi? Or wasn't he once in your

140

class at Columbia University? Or does he happen to know where the New York Public Library is? Or something like that?"

"Oh, I couldn't! Not that kind of thing. I just couldn't!"

"Why *couldn't* you? According to what you've said, this type of sweet, shy man you're looking for, and who is so rare apparently in these parts—he's not going to accost *you* on the street, is he?"

"Oh, no. I'm sure he wouldn't. And I know that people like that rarely even *go* to the sort of places I usually go to, the resorts and the dances and things like that."

"O.K., then. A man such as the one you want is not likely to be at the regular places you go to meet males. And he's also not likely to be bold enough to pick you up if you do happen to meet him at a bus stop. Obviously, you've boxed yourself in, and narrowed down your possible prospects to practically zero. Unless, of course, *you* are willing to be the more assertive one yourself, and to make the overtures when you do happen to meet one of these rare creatures in a situation where he's not likely to be formally introduced to you."

"But I couldn't! How could I? I've never done a thing like that in my life."

"No, you haven't. And where has *not* doing a thing like that in your life got you? Where you want to be? With the kind of rare man you crave?"

"No, it hasn't. But—well, you really don't think I could go out and, well, you know, actually, that is, *pick up* this kind of a man, do you? You really wouldn't expect me to do *that?*"

141

"I wouldn't *expect* it—not with your crummy, inhibiting upbringing in this silly society. But I'd certainly *advise* it."

"You're *serious* about that? You really *are?*"

"I damned well am. For what have you got to lose? If you go on the way you have been doing for the past several years, you're not likely to get any farther than you've got so far. You could, of course, change your goal: go for a different kind of man, one like your father, for instance, who is much more common than the one you do go for; and that might well solve your problem. But do you *want* to change the type—or do you want to keep going after the type you already like, and then have to change your tactics?"

"Do I have to do either? Can't I keep looking for the type I like and not change my tactics?"

"Sure you can. But as we just noted, what are your chances, under those circumstances, of succeeding—of getting what you want?"

"Hmmm. Pretty slim, I guess."

"All right: that's the point. The shyer the man you want, the *un*shyer, usually, you yourself have to be. The only logical way to increase your chances, if you keep going after your desired type of male, is to do *more* looking than the average girl would do—and to be more forward when you finally find what you seem to be looking for."

"Meaning—exactly what?"

"Meaning, that you should go where your type of man would be most likely to go—to museums, for example, or art galleries, or concerts—and then approach the good candidates you meet at these places and try to engage them in conversation."

"Like asking them for a match, you mean? Or making a comment on the painting we are both watching at the museum?"

"Exactly. I see you know *what* to do. Now, how can we get you to do it?"

"But how *can* I do it?"

"How *can't* you, if you want what you say you want?"

"But I just never *have*."

"You probably have never eaten whale steak, either. But that doesn't mean that you can't order one and eat it."

"Oh, but this is different! I wouldn't—well, feel ashamed about that."

"And you would feel ashamed for approaching a sweet, shy man, and asking him a question or two, or making a comment on a painting to him?"

"Why, yes. Wouldn't almost any woman?"

"I'm afraid you're right: almost any woman in this idiotic society of ours would. But that's *her* problem. Let's get you out of her class and on the way to solving *yours*. What are *you* telling yourself, when you see a desirable man and think wouldn't it be nice to meet him, and then you make no efforts whatever to do so?"

"What am I telling myself? Nothing, as far as I know. I just *feel* it's not, well, the right thing to do, to approach him. I wasn't brought up that way."

"Sure you *feel* it's not the right thing to do—*after* you tell yourself that it's not. Without convincing yourself, very forcefully and vigorously, that you just couldn't, no you just *couldn't*, approach a strange man, you never would *feel* the way you do. Now just look at the nonsense you're telling yourself to *make* yourself feel that you couldn't."

143

"You mean, I'm saying to myself 'Oh, nice women just *don't* approach strange men,' or something like that?"

"*Aren't* you? And: 'What would my mother ever think if she knew that I did a thing like that?' And: 'What would my girlfriends think?' And, even more: 'What would *he* think of me, if I approached him so boldly?' Aren't *these* the sentences you keep telling yourself, as you're standing there drooling to yourself about him—and then walking off and making no contact with him? Aren't they?"

"I'm sure you're right. Those *are* the sentences I'm saying to myself. But shouldn't I be saying them? Wouldn't my mother be shocked? And my girlfriends? And *would* he think well of me if I did speak to him like you're saying I should?"

"Suppose that's true? What have you got to lose? This way, by not trying to go after what you want, your mother and girlfriends don't think ill of you—and what does *that* get you? Let us even suppose that you meet the kind of man you want, and you boldly approach him, and *he* thinks badly of you—thinks you're a whore, or something like that. Have you *still* lost anything? The chances are, of course, that he won't think poorly of you at all—that he'll be delighted that you are making the overtures, since he's afraid to make them himself. But even if he does think you're a tramp —what have you lost? For if you *don't* make any approach, what chance have you got *then?*"

"I can see what you mean. This way, I'm *sure* not to get what I want. That way, I *might.*"

"Right. And even if your mother, girlfriends, and the

144

man you pick up at the museum *all* think badly of you at first—which isn't very likely, but let's suppose, at the worst, they all do think badly of you. What are they going to *do* with their poor thoughts of you: kill you with them? Maim you? And how *long* are they going to think badly of you?"

"They'll get over what they first think? Is that what you're saying?"

"*Won't* they? Take, even, a man whom you might pick up. Let us assume, again, the worst: that he thinks you're a tramp, who's only interested in going to bed with him, and that he has no respect for you at first. Will he, after he speaks to you for a half hour, and actually tries to plop you right into the nearest bed, will he *then* think you're such a tramp?"

"Not unless I act like one."

"Exactly. If, after you go off and have coffee or a drink with him, as he's most likely to ask you to do, you behave as you normally do, show him that you're not just interested in sex, but are looking for a permanent companion, the kind you almost had but didn't quite get in that Indian man you went with awhile ago, will he then think it awful that you picked him up like that?"

"No, I guess he won't."

"You know damned well he won't. And your mother and your girlfriends. Suppose you did get a man in this highly 'improper' way, and he turns out to be a truly fine person, and you end up by marrying him. Do you think that they'll *still* think it was terrible of you to have met him like you did?"

"I can see what you're getting at. No, they'll prob-

145

ably be telling the story of my famous pickup, in a sort of merry, joking, but still favorable manner, for the rest of their lives."

"I'll bet you're right. That's exactly what'll happen."

"But suppose it doesn't work out. I pick up a man, or a dozen of them, and none of them quite work out. Won't my mother then be quite upset by what I'm doing?"

"I'm sure she will. And your girlfriends, too. Just because *they* haven't got the guts to do what you're doing, they'll probably jealously pick on you and think how awful it is, you're doing what they would so like to do themselves (and avoid, incidentally, marrying the wrong kind of man, as your mother did when she picked your formally-introduced father!). All right: let's suppose that they will be upset. So?"

"You mean *I* don't have to be upset just because they are?"

"Well, *do* you? If you enjoy reading Henry Miller or dancing the twist, and they think that kind of thing is perfectly awful—do you let *their* views stop you? Do you always live exactly the way *they* think you should?"

"No. Sometimes I let them stop me, of course. And then I hate myself for it. But not usually."

"Right: you hate yourself when you sell your soul for their approval. And don't you think that that's just about what you're doing now, consciously or unconsciously, when you're refraining from going after the kind of man *you* really want because *they* wouldn't approve of the way you would have to go about finding and meeting him?"

"You think I really do? I hate myself for following what they think I ought to do?"

146

"Well? Doesn't anyone who plays the patsy role, and refuses to do what she really wants to do because someone *else* wouldn't like it, underlyingly hate herself? Can you really respect your*self* when you have no self, but are merely a reflection, in your acts and thoughts, of what *others* think you should be?"

"Hmmm. I guess you've got something there. I can see, now, why I've tended to become so depressed recently. Not just because I wasn't getting what I want, in the way of a man. But because I *knew*, I guess, that I wouldn't get it if I continued to look for it the way my mother and girlfriends think I should look, and I *knew* I couldn't bring myself to go against them and to do things the way *I* thought they should be done."

"Evidently, then, you've given some thought, on your own, to what I have been pointing out this session."

"Oh, yes. Everything you've just told me, I've thought of before. Because I could *see* that I wasn't getting anywhere, with these affairs I've been attending. I could see that the man I'm looking for practically will never show up at these kinds of gatherings. And I knew I had to do something else to find him. And I sort of knew what it was, just as you've been pointing out. But I couldn't see myself doing it, against the criticism of my friends, and particularly of my mother. But I see it all even more clearly now.

"And what you said about my mother is true, so true! She *did* marry Daddy, whom I'm sure she's hated for years, because she was so shy and withdrawn herself that she never could even think of doing what you're showing me I must do. And she knows, oh, she really does know, that she married him by default—her own default. And she even had a chance, a few

147

years after she married, to get what she really wanted, when one of Daddy's business associates who was just her type showed real interest in her and she was just dying to leave Daddy and go off with him. But she didn't dare speak up. She never even let him know, this other man, that she cared. And he went away, somewhat like my own Armandi did, though not to another country, and she never saw him again. And she's hated herself for not speaking up, ever since. But she couldn't—"

"You mean, *thought* she couldn't."

"Yes, you're right. She thought she couldn't. And she didn't. She didn't dare oppose *her* mother—my damned bitchy grandmother!—so she kept her mouth closed until it was too late. Then I came along, and she was stuck with my father forever. And she's been miserable ever since."

"See. That's what comes of living *other* people's lives and having no self of your own. And is this the example that *you're* going to continue to follow? Do *you* want to compromise, as you're apparently going to have to one of these days, if you don't find what you really want, for a man like your father?"

"God, no! Anything but that!"

"Well?"

"Hmmm."

"You can say that again! Hmm, hmm!"

It took a good many sessions more of therapy before I had Linda not only theoretically but actively convinced. She used every excuse in the books to keep following her mother's and her girlfriends' views. And I used every argument in the psychological books to

148

induce her to formulate and to act on her own philosophy of life.

At one point, I almost lost out completely, when she started to become attached to a man pretty much like her father, whom she had met through one of her girl-friends, and when she began convincing herself that, after all, maybe she was just prejudiced: maybe she *could* make it with this kind of insensitive, typical businessman-type person. Fortunately, she found that she just couldn't—or, rather, really didn't want to.

In desperation, she did go to an art gallery one day and started a conversation with an Indian-looking man (who actually turned out to be from Iran, and who was nothing like her lost Armandi, as she thought he might be). Though nothing came of this, she was surprised at the ease with which she carried off the pickup, and began to see that there really *was* nothing to be afraid of in this connection.

After that, there was almost no stopping her. Nearly every nook, particularly each highly cultured nook, in New York City became a potential place for her to find and actively work at getting the kind of a man she wanted. She still, at this writing, has not quite made it. But she most definitely will, I am willing to bet. In the last six months, she has come fairly close three times—and each time with males whom she never would have met at all had she not gone out of her way to ask them a question or otherwise introduce herself into their presence. It is only a matter of time, if she continues to do what she has been doing recently, for her to strike real pay dirt. I am sure that she will.

Must *every* girl, then, go out and literally pick up men if she is to find the male of her choice? No, not

149

literally: since some women manage, without such activity, to meet as many men as they can handle, and to be able to find, among the males that easily come their way, one or more who is exactly to their tastes. But the more selective you, as a woman, are, the more you will probably have to look and look and look—and act and act and act—to find what you really want.

If you were looking for an unusually interesting, well-paying job with a very kindly boss and with lovely associates with whom to work, you would expect to have to go through many, many job possibilities before you actually found such an opening. Similarly, if you are looking for an unusually interesting, fascinating man who will be most loving toward you and introduce you to lovely friends and adventures, you must expect to have to go through many, many marital possibilities before you actually find such an unexcelled opportunity.

And people *will* stare and criticize if you boldly go after what you want in a man: if you talk to strangers, flirt with men in public so that they feel free to approach you, or even if you brashly go around at a cocktail party introducing yourself to every interesting looking male present. So they'll stare and criticize!

Always remember that it is definitely not, nor can it ever be, what *they* say about you that makes you feel guilty, ashamed, or upset, but what *you* say about you in agreement with what they say. If you *agree* with your mother or your girlfriends that, yes, you really *are* a tramp for picking up strangers, then *your* self-depreciating evaluation of you will hurt. If you listen calmly to what they think, but politely and firmly (especially in your own head) *dis*agree with their views, then practically nothing that they can say or do will hurt you. *Your* internalized sentences are the ones that cruelly prick you. O.K.: what are you going to do about changing *them?*

Let's assume that you have been preparing yourself to go out to look actively for men, and that, whatever your close relations think of your tactics, you are determined to open your big mouth and go after what you want. Where shall you look? What are some of the best —and the worst—places? Let us look at some of the possibilities.

Friends

By all means, if you can, use your friends as a source of new dates. But if they are good friends of yours, really *use* them, rather than passively let them, in a sense, use you.

Tell your friends exactly what you want—and don't want—in a male. Don't merely say "I'm desperate for a date, please fix me up," or "Any suitable guy that you happen to meet, be sure to give him my phone number." This kind of promiscuous date-making will probably pay off very badly and leave you stuck many evenings on end with a horse's ass who you can see, about five minutes after meeting him, is precisely what you *don't* want.

Say, rather, to your married cousin, or the girls you know at the office, or your ex-lover who insists on staying with his wife: "Look, I really want to get attached to someone. But *not* anyone. I just don't like sloppy (or greasy, or stupid, or sports-mad, or overly-dedicated) men. Sure, they're great guys. But not for me. Now, what I really want is—" And detail, as accurately as you can, what it is you really do want.

151

Don't feel ashamed to be precise. Don't think that they think you a dope for being so choosy. Or even if they *do* think you such a dope—so what? If you have fetishes and anti-fetishes, name your poisons. And when one of your friends finally does come up with a fellow who just seems to be for you, don't hesitate to ask "embarrassing" questions about him before you actually make the date. Such as: "Does he still, at 38, live with his mother?" "Why hasn't he married up to now?" "What kind of work does he do?" "What is his financial condition?"

Questions such as these, if you can get good answers to them, not only help you decide whether to go out with a prospect known to one of your friends, but also give you leads as to what to talk about when you do decide to date such an individual. You can, of course, use such information in a defensive manner: to convince yourself that you should *not* see a man, ostensibly for good reasons, but actually because you yourself are afraid of dating.

So the general rule is: When in doubt, date. You have nothing to lose but a little time and energy. And even if your date turns out to be a dud, you can usually get some experience (about yourself and others) that will serve you well on future dating. If, however, you really do have sufficient experience dating, and are not in the least afraid of seeing anyone, then prior information obtained about him may well be a good reason for not seeing him at all.

The decision as to whether or not you should see a given friend of a friend should often be taken not merely with the immediate prospect in mind, but with a longer-range view. If you feel that a certain man your girlfriend wants to introduce you to will almost certainly be a poor marriage prospect, but you also feel that he has a wide circle of friends to whom he will probably introduce you and that he consequently may lead you to *other* and better prospects, dating him (at least for a few times) may have some value to you. Short-range hedonism in meeting males can be just as self-destructive as it often is in other aspects of living. The date of the moment may be of little interest or value; but the future prospects that it offers you may be considerable.

In general, there are certain rules of the dating game when you enlist the services of friends. If your girlfriend gets you a date, for example, and you and your date go on a double date with her and her boyfriend, don't try to make eyes at her boyfriend or date him yourself. Once he stops seeing her, you may then (especially, with her permission) see him; but while he is seeing her, you keep your eager little hands off! Although dating is a competitive sport, you normally do not compete with your friends and relatives —else you are likely to end up sans dates *and* friends.

Although some amount of caution is wise in dating people who have been introduced to you by friends, don't think that you must entirely walk on eggs in this respect. If you date your cousin's neighbor, you naturally do not tell him how awful you think your cousin's taste in clothes, furnishings, and friends is. At the same time, you do not necessarily act like the Duchess of Bloomsbury, because you are terribly afraid that, through your date, your cousin will learn something bad about *you*. Better you should let your cousin know, in advance, those "bad" things about yourself—and then be able to relax and be yourself with your date.

Double dates arranged by your friends (or by yourself in conjunction with your friends) are perfectly fine forms of entertainments—but don't abuse them and use them for self-protective devices. It's relatively easy to get along with a man, especially a strange one, when there is another couple or two present to help carry the burden of conversation. But any date that begins and ends with another couple present is almost certain to be lacking in intimacy, and will not help you really to know your boyfriend and yourself.

Moreover, double dates normally exclude any amount of sex intimacy, and are particularly frustrating to a male—if he is a true male! If you must have them regularly, therefore, at least see that they usually end up with an hour or more of being alone with your date. Otherwise, you are likely to have a pleasant time for months with a man and end up by marrying someone you hardly know.

Blind dates are fine—as long as you manage, as noted above, to find something out about the man you are dating blind before you actually make the date. Blind dates, also, are safer if you make them for cocktails, lunch, or some other function which is for a relatively brief period of time, so that you do not have to spend three or four hours with someone that you can see, practically at first glance, you are highly unenthusiastic about.

Blind dates are particularly good if you have any trepidation about meeting new males. For if you have such fears, and you use them as excuses not to have blind dates, you will help protect your fears forever; while if you throw yourself into having blind dates, in

154

spite of your fears, you can use them as excellent vehicles for working through these worries. As ever, it cannot be the blind date itself that you fear, but some assumed catastrophes that you are constructing in connection with it. And it is your own catastrophizing assumptions, rather than the date itself, which you must start attacking and attacking and attacking.

Thus, if your girlfriend has arranged a blind date for you, and you are terribly worried about what will happen when you finally meet your date, you are almost certainly saying to yourself the following kinds of sentences: "Wouldn't it be terrible if I met him and he immediately took a violent dislike to me?" Or: "Suppose I say or do the wrong things when I meet him. Wouldn't *that* be awful!" Or: "Maybe he'll be a bore, and I just won't be able to stand even a single evening with him!"

All these kinds of internalized sentences have a sane and an insane element. The sane element is the first part of the sentence: "He may take a violent dislike to me," or "I may do the wrong things when I meet him," or "He may be a bore." These are perfectly sane statements, since the boyfriend you meet on a blind date *may* be nasty or boring; and you yourself *may* very well do the wrong things when you meet him.

The insane part of these sentences is the second part: "...and it would be *terrible* if he took a violent dislike to me"; "...it would be *awful* if I did the wrong things when I met him"; "...I just won't be able to *stand* him if he's a bore."

These statements are insane because they are not based on any objective evidence, but are completely definitional. For, of course, it won't be terrible if your

155

blind date takes a violent dislike to you—unless you *think* it will be terrible. And it won't be awful if you do the wrong things when you are out on a blind date— unless you *imagine* that it will be awful. And you will be able to stand your date if he is a bore—unless you *convince yourself* that you're not able to stand him. There are no good *reasons* why being rejected by a blind date, or doing the wrong thing in his presence, or having him bore you for awhile, are terrible, horrible, or catastrophic. You just falsely *believe* that these things are frightful; and by believing them so, you *make* them so.

Obviously, therefore, if you are afraid of blind dates, you'd better examine your own beliefs, your own internalized sentences, that make you afraid. The dates themselves are innocuous, and at the worst can be somewhat unpleasant. Their so-called horror lies in your own irrational philosophy of living—and that is what you should forthrightly go about examining and changing.

Parties and dances

One of the easiest places to meet new men, in our society, is at a party or a dance: since it is accepted protocol to be friendly and open with strangers in such surroundings. Moreover, particularly at a dance, American etiquette states that the male should normally approach the female and ask her to dance. Which means that you, as a female, have to do little but be approachable.

Not that there is a law against doing more. There isn't. And if you *really* want to make out well at a dance or a party, you'd be wise to be doing a good deal of the approaching yourself. For men, especially after they have been rejected by a couple of girls in a row, are often loath to keep plunging in and risking more rejections. And if you can make the overtures, or at the very least indicate by a smile or a gesture that you are most willing for the male to make them, your chances of meeting a greater number of men at any social gathering will be greatly enhanced.

When a male does approach you at this kind of gathering, watch your own self-repeated nonsense! Yes, he may be ungainly looking, or a little too forward, or dressed peculiarly, or awkward in his speech. But are these the *real* reasons why you are remaining aloof, giving him no help, and finally rejecting him? Or is it not, rather, that *you* are so afraid that he will find out the depths of *your* inadequacy, that you would rather have almost *any* excuse to reject him than wait for him to finally discard you?

Watch, particularly, the garbage you tend to feed yourself when you are in the presence of the most attractive males you find at a party or dance. Are you telling yourself that they're too superficial? Or conceited? Or cold?

Don't you really mean, on a deeper level, that they could never possibly be interested in drab, shy, unexciting you? And have you any factual evidence, really, that they couldn't be? None of that crap, now! What have you got to lose? You know you came to this affair precisely because you might meet such an attractive man. Now why don't you barge in and try? If you can siphon him off from the crowd of other girls who are probably also interested in him, fine. If you cannot, and he never gives you another nod or takes your phone number and fails to call, what does that mean about you? That you're a worthless slob, a hopeless fool? Rot! It merely means that you have made a good effort and unfortunately failed.

Not that dances and parties may be the best of all hunting grounds for you, for they may definitely not be. The easiest place to meet a male is not necessarily the most satisfactory place. Perhaps the crowd that normally populates these kinds of affairs is too young for you; or too unintellectual; or too crude. Even then, you still may find *one* man each time who happens to be your special cup of tea. If not, too bad. Stay away, then, from parties and dances—as long as you don't stay away from everything else, too. For, unless your dream man is truly impossible to find, there must be *some* place where he hangs out. Find it and go *there*.

Organized groups

Another of the easiest places to meet suitable members of the other sex is in organized groups; such as political organizations, religious groups, poetry reading societies, school classes, country clubs, etc. The advantage of these kinds of groups is that they meet regularly, not merely at a single session; and if you keep attending their gatherings, you are almost certain to become friendly, at least in a superficial way, with most of their male members. This is fine: particularly if the group of which you are a member is one that tends to have people of your own ilk in it.

The trouble with most groups of this sort is that they are too limited in number. A college class, for example, usually only has thirty or forty students, and half of these are likely to be of your own sex. Of the other half, a good number will be married, engaged, or otherwise taken; and a good number will be too homely, too stupid, too disturbed, or too something else for your tastes. Consequently, you are lucky to find even three or four true eligibles in such a group; and during the four or five months that you will probably stay in this class, the number of eligibles will remain exactly the same (or even decrease, if some of the members drop out of the class).

In terms of numbers, therefore, organized groups tend to be distinctly limited; and for the amount of time that you may spend in such groups—perhaps thirty or forty hours a term, for example, in a class—you are not getting very many pickings. The same amount of time spent actively looking for men in more public places—in the college cafeteria, say, or in the library—will almost always bring you in contact with a much greater number of prospects, even though it may not be as easy to talk to these prospects as it would be in an organized group.

Organized groups also are often sexually or amatively constrictive. In a church group, for instance, you will naturally meet church-interested people: who in many instances will be puritanical, not overly bright, and perhaps fanatic individuals who may make great church members—but hardly great lovers or husbands. In a political group—especially an extreme right-wing or left-wing group—you may largely encounter dedicated men who are much more interested in the Cause than they are in you and a potential family life. In a ballet or modern dance class, you may meet many males who are homosexual.

159

If, therefore, you deliberately choose to join any group because of the possibility of encountering suitable males there, make sure that you carefully pick the kind of group where you are most likely to meet the types of males that you, personally, would be interested in— and to meet them in sufficient numbers to make your participation in regular group events worthwhile.

In making out well in a group situation, you have to follow some of the same bold and assertive patterns that would be necessary in less protective environments. For even in a class, where you see the same people over and over again, you can quietly stick to yourself, get into few intimate discussions with others, and remain so afraid of direct contact that the other group members hardly know you are there—or know you are there, all right, but are afraid to speak to you or get involved with you, since you behave so peculiarly.

Even when you get to know the members of a group well enough to talk to them, simply because you have seen them several times and they perhaps have made sufficient overtures to you, the eligible males in the group (particularly the brightest and most alert ones) are not going to look upon you with favor, in all probability *because* you are shy and withdrawn. The more you speak up; the more you courageously jump in where others often fear to tread; the more you frankly go after the intimate relations that you want with certain males in the class, the more you are likely to impress them with the idea that you are actually *worth* knowing.

So again: watch your internalized crummy sentences! Are you continually saying to yourself: "Oh, well, if I speak up, the members of the group won't like me,

160

anyway, and they'll just see what a dunce I am"? Or: "They'll think I'm too forward, and hate me for that"? Or: "What's the use of getting to know them: they're really not my type"? Are *these* your conversations with yourself? And, if they are, how much do they really hold water? *That's* what you must keep questioning and challenging if you are to take full advantage of any groups that you do join in order to make valuable heterosexual contacts.

Business contacts

Making sex-love contacts through your job decidedly has its disadvantages: since, if such contacts fail to work out well (which, statistically speaking, *most* social-sexual contacts do) you may lose your job, have to work closely with an ex-lover for whom you now have no love or even liking, or otherwise get into job difficulties. It is often wise, therefore, not to get amatively entangled with those with whom you work closely; such as your boss, your employees, or your fellow-workers.

Nonetheless, your job can still often be used as a good source of contacts with eligible males. If, for example, you work as an airline stewardess, travel agent, receptionist, or any one of a number of jobs that puts you into contact with a good many members of the general public, there is an excellent chance that ultimately you will meet someone, through this contact, who will be quite eligible as a boyfriend. If, on the other hand, you are cooped up in an office by yourself, or only working with a group of cantankerous females, your job is not likely to be any asset to your social life.

161

This does not mean that you should rush to take the first job that comes along that offers you some man-hunting possibilities. You probably could attract quite a few men if you worked as a ditch-digger or a road-mender; but I wouldn't exactly advise such occupations. Where, however, one job is pretty much the same as another, and one offers man-meeting potentialities while the other does not, you should carefully consider the one with the better male contacts, even though it may pay a little less money or have other disadvantages about it. Most of your leisure hours, if you are a working girl, you just will not have too much time to look for males. If you can do a good bit of your man-hunting while you are being paid for working, so much the better!

The fine art of the pickup

Let's squarely face it: the quickest, easiest, and in most respects best way to meet a man, if you are a resident of or work in a metropolitan area, is by the spontaneous pickup techniques—yes, I said by picking him up right where you first see him: on the street, in a restaurant, at the library, on a bus, or wherever else he happens to be. Why is this the best method? For several reasons:

1. It is unquestionably the fastest technique ever invented. Going to dances, parties, lectures, group discussions, etc., all are fairly time-consuming: since, at the very least, you must dress, go out, get to where you are going, and then usually spend some time there before you have any man-grabbing opportunities. But picking a man up on the street corner or at a bar where

you just happen, anyway, to be, is not at all time-consuming: in fact, it is instant companionship.

2. If you actively (rather than passively) pick up strange men, you are employing probably the most selective technique known. For when you are formally introduced to a man, or arrange through friends to go out on a blind date, or even meet a man at a dance, you are being relatively unselective: since your field of choice is strictly limited, and you can only select someone from within this constricted field. On a blind date or a formal introduction, you have literally one man out of one to choose from; and if he is not exactly your style, that's too bad, you are simply stuck with him, at least for the evening. At a party or a dance, you may have fifteen or twenty eligible males to choose from—but rarely more than that.

If, however, you go out on the streets of almost any sizable town in the country with the intent of picking up a strange man, you have literally hundreds, even thousands, of men to select from, and it is extremely unlikely, if you persist in your attempt, that within a short period of time you will not find one who is more to your taste than the one you are likely to get from a much smaller pool. The more highly selective you are, in fact, the more you should be picking up strange men: since you will obviously have to go through scores of males to find the one you really like, and the only way you can get such scores of males quickly is to meet them in the most casual sorts of ways.

3. If you pick up men correctly, your chances of getting the kind of person with the calibre of looks, brains, character, etc. that *you* want are much better than if you use more passive techniques of encountering males.

163

What do we mean by picking up men "correctly"? *Actively* seeking them out and *boldly* making the first overtures yourself.

Passive pickup techniques are much inferior. If, for example, you walk along the street, or sit around a museum waiting for some man to pick *you* up, you are first of all not easily going to get the person whose looks and attributes you especially want. Secondly, you may only get, this way, the brash, truckdriver types who specialize in picking up females. Thirdly, the man who picks you up may possibly be a murderer, a sex fiend, or some other kind of unpleasant character who is not really interested in your companionship, but who only has ideas that you aren't enthusiastic about. Getting the idea out of his head that you just *have* to sleep with him that night may be awfully difficult.

If, on the other hand, *you* are the one to do the active selecting and to make the first overtures, there is much less of a chance that the man you choose will be too peculiar or looking for a murder victim; and if you decide that you definitely don't want to go to bed with him that night, you will have much greater ease, in most instances, convincing him that a longer friendship is desirable before you do decide to do so. Men who pick you, in other words, may be out for no good; while men whom *you* pick are likely to be more normal human beings, whom you can more easily handle.

Aren't you *still* likely to get into some trouble if you go around promiscuously talking to strange men? Not if you handle yourself correctly. For there is no law that says that just because you pick up a man you *must* go to his apartment or take him to yours. All you have to do, usually, is go somewhere with him, some

164

distinctly public place like a restaurant or a bar, where you can sit and talk for hours, and find out various things about each other.

If, after several such hours of conversation have passed, you *then* feel you know him well enough to go to his place or ask him to yours, fine. But again: you don't *have* to end up in any overly-private tête-à-tête. In fact, if you find, after being with a given man for a short length of time, you just do not like him as you thought you would, and you don't even want to spend any more time with him, there is no reason why you can't plead a previous engagement that you have to keep, or say that you're not feeling too well, and insist on going off by yourself. If necessary, you can even give your non-wanted acquaintance a false telephone number and address, just before you fondly bid him adieu.

4. The art and science of picking up men gives you, of course, something to do almost any single minute that you want to do it. Even (hell, especially!) at three in the morning, if you are bored and lackadaisical, you can always go out and find a man to pick up somewhere. And talk about an antidote to loneliness—what could be better? Naturally, some of the men that you pick up will hardly be the most exciting or most fascinating creatures you ever met. But they will always be *new;* will tend to be somewhat *different* from the last man you were entangled with; can teach you *something* you haven't learned before; and can certainly fill up your time far better than your filling it up by moping around, feeling that you never can get anywhere in your love life, and wishing you were dead.

5. If the law of averages works—which it invariably,

in the long or short run, does—then the pickup technique is the one most divinely calculated to make it work for you. For if you stick to the usual sources of supply, you will be lucky if you meet, every year, twenty new males; and, on the law of averages, you will be damned fortunate if even one of these is your particular cupcake. But if you actively resort to the pickup technique, you should easily be able to encounter a dozen or more males every single month, or a hundred and fifty or more a year. Out of *that* supply source, you really do have a good chance to pick and be picked by at least a couple who are good love and marital possibilities.

6. The pickup method, of course, need not be used exclusively. There is no reason why, while you are employing it, you cannot use all the more "regular" methods, too—such as friends, parties, organized groups, and the rest. But when these are not working too well, when you have no good prospect in sight, and when you just happen to be out on the street, sitting in a park, or eating a sandwich at a lunch counter, and there just happens to be an attractive, intelligent-looking male within reach, what is the point in your *not* asking him the time, or commenting on the weather, or asking for a match, or otherwise making an innocuous overture to him?

"All right!" you say, "you've convinced me that if I did resort to the highly unorthodox method of selecting my own prospects in public places, and making some kind of verbal and gestural overtures to them, I would have a better chance to find the kind of a man I want than if I go along sticking to more formal means of

166

meeting men. But I just *know* that I won't do it that
way. I just *can't*."

You mean you *haven't*; and that you *think* you can't.
But, of course, you can. *If* you stop telling yourself the
dreadful nonsense that you've been telling yourself for
the last decade or more: that what would people think
if you picked up men? And what would the men think?
And wouldn't it be terrible if, after putting yourself
out to meet males like this, the males kept rejecting
you?

Bosh—pure bosh! And that's exactly the point: it's
not your society that's keeping you from efficiently and
wisely picking up men you think are desirable. It's not
your upbringing. It's not the men themselves. It's only
--and I mean *only*—the nonsense that you keep telling
yourself *about* your society, *about* your upbringing,
about the men you might talk to. This nonsense, of
course, you did learn from your society (especially
from your sainted mother) in the course of your upbringing. But it only remains, now, because *you* have
kept endlessly repeating it to yourself, ceaselessly convincing yourself that this crap is true. And you *still* are!

"All I have to do then," you ask, "is to *un*convince
myself that the conventional rules of manhunting are
the right ones, and then I shall be easily able to talk
to strangers in public places. Is that right?"

That's exactly right. All you have to do to give up
the political, economic, or religious views of your fore-
bears is to *un*convince yourself of the truth of these
beliefs and then to become active in different political,
economic, or religious groups than the ones they ad-
hered to. Similarly with choosing males. All you have

to do is thoroughly to *un*convince yourself that your mother and girlfriends have the right idea about man-hunting and then to become active in employing different techniques than they would recommend or approve. After just a few weeks of this kind of vigorous, activity-directed *un*convincing, you will almost certainly be so convinced of the *new* line of approach that it will tend to become second-nature with you, just as the old, crummy line of approach has now become.

"But it's not easy. It's very hard to do what you are trying to get me to do."

You're right, it's not easy. It's hard—at least for the few weeks that you're first working at it. But it's much harder *not* to—and it's much harder that way *forever*. So go back to your conventional ways of meeting men, if you insist that the unconventional ones are too hard. Continue to be the ninny you were raised to be for the rest of your life. You won't die of it. But you won't live very much, either.

Chapter 7

How to Get Along with the Men You Meet

Let us suppose that somehow or other, by hook or by crook, you have met a suitable man, and that your problem is how to get along with him well, so that he will think you a suitable companion and will be interested in prolonging the relationship with you. What are some of the things you can do to help yourself in this respect?

The art of conversation

"But when I do meet a man, I have absolutely nothing to say."

"I just lose all my wits, when I am with a man whom I really like. I sit there like a high school freshman, and can't think of a thing that's intelligent."

"I know that men like witty girls, those with snappy answers and bons mots. But even though I have a good sense of humor when I'm with my friends, I'm as dull and unwitty as I can be when I'm with a boy."

These are typical remarks that, as a psychotherapist, I hear all the time. Almost every unmarried female I see believes that she must be utterly clever and inordinately wise every moment she is with a potential lover or husband, and that she will most certainly lose him if she is not.

Like Ida R., who said to her psychotherapy group

members one evening: "I don't know. I'm just out of it. I keep going away to resorts on weekends and during the summer, in order to meet new men, and I just can't seem to get anywhere. The other girls stand around chatting gaily and talking ever so wittily to the boys they meet, while I just stand there saying nothing. I can't get out a clever remark to save my life. So naturally I don't get anywhere with the men I want to like me."

"What does that have to do with it?" asked Tom, another group member. "Since when do men want terribly witty and clever girls?"

"Don't they?" asked Ida.

"Not me!" said Tom. "When I see a very clever, always the one with a bright quip, girl, I run like hell. Who needs it?"

"Me, too," chimed in Fred (the one male member of the group who had no problems with girls, but who was pretty messed up in his business affairs). "I think I can say that I've had good relationships with many girls during the past several years. But of all of them, all that I really liked and got along with very well that is, I can't remember a single one who was exceptionally good at repartee. Oh, yes: there was one. But she was such a nut, who just *had* to be cleverer than anyone around her, that I just couldn't take it, and I soon had to break off with her. Hell, I couldn't open my mouth for a minute, without her making a joke of something I said. As Tom just said: Who needs it?"

"But *don't* men like witty girls?" Ida persisted. "From what I've always seen, they do."

"Sure they do," said Grace (who also had few problems with members of the other sex, but enough parental problems to fill a case book). "They *like* witty girls, especially right at the beginning, when a clever remark will help put off or cover up some of the embarrassment that usually goes with meeting a new person. Oh, I know it shouldn't and needn't, this embarrassment, and I must say that I'm getting better in that respect myself, ever since I started coming to group. But it is there with many of us at the beginning; and a little cleverness may go some ways to cover it up. So it may help. But it's hardly as *necessary* as you think it is. And some of the best operators I know, the girls who get further with the men in the briefest period of time, aren't witty at all. They just barge in, say whatever is on their mind—things that to me often sound very stupid, in fact—but the boys seem to love it. As long as they *keep* talking. *That* seems to be the thing."

"That's what I've found, too," agreed Marilyn (a group member who had been very shy several months previously, but was now improving in this respect). "I used to feel just the way you do, Ida. I sounded so darned *stupid*, whenever I opened my mouth in front of boys, that I said just as little as I possibly could. Of course, *they* then had a hard time talking to me, too. And soon there were long periods of almost dead silence, while I anxiously racked my brain for something brilliant to say. Naturally, the more I racked, the less it came."

"Yes, that's just what happens to me!" said Ida. "I know just what you mean."

"Yes," continued Marilyn. "I'm sure you do. Anyway, no more! I gave up, a few months ago, right after we spent the entire group session speaking about my problems; gave up trying to be so sparkling, and settled

171

down to being me, just me. You should see what a difference it has been making! I'm probably even *less* scintillating, now, than I ever was in my life. But boys seem to find me more *interesting*."

"But what exactly do you do?" asked Ida.

"Do? I just listen carefully to what *they*, the boys, are saying. And I think I listen for the first time in my life, this way, since before I was listening only, really, to myself, and the junk *I* was saying to me. Now I listen carefully to them. And I simply respond, the way I feel like responding. If a boy, for instance, says, or if he used to say, 'You know, that was really good acting,' after we've seen a picture or a play, I used to feel impelled to say something like 'Yes, but did you notice—' and then I'd make some funny remark; often, in fact, a not very appropriate funny remark. Now I just respond, 'Yes, it was good acting,' or 'Do you really think it was? What did you find so good about it?' I try to *feel* what he is feeling, rather than to put myself immediately back into the center of the floor and get him to be all absorbed in me and my witty remarks. It works out much better that way. The boys seem to like it. And *I* actually enjoy myself much more, because I am really being much more *me*."

"Do the rest of you men seem to feel the same way, too?" asked Ida of the males in the group. "Do you feel, as Fred and Tom do, that clever girls are not necessarily the best to be with? Or, as Grace does, that to be bright and wise-cracking has its advantages, but that a girl can easily get along without it?"

We took an informal poll of the male members of the group. Much to Ida's surprise, every single one of them said that he preferred a girl who was less brilliant but more interested in him and more honest about her own responses. In fact, the consensus seemed to be that the cleverer, at least at incessant repartee, a girl was, the less likely was she going to turn out to be a nice enough or stable enough person for the boy to get along with on a more permanent basis. As one of the group members, John, summed up:

"For just a fun date, with a girl I have no interest in getting seriously involved with, I must say that I have no objection to laughing the whole day away. But with a girl whom I really like and want to get to know, the laughing and joking often gets in the way, and at the end of a date I know no more about her, really, than I knew at the beginning. Cleverness undoubtedly has its place in life; but on a long-time basis, how big a place is it likely to keep?"

Ida finally began to be convinced that her problem was not her inability to be a supremely clever conversationalist with the males she met—but her worry *about* her lack of brilliance. She defined herself as good, and particularly as heterosexually adequate, when she was excellent at repartee; and because she defined herself in this manner, she actually became worse at intersexual dialogue than she otherwise would have been. This is what normally happens to people who define themselves as worthwhile in terms of some outside criterion: they then usually become worse at fulfilling that criterion. They are so focused upon "How am I doing at this thing?" that they fail to focus on "*What am I doing?*" and they lose instead of gain competence. When Ida, prodded by the group, started to follow Marilyn's example and to try to *enjoy herself* with her male companions, instead of striving mightily to *impress*

173

them with her cleverness, she began to do much better in her dating relationships.

The art of heterosexual (or any other kind) of conversation, then, rarely lies in the knack of being brilliant or scintillating. Most of all, you must be *interested* in your partner—rather than obsessed with what he is thinking of *you*. Ask him questions about himself: where was he raised?—how did he grow up?—what are his likes and dislikes?—how does he feel about marrying?—how does he react to your ideas?

As he responds to your questions, respond back. Don't merely say: "Oh, that's fascinating!" or "How nice!" Tell him what *you* feel about your parents, your hobbies, your work, friends, marriage, sex, etc. If you want to become intimate with anyone, the best rule usually is: confide yourself. The more of your own deep and dark secrets you let out, the more he is likely to tell you how many people he has killed and stolen from. The more precise you are about your sexual, religious, political, and other views, the more he will normally tend to tell you the gory details of his.

Conversation, in other words, largely consists of drawing out others and expressing yourself. If, in the process, you can get in a bon mot or two, and indicate that you have a sense of humor and some verve, fine. But don't overdo the glib line! And don't crack so many jokes that there's no time for serious interchange. Remember that if you really do get along well with this particular guy and he in turn is favorably struck by you, you are likely to be spending hours, days, even years together. And who can keep up a series of gags for *that* long? Or who would want to, if she could?

Accepting the male viewpoint

For both biological and social reasons there *is* a definite difference between males and females in our society. And if you are going to get along wondrously well with men, you must at least gracefully accept this difference, even though you may never get highly enthusiastic about it.

This means, in plain English, that you'd better fully accept the fact that most males are much more interested in sex than love, that they love *after* being sexually satisfied rather than (as females often do) in order to be, and that even their loving (or vital absorption in some person or thing) tends to be considerably less romantic and monogamous than is, in our culture, female loving. This also means that there is nothing *insulting* or intrinsically *nasty* about how the male feels about sex, you, and his outside interests. You may never greatly *like* the way he is in these respects; but it is pointless for you not to accept the fact that he *is* the way he is, and at best you're probably only going to be able to change him slightly.

You may, then, be fairly accurate if you find yourself saying, "Men are interested in only one thing—sex," or "Men are really only interested in their work and not in their home or family," or "Men are all selfish." To a considerable degree, if not entirely, these statements are true. So they're true! What's the *horror* of men being interested in sex, in their work, or in themselves? It might, perhaps, be a much better world if this were not so (though it might be a much worse world, too!). But it *is* so. And all the wishing on your part, and all the bitter demanding that men be different from the

175

way they are, is not going to change things very much.
Except for the worse!

If, then, you are interested in finding a man for your
true, true love, seek exactly for that: a *man*. Not a
mouse; not an angel; not a female; not a little boy; but
a man. And fully expect, if you find such a man, that
he will have, for better *and* for worse, some distinctly
manly traits. For the most part, in all likelihood, he
will be more sexually demanding, less devoted to the
children, more fickle, more absorbed in outside affairs,
less warm and romantic, less sociable, and more interested in some silly sporting events than you. Tough!
That's the way the sonofagun is. After all, he's a *man*.
And isn't that why you wanted him in the first place?

This does not mean, of course, that if he's the man,
you have to be the mouse in the family. As we stressed
in previous chapters, you can still assert and be yourself and get along with a bright, not too disturbed male.
Indeed, he'll probably like you, in the long run, better
that way. But your not acting as a patsy or a perennial
yes-woman does not mean that you have to go to the
other extreme and be a termagant.

Live and let live! Be yourself, as much as you can
be in any intimate human relationship—and let him be
himself as much as he can reasonably be in the same
relationship. You still don't have to *like* him for everything he is (for his forgetting to call when he stays
late at the office or reneging on his promise to take your
little brother to the ball game), but why can't you
learn to gracefully *lump* many of his meaner or pettier
characteristics? After all, he's going to have to accept
a hell of a lot of defects in *you*, if he is to stay peacefully with you for any length of time. Well?

In *A Man for Every Woman* (New York: Macmillan, 1959), Richard Klemer has written one of the sanest books on manhunting that I have ever read. At times, however, he goes a little too far in his espousal of what I call Florence Nightingaleism. Thus, he notes that "getting someone to love you isn't easy since it involves the most difficult sacrifice a human being is ever called upon to make. It requires the temporary suppression of the ever-burning desire for the satisfaction of your own emotional needs while you give your total attention to the satisfaction of someone else's needs."

Total? Perish forbid!

Dr. Klemer is quite right in pointing out that if you want to get a man to love you and to stay loving, you must very often suppress your desire to have him be terribly kind to you and must, instead, give considerable attention to *his* desires and (alas) demands. But *very often* hardly means *always*. Every once in a while your partner is going to want help and understanding, while ignoring your own wants. He is going to ask you, for example, to satisfy him sexually, but make very little effort to satisfy you when you are frustrated.

At such a time, instead of telling yourself, "That lousy bastard! Look what he's doing to me, when I've been so nice to him! How can he *do* such a thing?" you are going to have to stop and think: "Now isn't that too bad! Here, he keeps wanting to be satisfied, but he makes little or no effort to satisfy me. I wish that he were different and were more considerate of me, but he isn't. Now, why don't I keep being nice to him and see, by being so, if I can't induce him after awhile to think more about *my* satisfactions."

This kind of mature thinking and behaving on your

part is not sick self-sacrificism (or Florence Night-ingaleism) for two reasons: First of all, you may engage in it every once in awhile, but not *always*. If your man always demands his own sex satisfaction and never thinks of yours, then who needs him? Off to the divorce courts and the remarrying races for you!

Secondly, and even more importantly, you should temporarily squelch some of your own desires while giving in to some of those of your boyfriend or husband because you are basically looking out for your *own* interest and know that such good behavior on your part will *eventually* bring you return satisfactions. It is not *merely* that you love your mate and enjoy making sacrifices for him (though that is part of the game, *too*, and a rather rewarding part of it at times). It is *also* that, in the back of your mind, you want your relation-ship with him to continue *because* it has other rewards; and you therefore willingly surrender some of your present pleasures for future gains. As every sane person, and particularly one who is in the difficult relationship of going together steadily or of marriage, must.

Within *reasonable* limits, then, Dr. Klemer is right. If you want your man to love you *and* by his loving you to make certain moderate sacrifices for you, then you will have to cater to his desires, at times, even when you do not especially feel like doing so: satisfy him sexually when you are tired yourself, listen to his troubles when you'd really much rather talk about your own, etc. So far, so good. But not *too* much farther!

Treating your man as an individual

The first, and probably most important, psychological

178

principle is that although all human beings are surprisingly alike in many respects—since they are born of the same species and raised in a fairly uniform social atmosphere—they are also all significantly different from each other. Even identical twins, who are born from the same neatly divided cell, are never exactly alike, but have some different tastes, desires, and ways of responding. And non-twins, even when members of the same family brood, can be so dissimilar as to seem inhabitants of two different universes.

Any particular man you choose, therefore, is *not* exactly the same as all other men. Perhaps you intimately knew, before he came along, a father, a brother, a prior lover, or even a now deceased or divorced husband. Fine: you may well have learned some interesting and useful things about men from your association with these others. But he, your present man, is not the same as they were. Nor *should* he be. He is only himself; and must, if you are to understand him and get along well with him, fully be accepted as such.

All men, in other words, are *not* as protective of you as your father may have been. Nor as sexually disinterested in you as your brothers perhaps were. Nor as neat, nor as sweet-smelling, nor as carefree as the first sixteen-year-old who walked hand in hand with you on the dunes and talked to you endlessly of you and you and you.

Sometimes your present lover is surly. Sometimes he is a bore. Sometimes he is completely indifferent to you. O.K.: that's he. By the same token, he may at other times be maddeningly delightful or the best damned lay you ever had. Whatever he is, he is definitely not your mother's or your best girlfriend's man; he is the unique, good and bad, sugar and spice individual who is *yours*.

So stop the goddam endless comparisons, comparisons. Stop feeling that you are terribly deprived when some lack of his clearly shows up; or horribly hurt when, for the nonce, he insensitively ignores you. A flawless angel, he will never be; a perfect doll, rarely and, at best, intermittently. He is, as you are, an individual; and individuals are always exceptionally sweet —and painfully sour; unusually nice—and awfully nasty. How could they possibly, as individuals, be otherwise?

"But," you may sadly wail, "he is much *too* much of an individual for me. Other men play golf—but he just *lives* on the golf course. Or other men eye every lovely floosie who passes—but he actually gets up and follows them to their doorsteps. Who needs *that* kind of individuality?"

If that's the way you feel, I reply, fine. You are certainly entitled to your belief that your particular man is *too* much of an individual, and that you'd rather have someone who is more like the run-of-the-mill lover or husband. But if that's what you want, why don't you stop your silly wailing and go get it? Whatever the man of your choice now is, he is not to *blame* for being what he is. You don't have to put up with him, to be sure; but neither is there any necessity for his changing. If you will just calmly show him that you won't take him the way he is, and try to get him to improve somewhat, maybe you'll succeed. But not by wailing! Besides, what makes you think that some other man won't have *his own* pain-in-the-neck idiosyncracies, too?

"Are you saying that I simply must accept the man I

have, no matter how badly he behaves? That I must have patience and fortitude?"

No, I am saying that, if you are to act sanely, you must either *calmly* accept or reject him. *Agitatedly* staying with him (or agitatedly leaving him) will do you no good whatever. If he has too many traits that you consider to be bad, quietly leave him. If he has poor traits but is still, all things considered, the man you want, then unangrily try to help him change these traits for the better. If he cannot or will not change, but you still do not want to leave him, then your only sensible choice is to accept him with his deficiencies: to dislike his disadvantages, but nonetheless to continue loving *him*.

Patience and fortitude, then, are in order *after* you have decided that, in spite of his failings, you still want this particular man. Up to that time, you can afford to be somewhat impatient—since there are presumably plenty of other fish in the sea, and your desperately hanging on to this one may not be an act of wisdom.

Even under these circumstances, however, the general rule still is: Be as patient and as nice as you can be to your chosen partner for a period of two or three months, no matter how badly he behaves during this time. If persistent good behavior on your part still does not induce him to act better, then by all means start to pack your things, or his. If you still, at this time, have great difficulty in leaving, and want to take the risks of living with a seriously deficient or disturbed mate, you've really got a problem. Seek professional help yourself—and read the next chapter.

Chapter 8

How to Handle a Difficult or Emotionally Disturbed Man

Let us hope that you will never need to take serious note of this chapter, or at least will only have to resort to it temporarily. For the very best thing for you to do when you are involved with an exceptionally difficult or seriously disturbed man is to leave him. No matter how good his *other* qualities—such as looks and intelligence and bedmanship—may be, if he is really a most difficult or emotionally unstable person, your chances of being permanently happy with him are slim. With all the hope and work in the world on your part, they may be somewhat better. But still slim.

If, nonetheless, you insist on sticking with a distinctly difficult man, there are some things you can do to make life easier for you. Let us see what these things are.

Cultivating your own emotional garden

The more ornery the man with whom you are intimately associated, the saner you have to be in order to get along with him satisfactorily. Consequently, instead of spending too much time and energy in trying to change him, you must devote considerable thought and effort to changing you: to acquiring the kind of sensible

183

outlook that will enable you to live with a nut and like it.

Edna B. was a charming, vivacious girl who had had, in her twenty-four years of life, scores of boys who were interested in her, and several with whom she carried on intensive love affairs. But all of these boys, she complained, were weak and bizarre, and she would no more think of marrying any of them than she would think of giving up her chosen career as a teacher and settling down to a purely housewifey routine. They were nice boys, all of them, the ones with whom she became deeply involved, and she remained friendly with them for years, long after she had stopped having any sex relations with them. But they were hopelessly, helplessly weak—and that she just couldn't stand (especially since, as she well knew, she had more than enough lack of moral fiber of her own with which to contend).

Then Edna met Donald. One thing you could say for sure about Donald: he was quite unlike all the other boys she had gone with. Where they were nice, he was something of a real bastard. Where they catered to her, he catered to nobody. Where they had all the social graces, he was practically a friendless hermit. But he did, with all his bitterness and nastiness, truckle to no man—nor woman. Edna liked that enormously in Donald; and when he also proved to be exceptionally good in the hay (in contradistinction to the many impotent and semi-homosexual males she had previously known), that clinched it: she felt that Donald was really for her and that, with all his obvious problems and difficulties, she just had to make it with him.

I warned Edna at the start about what she was getting into. Granting that, so far, she had not met any males as strong as Donald, that was no reason why she would not in time meet one if she continued to look. I strongly advised her to keep looking. But her ears were already plugged with love batting.

"I know you're probably right," she said, "but I don't care. It's going to be awfully difficult living with Donald. But it's even worse being with any of those other weaklings that I've had all my life. So you just teach me to be able to take him, and even though my life won't then be perfect, it'll be much better than it's been before. Now, what must I do to be able to take him and not get upset when he gets so bitter and nasty, not only at me but at others, too. How can I not let that bother me?"

"How can you *let* it bother you?" I countered. "Here, you just told me that you know he's going to be difficult to get along with; but then in the next breath, you're really saying: 'But he *shouldn't* be!'"

"Am I really saying that? How? I don't see it."

"It's as clear as can be, if you only look at it. On the one hand, you're saying: 'I know he's difficult.' This means, if it means anything, that 'I don't want him to be as hard as he is to get along with; but he is; so I'll just have to accept him the way he is, since I also don't want to be without him.' Isn't that what 'I know he's difficult' really means?"

"Yes. I *do* know he's difficult. But I'm willing to take him that way."

"You *think* you're willing to take him that way. You *say* that you are; and you really *believe* that you are. But the very next second you say: 'How can I not let

185

that (meaning, his bitterness and his nastiness) bother me?' So clearly, you *are* bothered by his behavior.'"

"Yes; and that's what I want you to help me not be bothered by."

"Fine. But your being bothered by his behavior is just another way of saying to yourself: (*a*) 'I know he's difficult,' and (*b*) 'But I *can't stand* his being difficult; he *shouldn't* be that way.'"

"Is *that* what being bothered by anything is?"

"*Isn't it?* If you were saying to yourself, instead: (*a*) 'I know he's difficult,' and (*b*) 'So what? I *can* stand his being that way; I don't like it, but that's the way he is,' would you *then* be bothered?"

"Well—no, I guess I wouldn't be very bothered then. I wouldn't like it, as you say, but I wouldn't be bothered by not liking it."

"Exactly. Your being bothered is an *addition* to your not liking his bitter and nasty behavior—and an *unnecessary* addition to it. You can't very well help disliking the way he is acting—for who the devil would *like* it? But you can help bothering yourself about your disliking it."

"I could say: 'I don't like it. But that's the way it is. And I have come to terms with myself to accept the way it is. So I just have to accept what I don't like.'"

"Right. In fact, your final sentence, 'So I just have to accept what I don't like,' is really implicit in your very first sentence, 'I know he's difficult, but I don't care.' If you *really* don't care, then you must be *accepting* the fact of his being difficult; and if so, you can't possibly be bothered by it. Obviously, however, you *are* bothered: which means that you are just giving lip-service to the statement, 'I really don't care.'"

"I'm saying: 'I really don't care about his being the way he is,' but then I'm immediately contradicting myself, by letting myself be bothered, and telling myself: 'But I really do care; I *hate* the way he is; and he shouldn't *be* that way.'"

"Yes. The sentence: 'I really don't care about his being the way he is,' means: '*Even* though I don't like the way he is, I am willing to accept him—because of his other advantages.' But your feeling of being bothered therefore directly contradicts your feeling of supposedly accepting him the way he is. You have *two* diametrically opposed feelings—because you have two diametrically opposed beliefs."

"And I must rid myself of one of these sets of beliefs?"

"Yes. Either you must pretty fully believe: 'Even though I don't like the way he is, I am willing to accept him,' or you must believe: 'Because I don't like the way he is, I am not willing to accept him.' You can't slice the pie both ways and expect to come up with a perfect piece."

"But if I *do* have both sets of beliefs—that I am and am not willing to accept him with his faults—how can I get rid of one of them?"

"First of all, by admitting that you do have two opposed views and that you *can't* happily exist with both. You can't believe that the earth is flat and *also* believe that it is round and hope to get along well as a navigator. *One* of these beliefs has got to go."

"But in the case of the earth's being round or flat, I can find objective evidence to prove one of these views and disprove the other. Can I find such evidence in relation to my accepting or rejecting Donald?"

"No, not in the same way. You can find evidence of

187

whether or not Donald is a nasty person—just as you can discover whether or not the earth is round. But once you decide that he *is*, let us say, nasty, you then have your choice between liking him or disliking him for being nasty, and of accepting him or rejecting him for being dislikable, if that is the way you find him to be. That is to say: once the facts of Donald's being nasty are known, you can give a certain value judgment to these facts—and then you must live with your own value judgments. But you cannot very well give two opposing values to Donald's nastiness and expect to live comfortably with *both* these values."

"Are you implying that because my values—or what you previously called my beliefs—about Donald's nastiness are set by me, and are not necessarily related to the facts of his being or not being nasty, I can change them any time I want to do so?"

"Yes, essentially. Although it's not exactly as easy as all that. For once you set, let us say, negative values on Donald's being nasty, and you convince yourself that these *are* your values, you will then, naturally, have to do something to unconvince yourself in regard to these values if you later want to change them."

"But I probably didn't *consciously* convince myself that Donald's nastiness was unlikable and that I can't stand his being nasty, did I?"

"No, you probably didn't. Without even realizing that you were doing so, you convinced yourself that Donald's behavior was unlikable and that you couldn't stand it, or couldn't stand him for engaging in such unlikable behavior. But you could have convinced yourself consciously, too. And once you have unconsciously made yourself believe something, you can still

188

consciously see what you believe and get yourself to disbelieve it."

"Yes, you keep saying that—but *how?*"

"Well, let's look, first, at the process of convincing yourself of anything. In regard to objective facts, as we said before, you convince yourself that they are true or not true by looking at the empirical evidence. You check the curvature of the earth, for example, by going up in a plane or a rocket, or by sailing around the globe, and you finally conclude that it is round instead of flat. If you found that, when you were up in a plane or rocket, the earth did not curve, you might well conclude that it was flat. But you don't find this; so you base your conviction of its being round on the evidence that you do find."

"Yes, that's clear. But how about when there isn't any true factual evidence to base your conviction on?"

"You mean when there isn't any *indisputable* factual evidence. For there virtually always is *some* kind of evidence involved even in your purest value judgments. Take what we are mainly talking about: Donald's nastiness. Theoretically, your liking or disliking Donald's being bitter and nasty to you and others is a matter of pure definition: since you could tell yourself either (*a*) 'I like nasty people,' or (*b*) 'I dislike them,' and today you could tell yourself (*a*) 'and like Donald's behavior', while tomorrow you could tell yourself (*b*) 'and dislike it.'"

"Could I really do that—define my likes and dislikes in such a, well, haphazard manner?"

"Theoretically there is nothing to stop you from doing this; but actually there is."

"And that something that there is to stop me—what is it?"

"Several things: such as your inborn physiological tastes; the kind of community in which you were raised; the specific manner in which you were raised in that community; etc. Let us take one concrete aspect of Donald's nastiness, for instance: his hostility toward others, including yourself. Because he is hostile, you will be unable to keep certain friends who otherwise would be glad to keep seeing you. And since you have been born and raised in a particular manner and therefore *enjoy* certain people, it is unlikely that you are ever going to like Donald's antagonizing and alienating many of these people you normally would enjoy. Similarly, since you have been born and raised to enjoy a reasonable amount of agreement and rapport with people you are constantly with, it is improbable that you are going to like Donald's constant hostility toward you."

"But I *could* like it, if I really tried? I *could* enjoy his antagonizing others or fighting with me all the time?"

"Yes, since human beings are very creative, you probably could—if you really wanted to work on this problem. In spite of your biological and sociological heritage, you probably have the ability to convince yourself that alienating many of your friends is not a bad thing, in fact it has its advantageous aspects (such as, leaving you and Donald more time for other pursuits) and you might even be able to convince yourself that fighting constantly with Donald is more exciting and thrilling than living peacefully with him. You'd doubtless have a hard time convincing yourself of these things; but there is no reason why you couldn't."

"Just as some people convince themselves that hostile deities, such as Jehovah and Allah, are good, while others convince themselves that kindly deities, such as Jesus, are good, so, you are saying, I could convince myself that hostile people like Donald are not annoying, but that they actually have more advantages than disadvantages. Is that right?"

"Yes, you could. It's been known to happen among human beings that females have convinced themselves that their very hostile mates were better to live with than equally intelligent and cultured mates who were much kindlier and friendlier. But you can see that it's not very easy! And I'm certainly not advising you to start convincing yourself of that in regard to Donald!"

"No, I can see why you're not going to try," Edna laughingly responded. "And I don't think you'd easily succeed if you did!"

"Agreed. Anyway, what's probably more to the point is that because you were born and raised with a tendency to dislike nasty people, such as Donald, it would be very difficult to get you to change this tendency since all the evidence that you have at hand convinces you that it is uncomfortable for you to be with people like him. The evidence that you have, in other words, tells you that you *don't* like to lose friends; that you *don't* like to argue with your lover all the time; that it *would* be more pleasant if Donald were nicer and less hostile. This is not conclusive evidence—such as that which you could amass to show that the earth is round instead

191

of flat—but it is reasonably good evidence, considering your biological and historical backgrounds."

"But don't those same biological and historical backgrounds present me with the evidence that I can't possibly accept Donald when he is nasty, and hence to me dislikable, and that when I tell myself that I can accept him that way I'm just going against what is really *me*?"

"Partly; but not entirely. For, normally, you would *not* accept Donald when he is nasty, and would simply stay away from him—as, of course, you stay away from various other nasty people you encounter. But in Donald's particular case, you are also convinced that he is strong, very bright, a good lover, and possessed of several other traits which you find most advantageous, and which presumably make it worth your while putting up with his nastiness. Isn't that so?"

"Oh, yes. Otherwise, I'd have a complete hole in my head for accepting anyone who is as unnice as he often is."

"Exactly. All right, so presumably your biological and historical backgrounds have prepared you for (*a*) disliking Donald's nastiness and (*b*) liking many of his other traits. And, according to what you say, (*b*) in this instance is stronger than (*a*), so that you 'naturally' like rather than dislike Donald, even though you 'naturally' dislike rather than like his nastiness. Correct?"

"Uh—yes. I have no trouble disliking his hostile manner, but I have no trouble, also, in liking the rest of him, or parts of the rest of him, very much. So on the whole, I guess I have no trouble, or relatively little trouble, in liking *Donald*."

192

"O.K., then. We have now determined that for pretty good reasons—for evidence, that is, that is important *to you*, even though it may have no importance to anyone else—you value Donald fairly highly, while at the same time valuing his hostility and bitterness much less. But you do, do you not, have some kind of *evidence* for these value judgments? You do, in some semi-objective manner, find Donald advantageous but his nastiness disadvantageous *to you?*"

"Yes, I must. Otherwise, I would choose to remain with Donald by pure whim. And I'm sure that it's more than that. I'm sure that I have what you call some evidence behind my deciding to remain with him."

"Which means that when you ask yourself the question, 'Should I continue to stay with Donald?' and you convince yourself that you should, you really do this convincing by presenting to yourself, or re-presenting to yourself once again, the evidence that you have that it is more advantageous than disadvantageous to stay with him."

"Yes, now that you make me think of it, I can see that's just what I do. Whenever he's mean and bitter, I think 'Oh, hell! What's the point of staying with such a person?'—and then I quickly review his *other*, better points, and then I convince myself that there *is* some use in staying with him. So I guess that I do just what you say: I do review the evidence to confirm or deny my beliefs or values about staying with him."

"Yes, we all do this kind of thing. Whenever we make a value judgment, as a professor at Columbia University showed some thirty years ago, we consciously or unconsciously weigh the advantages and

193

disadvantages of our decision *to us* (rather than to the rest of the world); and if this evidence seems to point in one direction, we make a favorable value judgment, while if it points in the other direction, we make an unfavorable value judgment. The process of valuing is somewhat subjective rather than objective—since *we,* in the final analysis, must make the decisions as to whether a trait like Donald's nastiness *is* 'bad' or if his strength of character *is* 'good'; and we must also make a decision as to *how* 'bad' or 'good' his various traits are.

"Again, we are constantly evaluating the 'badness' or 'goodness' of Donald's traits in relation *to us* and not in relation to others. But the process of valuing is not quite as subjective as it sounds, since various prior events, such as what kind of genes we were born with and what kind of teachings our parents and others indoctrinated us with when we were younger, importantly *prejudice* our present valuings, and make them much more uniform and predictable than they theoretically would have to be.

"No matter how you look at it, however, we are always *weighing* our value convictions against *some* kind of evidence. And when we find that this evidence radically changes—if, for example, you first found Donald's sex potency a great advantage because you yourself were highly sexed, but later found it a great disadvantage because you lost your sex interest—we consciously or unconsciously, sooner or later change our values."

"The whole thing is much more premeditated than it appears on the surface, isn't it?"

"It certainly is. And even though much of our valuings go on unconsciously or semi-consciously, they are still fairly premeditated. Thus, you may begin to value Donald less highly and *then* realize that you no longer are thrilled by his sex potency. Actually, however, you first unconsciously noted that you were less thrilled by him sexually and *then* you began to value him less highly."

"I see. But you seem mainly to be saying, then, that if I want to change my values, when they are self-conflicting or are defeating my own ends, I must look for the evidence behind them, and then re-weigh that evidence."

"Yes. Let's take the main value involved in your case —that of accepting Donald even though he is distinctly dislikable in some respects. Let us suppose that we have established the value of his dislikability and that that's not going to change very much."

"You mean, that while he's nasty, I'm not going to like his *being* nasty."

"Yes. Let's suppose that this is 'naturally' your tendency, and that you don't see any good reason for changing it."

"Which I don't! Nasty people are unlikable to me— or at least their nastiness is. And I don't think it'll ever be different."

"O.K.: that's your prerogative to feel that way, to value them in that manner. And let's suppose you'll continue to do so. The point is, now: what about accepting Donald in spite of his nastiness? As we said before, you have two values in this regard: (*a*) 'Even though he is nasty, I love him and will accept him,' and (*b*) 'Because he is nasty, I can't stand him, and won't accept him.' From what we have said so far, it

195

would look like most of the evidence that you have about yourself, both physiological and historical, would support the first of these statements. Is that true?"

"I suppose it is. For my evidence tells me that although I don't like anyone's nastiness, especially when it is my lover who is being nasty, I also greatly dislike anyone's weakness, stupidity, and sexual impotence. And I'd rather have the former than the latter, while practically all the boys I have gone with before Don have given me the latter rather than the former. And I haven't thrived in the relationships with them at all, while I really have got a great deal out of my relationship with Donald. Therefore, if I am to go by the evidence, I can accept his nastiness, in order to get the rest of his advantages."

"Right. Though don't forget that there is other evidence that also tells you that somewhere in the world there must be someone for you who has Donald's advantages *without* his disadvantages."

"True. But the evidence also tells me that this someone is so rare that I haven't met him yet in my whole life. And I may not meet him until I am eighty—and when I no longer will want him!"

"Yes. So all the available evidence would seem to point to the fact that even though Donald is a pain in the tonsils in some important respects, other boys are an even greater pain, and you're not too likely to meet, in the near future, one who isn't. All told, therefore, the facts of your preferences and your history favor Donald."

"They certainly seem to. That's why I don't want

196

to give him up, but want to learn to live with him more comfortably."

"Fine. But you're actually living with him *uncomfortably* because of your *other*, conflicting value judgment: that even though he has more advantages than disadvantages, you *can't stand* his particular disadvantage —his hostility. Now, what's the evidence for *this* value judgment?"

"Uh—let's see. I want his advantages and am willing to overlook the disadvantages. Yet I also refuse to overlook what I say I want to overlook, and I convince myself that I *can't* overlook his hostility. That's what we're talking about, isn't it: my belief that I *can't* overlook this hostility?"

"Yes. What's the evidence for *that* belief?"

"Uh—none, I guess. No, none that I can really see. There's evidence that I don't *like* Don's hostility, as we said before. And evidence that I *want* to overlook it, so that I can still keep comfortably seeing him. But I guess that I'm using the evidence that I don't like it to 'prove' that I can't stand it. And it really doesn't prove it at all."

"Precisely. You're unconsciously translating your 'I don't like hostility' into 'I can't stand it'—even while, at exactly the same time, you're telling yourself that 'I *can* stand his hostility, because I get so many other good things from him.' Now, obviously, you can't have evidence, or at least good evidence, for *both* statements."

"I can't be able to stand and not to stand his hostility at the same time—is that what you mean?"

"Right. Either you can stand it or you can't stand it. But you can't do both at once. So you must change one of these values—and presumably the one that says: 'I can't stand his hostility, even though I want to do so.'"

"And I can change this value by questioning and challenging it, as you've told me in previous sessions; and, as you've just pointed out, by demanding the evidence that stands behind it, that proves it to be a valid value?"

"Right again. And what *is* the evidence that proves that you *can't* stand what you say you definitely do want to stand? Is there any such evidence?"

"No, I guess not. I *feel* that I can't stand it. But I know that feeling simply stems from my *belief* that I can't. And there *is* no real evidence supporting that belief. I guess I believe the belief without evidence."

"Exactly! You keep *telling yourself* that that belief is true, without ever asking yourself: '*Why* is it true? Where is the supporting evidence for it?'"

"I keep telling myself; 'I can't stand it!' without asking: '*Why* can't I stand it? Why can't I be happy with Donald, even though he continues to be nasty and mean to me and others?'"

"Do you see now the general principle of challenging, questioning, contradicting, and changing one of your own beliefs—one of your own value judgments that is getting you into trouble?"

"I think so. I must keep asking myself: 'What is the evidence behind this belief? What *makes* it true?'"

"Yes. And also: what will I *get* by continuing to believe this belief? Will it get me what I really want

198

out of life? Or will it only serve to defeat my main goals?"

"So I must ask myself: 'What will I get by continuing to believe that I can't stand Donald's nastiness? Will believing that I can't stand it get me what I really want—a good relationship with Don? Or will it help to sabotage that relationship?' "

"Yes. Ask yourself, right now, *will* believing that you can't stand Don's nastiness get you a good relationship with him?"

"No, it obviously won't. It, that belief, will only hinder me in maintaining such a relationship."

"Then why should you continue to believe it? Why should you keep bolstering this silly belief, and keep telling yourself that 'I just *can't* stand his nastiness?' "

"Yes, why should I? Damn it, I just won't keep bolstering that belief. Not any more!"

"Easy to say. But you're going to have to keep working, and working, and working at it. Because you have unconsciously been bolstering the belief that you can't stand Don's nastiness, and doing so for quite a period of time. Now you're going to have to keep facing the fact that that's what you've been doing. And you're going to have to keep questioning and challenging that belief, over and over. Asking yourself, that is: 'Why can't I stand what I don't like? Where is the *evidence* that I can't stand it?' And only after a good many days and weeks, perhaps months, of this kind of questioning and challenging will your belief that you can't stand his nastiness really begin to weaken, and ultimately stop plaguing you. But not till then."

"There's no easy way then, is there?"

"No: none. Only work and practice. Continual challenging and contradicting. Just as you must do with any superstition. Constant demanding of yourself: 'What is the evidence? Why *must* I continue to believe this self-defeating bosh?'"

"But it will work, won't it, if I do continually question and challenge myself in this manner."

"Yes, it will work. But you'll never know until you keep trying it. Why not try it and see?"

Edna did try. She was able to stand Donald and his nastiness so well within a few weeks' time that even he was quite surprised. Although he did not stop being bitter and disagreeable toward others, he did behave much more nicely toward her, and their relationship improved considerably. Eventually, seeing that she was getting along so well (since she was also able to stand other people's poor behavior, too, and to cease to make herself terribly unhappy about it), Donald decided to go for therapy himself: after which he also became much less hostile to others.

Whereas Edna had not been able previously to induce him to get therapeutic aid, as soon as she stopped trying to coax him to do so but merely showed him by her good example how much *she* had been helped, he saw the possible value of therapy for himself, and was more than willing to try it. This is what often happens when one member of a pair buckles down to work on herself: the other member sees what *can* be done, and likewise gets the idea that he can aid himself. Actions, in this respect, speak much louder than words—as Edna has, by her own example, now learned.

The moral of this tale is: before you would seriously

undertake to live with a neurotic mate, and especially to help him overcome his disturbance, first spend some time and effort cultivating your own emotional garden. Which means that whenever you find that you are intensely anxious or hostile, you must assume that you, just before becoming so, must have told yourself some awful nonsense: you must have *defined* something as being catastrophic or horrible, when it really wasn't, and made yourself upset by your unsupportable definition.

As I continually show my patients in the course of the rational-emotive method of psychotherapy which I practice with them: it is never the stimulus A which causes us to be emotionally disturbed at point C; rather, it is the negative, moralistic interpretation B, which we give ourselves, which *makes* us upset at C. Edna was upsetting herself, at point C, by convincing herself that she couldn't stand Donald's nastiness, when she thought she was convincing herself that she didn't like it but that she could stand it. And, of course, she kept feeling that it was his bitterness and meanness that upset her —rather than her own conviction that she couldn't stand this meanness.

That's what practically all disturbed people do. They upset themselves, at point B, by telling themselves something catastrophic about what's happening to them at point A. Then they completely convince themselves that it *is* the happening at point A that is really upsetting. Thus, in a typical case of a severe anxiety reaction, Susan L. kept worrying all the time that her boyfriend, Anthony, would not show up for their wedding—since he *wasn't* completely reliable (every few weeks he lost a greater sum than he could afford at poker) and he *had* once left her waiting for him for an hour at a movie date, before he unapologetically appeared. Susan was utterly convinced that it was Anthony who made her anxious, because with someone else she wouldn't have been so worried about his showing up at the wedding.

This, I quickly showed her, was nonsense. She had been anxious virtually all her life about all kinds of similar things—about whether she was going to pass tests at school, about whether her parents were going to ever return when they went out visiting, about whether her new dress was going to arrive in time for the special affair she was going to on the weekend, etc. And certainly Anthony had nothing to do with *those* anxieties.

No, I insisted: she had to face it. She, by continually telling herself (at point B): "I *must* pass this test at school; it will be *terrible* if I don't," or: "If Anthony *doesn't* show up at the wedding I shall positively *die* of mortification,"—she herself, by these internalized thoughts, was creating her own anxiety; and unless she saw what she was doing, and stopped herself from doing it, Anthony could become the most reliable person in the world and she would still remain terribly anxious.

Susan was a tough nut—and I mean nut!—to crack; but I finally convinced her. When she was able to see clearly what she had been saying to herself, and to change her internalized sentences at point B to "Suppose he doesn't show up at the wedding. I won't die! And I *will* know, by that kind of behavior, that he *is* totally unreliable and will be much better off *not* being married to him," she became quite unanxious. She went

202

through with the wedding—yes, Anthony did show up, though *he* was more anxious than she was and almost didn't make it out of fear, rather than unreliability!— and she is now getting along with herself better than she ever did before.

Largely as a result of her being able to handle her own anxiety, she has been able to help Anthony with many of his problems, and it looks like they will have a better than average marriage. If she had not tackled her own anxiety-creating sentences at point B, the chances are enormously high that she would have kept blaming Anthony for making her disturbed, and that if they had married they would have had a miserable relationship.

So don't fool yourself. Others do *not* upset, hurt, or seriously bother you. *You* do. They, to be sure, often act badly: which is their problem. Then you, instead of philosophically accepting the fact that that's the way they are, tell yourself that you can't *stand* their acting badly, you can't *take* their words, gestures, and attitudes. Hogwash! If there's anything you can't take, under the circumstances, it's the tommyrot you are steadily feeding yourself. That *is* nauseating and indigestible. But you don't *have* to self-feed it.

If you must, then, remain intimately associated with a difficult or seriously disturbed man—and I still would usually say, "The hell you must! DON'T"—you'd better cultivate your emotional garden so well that virtually nothing, and especially not he, can depress or upset you. For difficult people invariably will do mean, crazy, undesirable things. And if you insist on being the brunt of their attacks, you'd better be in the best possible

203

emotional health while you are serving as their targets. Get all the professional help you can afford yourself— and work your goddam head off to stop telling yourself perfect nonsense and contradictory value judgments at point B.

Helping a man overcome his emotional problems

Can you, as a non-professional person yourself, actually do anything to help the man you care for to overcome his severe emotional problems. Definitely, yes. The major portion of my book, *How to Live with A Neurotic* (New York: Crown Publishers, 1957), is devoted to showing the reader how he or she can help a loved one become less disturbed; and literally hundreds of persons who have read this book have written to tell me that they learned a great deal from it and actually were able to help both themselves and their mates by putting into effect some of the techniques I recommended.

What are these techniques? Let me plagiarize myself a little, and briefly expound them here.

1. The first thing that you can do to help a man become less neurotic is to recognize clearly and, even more importantly, to *accept* the fact that he is disturbed. Don't pretend that a neurotic is well-adjusted, nor try to treat him as if he is. Fully acknowledge, at least to yourself, that he is distinctly maladjusted and that, as such, he is absolutely *bound* to do many silly, peculiar, inconvenient things.

2. Accepting a neurotic, in the full sense of the term, means never *blaming* him for being disturbed. Though he may be *responsible* for what he does—in

the sense that he, and not the Man in the Moon, causes his own actions—he is not a blackguard or a bastard because he is responsible. Even non-neurotic human beings are always fallible, and continually make minor and serious blunders. Neurotics are much more fallible: are consistently defeating themselves and annoying others, even when they try not to do so.

All right: that's the way they *are*. It's not good that they're this way; but it's not horrible, either. It's merely damned inconvenient. And blaming neurotics for being the way they are will almost always serve to make them more disturbed: since, at bottom, they are invariably self-blaming individuals, who cannot accept their mistakes philosophically, and who denigrate themselves when they do the wrong thing. So accepting a neurotic for what he is means (*a*) seeing clearly that he is emotionally unstable, and (*b*) giving him the right to be as disturbed as he is without showing him that you think him a louse for being so.

3. Teach yourself to distinguish clearly between a disturbed man's *actions* and his *self*. You can very legitimately deplore what he does, and even (calmly, calmly!) be able to tell him that you do not approve of his behavior. But make sure that you do not hate *him* for behaving in this manner—that you do not condemn his *self*. The neurotic's deeds are frequently bad; but *he* is not a bad person. Show him (quietly, quietly!) that he *is* behaving poorly at times; but that he *can* behave better; and that even while he is now doing poorly, you still do not loathe or despise him.

4. Try to show your neurotic friend that *nothing* is terrible, *nothing* is horrible, even though many things

205

are an awful nuisance. Try to indicate to him (as we explained in the first section in this chapter) that things *appear* frightening and dreadful to him because he, at point B, takes what occurs to him at point A, and *makes* them "awful." Try to show him that he feels worthless and hopeless because he *defines* himself in that manner. Try to help him see that whatever are the frustrations and insecurities of the world around him, he doesn't have to take these too seriously, nor inflate their nuisance value. Speak to him logically, uncritically, just as a rational therapist would speak to you; and do so, preferably, while you yourself are getting some therapeutic guidance and supervision.

5. Endeavor to induce your neurotic partner to engage in de-propagandizing actions and homework assignments. If he is neurotically afraid to ride in automobiles, try to get him to ride, and ride, and ride in autos until he begins to *see* that there is nothing fearful about them. If he becomes terribly angry at his mother, try to get him to maintain contact with her and to note, during this contact, how he *can* refuse to take her seriously, how he *can* accept her the way she is even though she says or does the wrong things.

If he paranoically accuses you of being against him, try to show him, by your calm actions as well as words, that you are really on his side, and that you do not even blame him for wrongly thinking that you are against him. Try not to let him retreat into neurotic ideas that he thereafter refuses to test and can consequently never disprove to himself.

6. Adopt the general attitude of *firm kindness* toward your emotionally disturbed partner. This means

206

that you must be consistently pleasant, warm, and accepting toward him, but at the same time must set definite limits as to how far he may impose on you, and firmly stick to those limits. If you take the attitude of *un*firm kindness, and let your neurotic beau take consistent advantage of you, you will then be giving him an excuse to remain the baby which he (and every neurotic) is; and you will be setting him a poor example by showing lack of respect for yourself.

If you take the attitude of firm *un*kindness, you will be, as we noted before, blaming him for his poor behavior, and encouraging him thereby to blame himself and make himself more neurotic. *Firm kindness* is exactly what it implies: an attitude where you are most unblaming and understanding; but where you refuse to let your mate walk all over you and do whatever he neurotically wants.

7. In following a policy of firm kindness with your disturbed boyfriend or husband, you can frequently attack his ideas and his behavior without attacking *him*. If you show him that you consistently love him, even (or especially) when he is behaving badly, he will come to feel that at least one person has true respect for and confidence in him, and that he has a real helper on his side. Then, *because* he knows that you can see things from his frame of reference, and lovingly accept him in spite of his wrongdoings, he may be able to accept your firm disagreements with many of his thoughts and actions, and he may (for his own sake as well as out of his return love for you) be able to help himself change.

8. Try to induce your neurotic mate to distinguish clearly between wrongdoing and sinning. Show him

that he indeed makes many mistakes and commits individual and social misdeeds—as we all do. But try to convince him that blaming himself for his mistakes—instead of calmly acknowledging them and focusing upon what he is going to do to make fewer errors *next* time—will only make him more and more disturbed.

9. At times, especially when your neurotic lover or husband is under undue stress, help remove some of his strain by lightening his load, and not expecting him to do as much (job-wise, socially, or in other aspects of his life) as you would normally expect him to do. When conditions, however, are relatively good, that is the time to try to show him (without blame!) that short-range hedonism, or only going after the satisfactions of the moment, is usually a poor plan of action, and that if he is to become stronger and less disturbed, he must take a longer-range approach to life, and often put off the pleasures of the moment for future gains.

10. Quietly and uncritically show your disturbed inamorato that others are not necessarily doing him in, and that even if they are he need not take them too seriously, but can understand *their* disturbances. Indicate to him how he misinterprets others and fails to make necessary allowances for them, and show him how he can get along better with them and at times develop real social interests. Encourage him to initiate and maintain intimate contacts with others and thereby fulfill himself creatively as a social being. Also, if you can help him to achieve some vital absorbing interest—whether it be in people, in some project, art form, or anything else—such an interest will usually do much

to keep his mind off his self- and other-blaming tendencies and to keep him thinking along healthier channels.

11. If at all possible, see that your neurotic beloved eventually gets some kind of professional help. Show him that you yourself believe in psychotherapy, and perhaps have made some use of it in your own life. Introduce him to the kinds of people who are not in the least ashamed to see a psychologist or a psychiatrist when they are in emotional difficulties. Encourage him (without nagging!) to go for help; and occasionally, as a very last resort, insist that you will not maintain your relationship with him unless he does so. If you are calmly determined that he obtain some intensive psychotherapy, you should somehow be able to induce him to obtain it.

How to live with a neurotic man

Let us suppose that you have done everything possible to help your emotionally disturbed partner overcome his deep-seated anxieties and hostilities, but that there is just no moving him. He remains terribly neurotic and—naturally!—you as well as he suffer because of his irrational, self-defeating behavior. Then what?

Then, in most instances, you should do yourself a great favor and leave. Delude yourself, if you will, that he's really not *that* sick; or that he will somehow magically get better; or that even though he is that sick and will not get better, there is just no other possible man in the world for you. Twaddle! You're lying, lying, lying; and you'd better look for much better reasons than these for staying.

209

Nevertheless, with good reasons or bad, you insist that you *are* going to stay with a seriously disturbed mate. What *then* can you do to handle him intelligently and to minimize, if not actually remove, the difficulties that are bound to ensue because you insist on seeing or being married to such a neurotic individual?

First of all, as we noted previously, you must *fully* and *unequivocally* accept the fact that your lover or husband *is* disturbed and that, because of this fact, he will positively, certainly, and no two ways about it, do crazy, mixed-up, and often downright mean things.

Almost every day in the week one of my patients comes in and tells me, with an utterly anguished and bitter tone, that her boyfriend did this or her husband did that—and how *could* he possibly have acted this way to such a loving, kind, positively angelic girl as she?

"But didn't I tell you," I say to these complainers, "that he is seriously disturbed and that people who are as self-hating and hostile as he *do* act in the manner you are now describing?"

"Yes, I know," they invariably reply, "but how could he possibly do a thing like *this?*"

They do *know* that their men are neurotic; but obviously do not *accept* what they know. For if they did accept this, they would also accept the fact that neurotics behave neurotically: meaning, invariably, badly, nastily, insanely, and unlovingly.

So if you must live with a neurotic male, for the sake of your potential ulcers and high blood pressure, please accept him fully and unequivocally as what he is: an unusually fallible human being who definitely well *will*

210

do, and keep doing, exactly what you wish he wouldn't. What do you expect a neurotic to be—nice, loving, and sane?

While accepting your neurotic partner the way he is, you must take great care not to personalize his negative attitudes toward you. Almost certainly, just because he is disturbed, he will treat you (as well as others) in a harsh, unfair way. Sometimes, he will unwittingly do so, because he is so absorbed in his problems that he just doesn't see that he is being unjust to you. But at other times he will actually deliberately, viciously try to harm you: for that is what neurotics almost always are—hostile and vengeful when they become greatly upset.

All right: so your man is sometimes deliberately vicious. But that *still* is no reason for you to take his behavior personally and to bewail his being nasty to *you*. For he is driven, by his neurosis, to be hostile; and whether you are around or not, you can bet that he will display his hostility toward *someone*. You, just because you happen to be around more than others, will very frequently be that someone.

Besides, even if your lover or husband, because he is emotionally unstable, is specifically mean to you, and even if he makes it perfectly clear that he hates you alone at the moment, why should you still personalize his attack? So he hates you. And after all you've done for him—after all the sacrifices you've willingly made. What does that mean *about* you? That you've made a mistake in remaining with him? Possibly. That he really doesn't care for you, as you thought he did? Yes, could be. That you're utterly no good *because*

211

you made a mistake in staying with him or *because* he doesn't love you the way you thought he did?

Nonsense! However badly he (or anyone else) may act toward you, it at worst means that you have made some serious blunders in handling him. But it never—no, *never*—means that you are worthless for *making* those blunders. This is purely definitional interpretation —and very neurotic interpretation at that.

To live with a neurotic and *not* personalize his poor behavior toward you, in other words, means that you yourself must be quite unneurotic, and must be able to accept yourself as a perfectly worthwhile individual whether or not he cares for you, whether or not you have made some mistakes in your relations with him. It is bad enough living with a disturbed man when you yourself are emotionally healthy. But if you live with one while you are yourself sick, then you will inevitably suffer. Not because *he* is out of his head, but because *you* are.

The main thing that you need if you are to live successfully with a disturbed partner is exceptionally high frustration tolerance—which, you will recall, we have several times mentioned before in this book. For neurotics *are* frustrating; they *do* perform acts which are distinctly irritating and annoying to practically everyone; and if you are to avoid getting upset by their behavior, you must be able to *take* their annoyances and gracefully, oh so gracefully, lump them.

Most of us, as I have pointed out in several of my recent books on rational living, are easily upsettable in the course of our relations with others not merely because we become annoyed at their actions, but because we foolishly allow ourselves *to become annoyed at being annoyed*. That is to say, we not only get irritated by someone's doing the wrong thing (such as, his coming late for the appointments he makes with us, or saying that he cares greatly for us and then showing, in actual practice, that he is most inconsiderate), but we tell ourselves something along these lines:

"I can't *stand* his annoying me like that! Imagine!— telling me one moment that he hates people who keep others waiting, and then keeping me waiting for a full hour! How can he possibly *be* that way?"

By telling ourselves this nonsense, we are saying two things, one of which is true and the other of which is ridiculously false. The true thing is: "He is annoying me, and I don't like it." The false thing is: "He *shouldn't* be annoying me. He has no goddam *right* to do what I don't like him to do. He is totally unfair, and I can't *stand* his being unfair."

The false sentences are false because there *is* no real reason why a neurotic *shouldn't* be annoying, even though there are many reasons why *it would be nice if he weren't*. And a disturbed person *has* every right in the world to be disturbed and, because of his disturbance, to do the things you don't like him to do. And even though it may well be unfair for your neurotic true love to be unkind to you when you have presumably been so nice to him, you *can* stand his being unfair; in fact, you'd better!

Although, then, it well may be terribly annoying for your man to behave badly toward you, this is how he behaves, this is what he is. Either you should calmly

213

leave him (which I *still* think is the most sensible thing to do if he is hopelessly disturbed) or should, with quiet determination, decide to stay with him. But annoying yourself *because* he annoys you will merely add enormously to your original, and presumably unavoidable, irritation; and *you,* not *he,* will be the one who is creating this twofold or tenfold irritation.

If you truly accept him as being neurotic—which, remember, we insist is the very *first* rule you must adopt if you are to live with such a crazy partner—then you will stop annoying yourself *about* his annoying behavior. If you continue to annoy yourself about this behavior, then you are conclusively proving that you are unrealistically refusing to accept him as he is— as an emotionally unbalanced person.

The best way to live successfully with a seriously disturbed individual is to withdraw somewhat emotionally from him. Thus, if your father or your brother is quite aberrated in his behavior, and in consequence acts badly toward you or others, you can, without actually hating him or thinking of him too unkindly, emotionally withdraw, accept him on a less intimate basis, and get along very well with him during the relatively little time that you do spend with him. What you really do, in such cases, is continue to love the disturbed person, but to love him from a kind of distance, and perhaps to love him with less admiration than you previously did.

This kind of self-protective withdrawal from a neurotic intimate has, of course, its distinct limitations when you apply it to a lover or a husband. You can take such a person, once you accept his disturbance, much less seriously than you previously did. But you have to face the fact that the less seriously you take him, the less actively and intensely you are also likely to love him. Consequently, although you can use the technique of emotional withdrawal to a moderate degree with a loved man who is most difficult to live with, if you take it to any considerable extremes you will soon find yourself to be accepting but unloving, and will want to go off and love someone else who is not that difficult.

A technique that is perhaps better in this respect is that of your acquiring a more realistic, more stoical philosophy of life. If you rationally and stoically accept the fact that the world is the way it is, and that even when it is a bad world there is no point in crying or upsetting yourself about the way it is, you may then be able to live with exceptionally neurotic individuals and still love them. Or if—looking at this same phenomenon from a slightly different standpoint—you fully come to accept the fact that *all* human beings are distinctly fallible and that *none* of them is a perfect doll to live with, you may be truly able to accept the neurotically-based fallibilities of your particular beloved, and be much more loving than you would otherwise be inclined to be toward him.

Which brings us—as usual—back to the point we have to keep making in this book: that the only good way to get along with others is first and foremost to get along well with yourself. If you have a poor philosophy of life, including all kinds of irrational premises about reality which are bound to get you into difficulty—such as the premise that you *must* be approved by others or *must* be successful in life in order to be a worthwhile person—you will certainly get into serious difficulties with even the most "normal" of males. With psychologically disturbed males, your self-defeating philosophy will hold you in much poorer stead. In fact, it will royally discumbobulate you and leave you in constant emotional shreds. Your main work, then, is invariably on you and not on your mate. Sweetheart, heal thyself! *Then* you can think about saving the souls of others.

Chapter 9

How to Be a Sexpot

Good sex relations, as we have been noting throughout this book, are as essential before as after marriage. You may get a ninny or a fairy to marry you in spite of (or, alas, because of) the fact that you retain your pristine purity or lie like a log and refrain from wriggling your butt when you finally do allow your boyfriend to get you between the sheets. But your chances of getting a real, live, swinging Joe this way are infinitesimally small.

Moreover, if you do, by sheer accident, get a good man to the altar by dint of avoiding the issue and defending your hymenal tissue, what *then*? Are you *still* going to maintain your ignorance and aspire to copulative bliss? Or are you going to consider sexual aptitude at least as important as cooking and shopping, and take a few lessons in the art of satisfying yourself and your mate with no nonsense about it?

Although this book does not purport to be much of a sex manual, let me crib a little from some of my other works in that area (particularly from my magnum opus, *The Art and Science of Love*. New York: Lyle Stuart, 1960) and outline some of the main methods by which you may achieve sexual adequacy. If you want to wait to read this chapter until *after* you are safely wedded, that is your prerogative. But I have to warn you that what you will read herein is hardly ungermane to the marrying process, too. In fact, it could be one whale of a big help.

Arousing and satisfying a man

Normally, it is not very difficult to arouse and satisfy a virile man. In fact, it is often a little too easy: since before you know it, any man who is attracted to you is likely to have a vigorous response; and, if you engage in almost any kind of sex activity with him, he may quickly come to orgasm. The younger he is, the more easily this is likely to happen; and the earlier it is in your sexual relationship, when you are still a considerable novelty to him, the more again he is likely to become quickly aroused and satisfied.

But not always! Many quite young males have difficulties in obtaining full sexual arousal. Either they are fearful, especially of sex failure; or they are diverted by certain existing conditions (such as the possibility of your parents or your roommate walking in on the two of you any second!); or they are sexually unsophisticated and are not focusing on the proper arousing ideas; or they just may not be too highly sexed, and may naturally have some difficulty in responding to your attractions.

What is to be done under such circumstances?

Well, the first thing is: Don't panic! Don't quickly say to yourself: "Oh, my God! What have I done wrong now? It surely must be me. Probably he doesn't really like me. Or I'm not pretty enough for him. Or he finds me less stimulating than the other girls he's known. I might as well give up and get me to a nunnery!"

Balderdash! The chances are nine out of ten that it's not you at all. He's merely got minor or major sex problems—as millions upon millions of men have. And that's too bad. But it's hardly catastrophic. Now, if you will only calmly accept the fact that there's a problem to be solved here, and exert more effort at solving it than wailing about it, a fairly easy solution will probably soon be available.

First of all, ask your man—yes, *ask* him, with no beating around the bush—whether he does not have any kind of sex problem. Is his present state of non-arousal normal? Does it happen under certain specific circumstances? Is he afraid of anything in particular? Does he usually require any special kind of preliminaries or technique of excitation before he gets going on all cylinders?

In other words: what goes with your friend? Open your trap and find out. Don't *assume* that you know the answer; in fact, don't assume *anything*. Just because your last boyfriend needed you to wear black stockings and high-heeled shoes before he could get going does not mean that this one necessarily has the same fetish. Maybe, in fact, he *hates* black stockings and high-heeled shoes. Who knows? Who will ever know, without asking. So ask!

Whatever the reason for your man's unarousability, keep cool. It's not horrible, nor perhaps even very unusual that he is the way he is. At most, it's a problem. And one that, if it really is too bad, you don't even have to solve: since there are other males, no doubt, with lesser problems. But if it's a problem, so it's a problem. Almost any difficulty can, with a little effort, be solved. Most of them are even fascinating to figure out

219

answers to. So accept his unaroused sexual state calmly, uncatastrophically. And *think* about how you might go about helping him solve it.

How about, for one thing, his erogenous zones? Almost all human beings have parts of their anatomies which are more susceptible to sexual stimulation than other parts; and these differ widely from person to person. The male of the species, usually, has one main erogenous zone: and it isn't ordinarily his lips, his forehead, or his big right toe. Right: it's generally his male organ, his sacred penis. You can frequently kiss and caress a man from now till doomsday, and very little will happen. But just make a few passes at his membrum virile, and lo! the situation changes rapidly.

What kind of passes? Well, not just any kind. For the easily aroused male, practically a single glance at his main source of delight will do the trick. But for the less easily aroused one, not only the correct touch, but the exact right touch in the exact right spot may be necessary to arouse him. The penis, except in rare instances, is not equally sensitive in all areas. Much of it, especially the back parts which are closest to the body, are relatively deadened in sensitivity. Other parts, such as the glans or front part of the organ, and the underside of it about one inch in back of the glans, are usually much more sensitive. Just a small amount of stimulation in these areas will go much further in arousing your man than a considerable amount in other parts of his penile anatomy.

Nor will any kind of touch or caress necessarily serve. Some men require an extremely vigorous kind of massage, and simply do not get aroused at all if they do not have this kind of forceful stimulation. With other men, however, such vigor is merely painful or neutral; and only the lightest strokings or kissings will get them truly raring to go. Since the man you have chosen is a unique individual in his own right, you must never assume that what is good for others is also good for him. Find out. Experiment. Try a variety of strokings in a variety of ways. You may well discover something about him and his sexual excitability that he himself never knew before. And if you do, your discovery will usually be most appreciated, and will do much to help your rapport.

Caresses and kisses, moreover, need not only be genitally oriented. Some men, particularly after they have had one or more orgasms, find that their penises are overly-sensitive and cannot very well be stroked or touched. Instead, non-genital manipulations—of the thighs, buttocks, breast, lips, shoulders, or almost any imaginable part of the body—may be the thing when more direct stimulation fails to achieve your arousing purpose.

Nor is physical contact, of course, the only avenue to arousal. What you *say* to a man—particularly if you are able to employ vigorous, down-to-earth sexual language, or to tell him sincerely how much you *enjoy* making love to him—can be exceptionally exciting. Sometimes stories or verbalized fantasies will help. You can read him erotic literature; or encourage him to use his memory and imagination to review sexually stimulating events.

Don't forget eye-appeal, too. Maybe the black stockings and the high heels *will* work with your present lover. Or clinging negligées. Or nudity in a bright, bright light. Or the reflection of the two of you in a sizable mirror. Or looking at sexy pictures or films. Or the devil knows what! Anyway, exercise your imagination and see if you cannot think up something when arousal becomes difficult.

All sorts of things may help in individual cases. Some men like musky perfumes. Or unusual sex positions. Or copulation under different conditions: such as on a grassy hill, or in the shallow waves of the ocean. Explore. Try. What have you got to lose?

Don't hesitate to take the initiative. If your partner expressly gets upset by your doing so (since he has some Victorian ideas about its being the male's prerogative, and his alone, to start things going), then you may at first have to tone down on priming the sexual pump. But if you calmly keep persisting, and make sure that you yourself feel no hesitation or shame in doing so (including no false pride about his not caring for you enough to take the initiative himself), you will almost always gain what you want in the long run.

Unless your man is really devoid of sex arousability, persistent and patient attempts to arouse him will sooner or later begin to pay off. The very fact that you *want* him (as long as you do not show hostility when you can't have him) will be exciting to him in most instances; and even though he *thinks* that he is incapable of being aroused—on nights, for example, when he feels tired or believes he has had sex too recently to have it again—he will often be amazed to find Old Roger startlingly at attention and ready to go when he just the minute before felt that he couldn't possibly be sexually interested.

The experiments of Dr. Lester A. Kirkendall are particularly instructive in this connection. Dr. Kirkendall asked many young males what they thought their maximum sexual potency was, and then got them to try to have orgasms more often than they thought they could. In virtually all cases, he found, the male was considerably more capable of arousal and fulfillment than he thought he would be. His sexual *capacity*, in other words, was much higher than his actual *activity*.

So it probably is with your man, if he does not have sex relations with you as often as you would like him to have them. Left to his own devices, he may be a once-a-weeker or even a once-a-monther. But why should you leave him to his own devices when you're right there, handy-like, in bed with him? Let's not go to any extremes in this regard, now—such as waking him out of a sound sleep each night to begin all over again when you've both been satisfied before you dozed off. Or raping him as you're driving him to meet the 8:15 in the morning! But, within reasonable limits, you can certainly get him to see that he *has* more sexual capacity than he normally thinks he has—and that he can beautifully enjoy using some of that extra capacity.

Another point to watch is timing. Just as many women are not particularly aroused at certain times during their menstrual cycles, males may have some degree of periodicity too. Sometimes they are too physically fatigued; or too worried about how things are going at the office; or recovering from a debilitating illness; or on a working schedule that makes it awfully difficult for them to have very regular coital relations. If so, make all due allowances and try to beat these kinds of limitations.

Having intercourse in the morning, for example, instead of always in the evening, is much better for some early-to-bed-and-early-to-rise individuals. Or massing your sex relations mainly on weekends, while keeping the midweek for more workaday activities, is sometimes a practical solution. Or getting completely away from your regular environment (especially if you have children and they are a part of this environment) may be an excellent idea. Almost every man has some kind of timing which is best for him and his sexuality. It should not be too difficult to discover what your particular man's bent is in this connection, and to plan and plot a little so that you are better able to cater to it.

Intercourse itself can sometimes be arousing, even though you and your mate are not especially excited when you begin to have it. As long as he is able to effect an even passably good entry in coitus, the continuation of the act may do more, after a while, to get him fully and eagerly aroused than may any other kind of caressive or manipulative foreplay technique.

The more difficult it is to arouse and satisfy the man of your choice, the more it may be necessary to resort to unusual, dramatic, and so-called perverted sexual methodologies. As I note in *The Art and Science of Love* (New York: Lyle Stuart, 1960):

"It should go without saying, in this modern day and age, that some of the most sexually arousing and orgasm-producing methods are those which for centuries prior to this have been taboo in our society but are now more widely accepted. Oral-genital contact, anal insertion, mild sado-masochistic forays, and similar so-called perversions are essential for the maximum arousal and satisfaction of literally millions of individuals in today's world.

"Consequently, any person whose husband or wife

is difficult to arouse or satisfy should be especially unshy about trying all possible techniques, including many of those which were erroneously considered perverted in the past, but which are now commonly accepted as a normal part of human sex behavior."

Don't, under any circumstances, be misled by the propaganda in favor of simultaneous orgasm which is still rife in many of our leading sex manuals. It is indeed nice and convenient when you and your mate can come to climax at exactly the same time; but *nice* is far from meaning *necessary*. The main thing is that, if both of you want to achieve orgasm, you do so at *some* part in the sexual proceedings; and that you do so in *some* satisfying manner. You definitely need *not* have your orgasms during intercourse; and if you do have them coitally, you do not need to have them at the same moment in time.

The goal of striving mightily to achieve orgasm during penile-vaginal copulation and to achieve it simultaneously often defeats its own ends: since both partners are so over-concerned about such a "necessary" achievement that they shift their sexual focus from "What shall I do to enjoy myself?" to "*How* am I doing at what I am doing?" This latter focus clearly implies that if I am not doing well at what I am doing, I am then a no-goodnik, a complete failure, and I might as well give up what I'd like to do and dig ditches instead.

The main reason for having sex relations, then, should be your own and your partner's *enjoyment*—and not achievement, "ego-bolstering" or anything of that sort. As a female, you will want to obtain the fullest satisfaction of which you are personally capable—which will differ widely from person to person; and you want your partner to be as satisfied, generally, as he possibly can be.

This does not mean that either or both of you must have the greatest orgasm under the sun every single time you copulate. Nor does it mean that you should have as intensive or extensive sex gratifications as John or Jim or Sue or Mabel—all of whom may be biologically and psychologically quite different from you. It simply means that you and your mate should be eager to learn what individually and mutually satisfies *yourselves*, and then should be more than willing to employ any experimentally discovered pleasurable approaches to sex that you cooperatively discover.

Arousing and satisfying yourself with your man

If, as noted above, it is relatively easy to arouse and satisfy the average male sexually, it is often exceptionally hard to achieve the same degree of arousal and release for the average female. Males have such large and easily accessible genitals that they usually can be excited and gratified within a few minutes of active sex play. Females, on the other hand, have genitals that are relatively hidden and inaccessible and that often make it difficult for them to achieve full psychosexual release.

This is especially true when girls are distinctly puritanical or when they pretend to be sexually liberal or free but actually cover their sexuality with blanket after blanket of deadening and stultifying romanticism. Not that romanticism doesn't have its advantages, for it does. Relatively low-sexed females can sometimes, by

226

focusing on love rather than sex, work themselves up into a high emotional pitch, and thus help themselves to become more sexualized.

But the reverse is probably often just as true. The average female is quite practical and unromantic about her masturbatory practices. She experiments with the various parts of her anatomy, usually finds that her clitoris is the most sensitive part of her genitalia, and then (with considerable further experimentation in a most down-to-earth manner) she discovers exactly what kind of physical manipulation and what kind of mental imagery is necessary to bring herself to full orgasmic release in a relatively brief period of time.

Often, she tries various sorts of external devices—such as hairbrushes, running water, electric vibrators, etc.—to heighten her pleasure; and frequently, she employs most concrete fantasies to help herself become sexually aroused and satisfied. In the course of this procedure, she is usually most practical and unromantic and quite properly does not permit any high-flown idealizations to get in the way of her sexual self-expression.

Not so, unfortunately, when this same girl starts to pet or copulate with a male with whom she is enamored. Under these circumstances, she more often than not insists that love conquers all, and expects him telepathically (just *because* he presumably loves her) to divine exactly what she requires sexually and to go about satisfying her in the most approved manner. And, since her romantic conceptions in this connection are almost entirely unmitigated hogwash, she soon finds that she is *not* enjoying heterosexual relations as much as she previously enjoyed masturbatory forays, and she

227

becomes disillusioned with her boyfriend and perhaps with heterosexuality itself.

What should she do, instead, if she is fully to enjoy sex with her best loved male? Obviously, speak up and *communicate* her wishes. If she requires, for her fullest pleasure, a soft or a hard stroking, a massaging of her clitoris or her vaginal orifice, a copulative or a non-copulative approach to sex, for Pete's sake *let her say so!* No man, no matter how much he may love a woman and be eager to please her, is a mind reader.

Moreover, he has sexual prejudices of his own which tend to make him feel that the woman is pretty much the same way he is. If he, for example, likes vigorous massaging of his penis, he will tend to think that she enjoys equally vigorous stroking of her clitoris. Or if he thinks that intercourse is really the end, brother, yes, really the end, he will tend to believe that she feels exactly the same way about it. Unless she unbuttons her lips and informs him to the contrary, how is he possibly to know exactly how she *does* feel?

Honest, forthright sex talk and shameless mechanical appositioning of a man and woman's body until they both maximally enjoy sex does not destroy human romance—unless you, by senseless definition, happen to *think* that it does. Loving, particularly in the male, frequently stems *from* good, solid sexual enjoyment; and literally millions of couples throughout the world stay together in unwedded or wedded blessedness mainly or partly *because* they have empirically determined what satisfies each other sexually and are unashamedly doing what they have determined works best. Not only do many of these couples merely stay together, but they *lovingly*, even *romantically*, maintain their ties because they have found, in their mates, at least *one* person with whom they can be sexually honest and with whom they can do exactly what they most like to do.

Let's then, not louse up sex with super-romanticism. Sure, it's nice to go to bed with your lover or husband when the moon is on high, violins are singing through the trees, and he is whispering endless sweet nothings of love into your enchanted ears. But do you really *need* this stuff to have a hell of a good roll in the hay? Is he truly a bastard and a boor when at times he *doesn't* behave with romantic ardor, but more matter-of-factly takes twenty minutes of distinctly mechanical maneuvering to bring you to a high ecstatic pitch, and then focuses on his own supreme enjoyment while you go to work in an equally "mechanical" manner on him?

What, in fact, *is* romantic about not bothering to discover precisely what is most satisfying to your mate, or discovering it and then refusing to do what he or she wants because this is "too premeditated" or "too practical"? Is the man who brings his girl a box of chocolates unromantic or unloving because he has made sure, before he buys them for her, that she actually likes chocolates or is not allergic to them? Is the husband who purchases a new car for his wife on their tenth wedding anniverasry unromantic because he has premeditatedly determined, beforehand, precisely what kind of a car she wants and what color she prefers? Naturally not. Then why should we look upon a sex partner as unromantic because he bothers, quite lovingly and considerately, to discover what his mate wants and to go to some amount of time and effort to fulfill her particular (or even peculiar) sex preferences?

229

The mutuality bugaboo works both ways in human sexuality; and it is just as important for the female as the male. First of all, there is no reason why you *must* get an orgasm every time that your lover does. Men, on the whole, tend to be more often in a sexual mood than women do, and to require climax every two or three days. Females, on the other hand, are frequently more episodic in their desires, and can live without fulfillment for a week or two or even three or four on many occasions, without feeling undue deprivation. Even when they are reasonably well-aroused sexually, they still do not require orgasm in each case of arousal and may be well content with petting or copulation that does not lead to climax.

If you are this type of female, stand by your guns, and let your partner know, in no uncertain terms, that you don't *need* a climax every time he does, and that your not achieving one does not mean that you do not love him, that he is not really a good lover, or any of that other bosh he may be thinking. It merely means that you are different from him. And both you and he can learn to live comfortably with this difference.

On the other side of the fence, you may well have a male partner who only occasionally requires sex relations, while you have distinct urges much more often than he. So—what is wrong with *that*? If he wants to eat oftener than you, you normally feed the brute as often as he wants. Similarly, if you want to come to orgasm more often than he, why should he not be persuaded to help you fulfill your desires as often as *you* want? If either of you is just about insatiable in regard to food, sex, or anything else, that may be truly onerous

230

for the other, and full cooperation in satisfying the insatiable one's wants can hardly be expected. But if one of you wants *somewhat* more food, or sex, or almost anything else that the other can fairly easily supply, why should not this other do, in the spirit of full loving, the supplying?

Recently I had two patients on the same day who had basically the same problem. In the morning, Gerald K. came to see me, to complain that his wife was a great housewife, mother, theater companion, and so on, but that she only wanted to have intercourse about once every two weeks while he literally was raring to go every single day of the week. He was easily satisfied by almost any kind of sexual stimulation, and he didn't quibble about how his wife gave him an orgasm. He didn't care, moreover, whether she had one herself, or whether she was even romantically or sexually involved while she satisfied him. But he did care, and mightily, when he was not satisfied, and found that his unfulfilled desire interfered with his work, his behavior to the children, his recreational activities, and almost everything else in life. Could I, therefore, prevail upon his wife to give him a sexual release about once a day, and no nonsense about it?

That same afternoon Mrs. Nina T. came to see me, with the much more hesitantly presented tale that her husband seemed to be satisfied with having intercourse about two or three times a year—yes, a *year!*—while she had always, up to the time of marrying, masturbated two or three times a day—yes, a *day*. Since marrying, she no longer wanted to resort to masturbation; so could I—well—er—that is, could I—well—show her hus-

231

band that—er—just a few minutes petting her each night would please her and—well—make her a much calmer and less irritable wife and mother?

I saw Gerald's wife only once. Although she at first objected that she was just too tired, by the time they got to bed, to satisfy her husband sexually on most occasions, I quickly got her to admit that she did all kinds of household chores, from morning to night, that were much more onerous than the five or ten minutes she would have to spend giving Gerald a daily orgasm. Since this was the only objection she raised, and I soon reduced it to shreds, she said she would see what she could do about giving her husband more regular satisfaction.

Being a woman of her word, she followed up this session by definite action, and when I next saw Gerald, he said that the problem was completely solved, that their marital relationship had never been so good in the eight years they had been together, and that even their two young children seemed to be benefiting greatly by their newly regularized sex acts. Also—as I had half-predicted, his wife was now getting stimulated herself about half the time she started out by just wanting to satisfy him; and her own sex pleasures had increased considerably.

Nina's husband was a much more difficult customer. In the dozen times I saw him, we debated endlessly over why he should satisfy her even though he himself had few sex urges. He used every argument in the book: that only intercourse was the proper sex method, and he wasn't often capable of that; that having sex as often as his wife wanted it would make him a most unspontaneous participant; that he was so tired by the time he went to bed with Nina that he literally couldn't lift a finger to help her; that it was abnormal and un-natural for a woman to be as sexy as his wife was; that sex was largely designed for procreation rather than for mere pleasure; and so on and so forth. I calmly batted down all these arguments, and showed them how il-logical and unscientific they were. He would admit most of my points, but still not change his antisexual behavior one jot.

Finally, it became apparent that he was rigidly and compulsively sticking to his guns mainly because he was terribly afraid to be forced to do anything, even to his own advantage, and that he construed such force as a direct impingement on his integrity. Although he would not admit that his fear of being dominated by people and outside forces stemmed from a seriously disturbed state of mind, it became more and more evi-dent to Nina that this was true, and she finally gave him an ultimatum: either try to satisfy her sexually or she would leave him. He still refused to change his ways and they eventually got divorced.

The main point here is that either a man or a woman in an intimate relationship with each other may be sexually deprived because of the other's physical or psychological peculiarities; and that unless some clear-cut adjustments are made so that the deprived mate receives at least a moderate amount of sex satisfaction, their relationship is not likely to last too long or too well. If you, then, are on the non-receiving end of sexual gratification, do not hesitate to express your dis-satisfaction and to try to induce your mate to do every-thing possible to place you on the receiving end. This does not mean, of course, that you should *blame* him

233

for not giving you more pleasure, but merely that you should call to his attention, politely but firmly, that he is not giving it. Show him, by mental and physical guidance, exactly what it is you require for full sex gratification; don't accept his easy excuses for not doing what you want.

And don't, under any circumstances, blame yourself for not being easily satisfied! There is nothing great or marvelous about a woman who, after her man looks her steadily in the eye or kisses her softly on the lips, goes into a string of powerful orgasms. This is simply her nature; and she probably would act similarly with almost any man with whom she had some degree of psychosexual rapport. Even though she may find it highly convenient to be the way she is—just as you may find it convenient to be tall, or beautiful, or large-breasted, or brainy—you are not, in comparison to her, a total loss.

If you never achieve the kind of quick and intense sex pleasure that she achieves, that is too bad—but that's all it is: too bad. And if your man demands that you be in her class, that is too bad, too: for most probably you'll never make it (any more than you'll be as lovely as Helen of Troy or as good a novelist as Jane Austen). But just because you are not the greatest bedmate of the century doesn't mean that you are no good whatsoever in this respect, nor that you can't show your lover or husband a trick or two. You probably can. If you're not too perfectionistic or over-romantic.

If you do find yourself somewhat deficient sexually, in that you do not get easily aroused and have a difficult time achieving climax once you are aroused, the chances are that you are not focusing as well as you might on sexually exciting stimuli. The main art of sexual arousal and satisfaction, particularly in relation to satisfying oneself, consists of proper focusing.

Females, for some reason which is still not entirely clear but which may well be related to their antisexual upbringing in this society, are notoriously poor at sexual focusing in innumerable instances. Even when they are actively engaged in intercourse, and presumably enjoying it, they are able to think of a host of nonsexual things, such as cooking, shopping, the laundry, the dress they saw in Bonwit's window yesterday, and (literally as well as figuratively) the kitchen sink.

This kind of nonsexual or antisexual thinking enhances your sex pleasure just about as much as thinking about murdering your neighbor and cutting him up into little pieces is likely to add flavor to the roast beef you are eating. Sexual excitation is largely meditated by (a) signals or thoughts from the cerebral cortex of the brain to the sex centers of the body (especially those located in the lower part of the spinal cord), and (b) direct and indirect physical manipulation of the sex organs themselves.

If only the second of these two main forms of arousal is being employed, lots of people can become sexually aroused—but they have the devil of a time helping themselves to experience orgasm. And one of the main reasons why women so often become sexually aroused without achieving orgasm is that they are getting the proper kind of physical stimulation of their erogenous zones, but are not using their brain power to give themselves sufficient additional stimulation to propel them to climax.

Matters become much worse in this connection whenever an individual who wants to become aroused and satisfied is worrying mightily over whether she actually will succeed. For the thoughts: "My God! it looks like I'm not going to succeed this time, and then he will think I'm a dud in bed," or: "Will I make it? Will I make it? Will I make it?" are as antisexual as they could possibly be. They sometimes seem, these worrisome internalized sentences, to be about sex; but really they are about personal worth: about how am I *doing* at sex? And no matter how close to orgasm a woman may be, if she at the last minute starts thinking, "Will I actually come? Won't it be awful if I don't!" she is very likely to stop her entire sexual processes and to wind up completely frustrated.

What *should* you do instead of focusing on nonsexual or antisexual thoughts? Obviously, you should think of whatever is most arousing to you, and avidly and concertedly concentrate on whatever that is, until you finally impel yourself to climax. You may think, in this connection, of your lover or husband; or the handsome man you saw on the street yesterday; or your favorite actor; of some particular kind of sex act, even a bizarre or peculiar act; or of literally *anything* that excites you. If love and romance work for you, think loving and romantic thoughts. If sheer, unadulterated sexy thoughts work, use them.

"But is this really cricket?" you may ask. "Here I am trying to achieve full satisfaction with George, and you tell me I may have to think of Jim or Donald or Guy. Or of some sado-masochistic fantasy. Isn't that unethical? Isn't that pretty crazy?"

It may be crazy, say I; but that's the way millions of

perfectly "normal" human beings are. Even though they madly love George, and are having sex relations with him, thinking of him is no longer exciting to them; while thinking of Jim or Donald or Guy is. It seems a pity that this is so; but it *is* so; and if it is so in your own case, you'd better calmly accept it as one of the facts of life and use it to your own advantage.

Similarly with other kinds of sex fantasies. Both men and women, I have found in my clinical practice, think of the damnedest things when they want to arouse and satisfy themselves sexually. If they ever carried some of these things into practice—if, for example, they actually allowed themselves to be beaten with a whip in order to bring on orgasm—they would have weird kinds of sex lives, and we would have to consider them deviated or perverted. But as long as their fantasies remain precisely that, and are not carried out into any actual practice, there seems to be nothing unusual about them; and such fantasies are so common among otherwise sane people that it seems fanciful to call them deviated or perverse.

Focus sexually, then, without any guilt or self-castigation. It would be nice if you could merely think of your man's wavy blond hair or huge genitals, and thereby bring yourself to a peak of sexual excitement. But suppose he has black hair and small genitals, which just do not send you. Or suppose he has the right kind of physical features that match your own prejudices but you *still* are not enthusiastic about focusing on these features, and you find your mind straying excitedly to someone or something else. Too bad; but hardly catastrophic. Do the best you can with the fantasies that work for you; and your relations with your lover or

237

husband, as well as with yourself, are likely to be much better than they otherwise would tend to be.

Try hard, then, to discover what uniquely satisfies you, physically and mentally; and do not prudishly or romantically hesitate to use the information you thereby discover. Don't, at the same time, *over*-try for perfect orgasm, since there is no such thing; and women (as previously noted) can have very pleasant relations on many occasions without ever coming to climax. If you don't, at certain times, reach the highest summits of sexuality, that is somewhat regrettable but that's all it is—regrettable. It does not mean that you are sexually incompetent; nor that you are personally worthless; nor that your man will quickly leave you; nor that you have missed the only true joy in life. It merely means that this particular time you have not got your piece of taffy; and that next time you'll have another chance to get it.

Chapter 10

How to Get a Reluctant Man to Marry

Let us assume that you have been getting your money's worth out of this book and have looked for a man, found a suitable one, and are getting along well with him sexually and otherwise. Unfortunately, however, the particular man you have chosen does not seem eager to marry you, but is more than willing to go along forever having an extramarital affair. Perhaps he is now married and balks at divorcing his wife; or perhaps he has had several marriages already, and is not joyful about adding another legal notch to his belt; or perhaps he has never been married, and just does not see why he should ever be.

What can you do about *these* difficult circumstances? Let us see.

What not to do about a reluctant man

The main thing you should *not* do when your chosen man will not, for the present, marry you is to become exceptionally resentful and vengeful. For one thing, he has a perfect *right* not to marry—no matter how strong your own urge to be legally wedded may be. Certainly he enjoys your company, your cooking, your love-making, and many other aspects of your relationship with him. But how does *this* prove that he therefore *should* marry you and is a bastard if he doesn't? Does a man necessarily have to *pay* for every advantage he gets with a woman? Does he have to be made to *suffer* for the benefits he gains from a heterosexual relation? If *this* is what you think, then you have a deadly, commercialized view of love and marriage yourself—and it is highly doubtful whether you should marry with that kind of distorted viewpoint.

If, moreover, a man is not marrying you, in spite of the fact that you are getting along splendidly with him in most respects, there is a good chance that he still has some fear of becoming legally bound to you. Perhaps he thinks that you're treating him very well right now, but that who knows what you will do after the marital knot is more firmly tied. Perhaps he feels that you are underlyingly hostile, nasty, or vengeful, and is afraid of what will eventually happen to him if he marries you.

If these are the kinds of fears he may have about marrying, then your now becoming terribly resentful and backbiting when he balks at proposing will almost certainly confirm his worst fears. By your negative behavior you will give him the best possible kind of ammunition with which he can convince himself that he is as right as he can be about avoiding marriage with you.

Resenting a man for not marrying you, moreover, is to tell yourself the sentence, "Because I *want* him to marry me and *dislike* his not doing so, he *should* marry me and I *can't stand* his not proposing to me." This sentence is both grandiose and anxiety-provoking, and it entirely follows from *your* irrational assumptions rather than from *his* poor behavior. You would be much wiser (in regard both to marrying the man you want

240

and to living a good life in general) if you questioned and challenged your *own* nonsense in this connection rather than unjustifiably blamed your boyfriend for being the (admittedly regrettable) way that he is.

While you are trying to keep yourself from becoming terribly resentful if your man is not in any marrying mood, you must at the same time not go to the other extreme and act in an unusually weak, namby-pamby manner. Don't just let your relationship with this man drag on endlessly, without ever bringing up the issue of marriage. Let him know, in a frank and direct manner, that you are most interested in getting married, and that you hope that you will be able to marry him in the not too distant future. Don't pretend that you *like* going on for a long time in an unwedded state when you definitely do not like this. Tell him, instead, what your real feelings are.

This does not mean that at certain special times you should not keep your gentle trap shut about your urges to marry; for at times you should. If, for example, your boyfriend is obviously in a poor financial situation and is therefore in no position to marry; or if he has a bitchy wife who at the moment clearly will not divorce him; or if he is still smarting from the unpleasantness of breaking up with his last wife—at times like these, it would be wiser if you kept reasonably quiet about your marital goals and let him first work out some of his own problems.

If, however, there is no good or special reason why the man you want cannot now marry you, and if he nonetheless seems to be dilly-dallying as the precious months go by, don't be a coward: tell him, in a very nice way, exactly what's on your mind, and let the

241

chips fall where they may. Perhaps, when you bring up the question of marriage, he'll be most surprised, and blurt out that he has no intention of ever marrying you (or anyone else). Perhaps he'll quickly lose interest in you, after you raise this issue openly, and stop seeing you again. Perhaps he'll scream and sulk and lament that you don't really love him, but are only selfishly interested in making your own future secure.

Good! If any of these or similar negative reactions break out on the part of your boyfriend after you have nicely let him know that you aren't getting any younger, that you may well want to raise children, and that in one way or another you intend to end up by marrying some man, you have done yourself a real favor by bringing them into the open so soon. For there is every reason to believe that if you had waited a month or a year or a decade longer, these *still* would have been his basic reactions; and where would you have been *then*? A month or a year or a decade further behind the eight-ball.

How long, generally, should you wait until you gently and sweetly convey to a man the notion that love and sex are great stuff, honey, but a girl normally wants something more than that? That depends partly, of course, on extenuating circumstances.

If you are fifteen or sixteen years of age, you can afford to wait quite a few years before you encourage your male to point his toes toward the altar. If you yourself have something to do that is most important in life—such as to finish medical school or tour the world with a ballet company—you may also be more than willing to put off legal wedlock for months or years to come. If your man is already married, but is making every possible effort to get away from a wife who is most reluctant to let him go, you will of course have to wait until his prior legal entanglements are no longer existent before you dulcetly persuade him to pop the question.

Suppose, however, that no such impediments to marriage as these exist? Then, as I tell most of my female psychotherapy patients and premarital counseling clients, the general rule of thumb is: If you have intimately known a man for from three to six months, and have spent considerable time with him during this period, your relationship with him should be distinctly heading in a marital direction, or else there is something radically rotten in Denmark.

This does not mean that every one of your beaux should have formally proposed to you by April Fool's Day, assuming that you met on New Year's Eve. But it does mean that by the time a quarter of a year or more of dining, wining, and monkeyshining has amiably passed, your current boyfriend should be indicating very strongly that he cares for you, that he would like to live with you, and that he is at least seriously thinking about the possibilities of visiting City Hall on your behalf. If he is not even *thinking* along these lines, and you definitely are, then you'd better jog his cognitive processes in this respect and let him know that you are eagerly awaiting some kind of a decision.

Should you play games to get your boyfriend to do his duty by Our Nell or else get off the pot? You can, if you wish—but not on my advice. I see no particular point in your pretending to have other dates when he wants to see you, refusing to see him very often even though you are just dying to be with him, or keeping him away from you sexually until he pops the question. I am sure—as women have often told me—that these kinds of games sometimes work. But they also frequently backfire. Thus, they may induce the man of your choice to marry you, all right—but to marry you against his own will, and perhaps to hate your guts for the next thirty years just because you have tricked him into getting hitched.

I am seeing at this writing a man who has been married for eight years and who gets along reasonably well with his wife, but who has been carrying on a series of extramarital affairs since he was married, and who keeps wondering whether he should divorce his wife and marry one of his adulterous inamoratas. One of his main reasons for this kind of behavior is that he discovered, shortly after marriage, that the man he thought was his greatest rival for his wife's hand, and whom she had been using to make him jealous and to induce him to propose to her, was really her cousin in whom she had never been seriously interested. He has been so resentful of this premarital trickery that he has never really buckled down to trying to make a good monogamous relationship with his wife; and it will probably be some time yet before I can help him overcome his childish resentment and rebelliousness.

So forget the coy games and stick pretty much to the truth. Calmly and nicely show your boyfriend that even though you do care only for him, and have no intention of baiting him with other men or seeing him more seldom, you are just, in a self-protective manner, going to *have* to stop being intimate with him and to seek other affairs if he remains adamant about marrying you.

244

If, moreover, you can have this kind of serious, heart-to-heart talk with your man *after* you have, for a period of at least many weeks, been unusually nice to him and have definitely not nastily beaten him over the head for depriving you of wifehood, you have a much better chance of getting him to say yes. In fact, if this kind of behavior will not work, I doubt whether anything else will.

Mary D., under my guidance, followed this kind of procedure and found that it worked beautifully. Mary although only twenty-seven, had already been twice-divorced and had two young children when she began going with Roger S. Roger came from a highly conservative, well-to-do family which was loaded with clergymen, army officers, and politicians. Almost no one, least of all Mary, expected Roger to rush into marriage with his twice-divorced beloved; and their relationship went on and on, every Wednesday and Saturday, with no sign of Roger's even getting close to a proposal.

Mary's mother, who was even more eager than Mary to see her daughter's nuptials concluded, kept strongly pressuring the young woman to keep far out of arm's reach of Roger. For Mary was unusually comely of face and figure; and the mother figured that if it were made known to Roger that he could get his sexual due with Mary only after he had given her a wedding ring, he would then be willing to overlook her previous marital history, as well as the objections of his family, and take on husbandly and fatherly responsibilities with her.

When I first saw Mary, she was dutifully trying to carry out her mother's best laid schemes—and there was a bit of hell to pay. Roger, though obviously most attracted to the girl, was getting more and more jumpy, overtly complaining that she clearly did not care for him as she kept saying that she did, and beginning to get soused and wind up with other girls on the nights when he was not seeing Mary. As a result of one of these extracurricular affairs, in fact, he had got one of the other girls pregnant and, out of a sense of guilt, had come within a hair of going off and marrying her. This affair had blown over; but Mary was not sure when a similar crisis might not rise again; so she was just about as jumpy as was Roger.

I quickly put a stop to all that. "Look," I said to Mary during one of our first sessions, "what do you really *want* to do with Roger? Do you want to go to bed with him and enjoy yourself—and, incidentally, see how the two of you really make it that way, and get some kind of a preview of how it might be after marriage—or do you want to keep as far as possible away from premarital sex relations, because sex is not your particular entrée?"

"Oh, no," she replied, "that's not it at all. I *do* like the sex. I liked it even with my first two husbands, neither of whom I got along with too well in other respects. And I almost pop off at the loins when I just let Roger kiss me goodnight. So there's no doubt about my wanting it. But my mother keeps insisting that if I do give in that way, that'll kill everything, and he'll never marry me."

"Damn your mother!" I said. "She's apparently been pulling that 'I must be pure until married' line ever since your father divorced her twenty years ago; and how come, if that approach is so good, that she hasn't married again?"

"Yes, I can't help wondering about that myself. Mother's had plenty of suitors ever since the divorce. She's one of the most beautiful women I know. And she says she wants to marry again. So I wonder."

"Well, that's her problem, and we aren't here to get her straightened out. But it does look as if her advice doesn't work too well for her, so why should it work that well for you?"

"But *won't* Roger lose most of his incentive to marry me if I have sex with him now? You know the old saw: 'Why buy the cow when milk's so cheap?'"

"Not so. The assumption there is that one *only* wants milk from the cow—and that, of course, is not always true. Some people *like* cows: like their looks, like to raise them, to milk them, to own them. And most men don't *only* try to get sex from a woman. They want other things from her as well—such as steady companionship and family living—which are more compatible with marrying than with not marrying her."

"But how about my handicaps in this case. You know: my two previous marriages, and the children?"

"How about them? As you say, they probably are handicaps. Especially from the standpoint of Roger's relatives. But what woman *doesn't* have known handicaps to the man who marries her?"

"Then you think I should do what I really want to do, and have sex with Roger?"

"I think that you should stop playing games and truly be *yourself* with him. Not only yourself, but your *nicest, warmest* self. Since you do, we know, have those handicaps; and you have to show him some good reasons why he should marry you. If, therefore, you treat him exceptionally well, including sexually well,

247

for the next few months; and if, after treating him in such a beneficent manner, you then frankly tell him that you can't very well go on that way forever, since you *do* very much want to marry again—if that kind of relationship with him doesn't make him want to accept you in marriage with all your real handicaps, I can't imagine what else will make him want to—and I mean really want to—do so."

"You are sort of saying that I might possibly get Roger by the kind of game my mother is trying to get me to continue, but that even though he would want me if I played such a game, it isn't exactly *me,* or me in *marriage,* he would want. Is that right?"

"Yes, I think that puts it pretty well. That if you get him by a cat-and-mouse game, what you are really getting is a game-lover. While if you get him by being exceptionally nice to him—which presumably you will continue to be to some considerable degree after you are married—then you get a you-lover or a marriage-lover rather than a game-lover."

"I can see what you mean. And of course I *do* want to be nice to him after marriage, and not merely before, as a technique to get him. If I didn't want to be, I would be marrying mainly for the sake of marrying, and not for the pleasures of being married."

"Exactly. So why don't you, right now, kind of pretend that you *are* married to Roger, and treat him the way you would if you were married. This gives both of you an excellent preview of the marital state—and you can see whether it's worth entering."

Mary followed my suggestions and began to have a full-blown affair with Roger. Her mother almost had

248

a fit about this, but she nevertheless stuck to her guns and within a few weeks was practically living with her lover. For the next ten weeks she gave him as much of herself as she could; and whenever she began to feel badly again, because he still was not proposing, she strongly reminded herself, as I kept teaching her to do, that he had a perfect right to be the way he was, and that he was not a louse just because his wishes did not perfectly coincide with hers. Consequently, she was able to be unresentful toward Roger even when she felt somewhat saddened by her insecure position with him.

At the end of this time, when Roger had still made no mention of marriage, she sat down with him one night and calmly but firmly told him that she loved him very much, and was now more than ever convinced that he would make a fine husband and a good father to her children (with whom he had been getting along splendidly during the last ten weeks); but that the only love relationship in which she could find prolonged satisfaction was marriage.

Therefore, she simply owed it to herself to discontinue their affair, if he did not feel inclined to marry her, and look for another man who would be highly motivated to do so. She doubted, she said, that she would ever find anyone who was as much to her liking as he was, and she was most sorry to have to end this relationship with him; but what else, under the circumstances, could she sanely do?

Roger was at first taken aback by her sudden confrontation—since apparently he had just put out of his mind the fact that time was passing and that they could not go on this way forever—but he was able to see that she was not merely trying to put him over a barrel, and that what she was saying was wise and true. He told her that he had no doubt whatever about his love feelings for her; but he admitted that he could not see his way to marrying her as yet, because of the great to-do that would arise in his family. He hoped that he would be able to marry her one day, but was most indefinite when this day would be. He agreed, therefore, that it would be sensible if she did stop seeing him, even though both of them would suffer for awhile.

Roger's answer was most disappointing to Mary, since she had naturally hoped that he would be so averse to giving up the happiness they both had been experiencing that he would simply disregard the opposition of his family and any other objections that there might be to marrying her. She was so torn by the prospect of losing him forever, that she came within an inch of reneging on her position and of agreeing indefinitely to continue their affair. She pulled herself together, however, and steadfastly, if sorrowfully, held her ground. They agreed to part, sadly kissed goodnight for what was supposed to be the last time, and Roger left.

Early the next morning he was on the phone, saying that he hadn't slept a wink that night because, in thinking things over, he couldn't find any objection to marrying her *other* than the displeasure of his family. And if that was all that was standing in the way of their permanently getting together, to hell with it!—he was not going to be ruled by the opinions—not to mention the bigotries—of even his closest family members. How soon could Mary meet him to go with him and select an engagement ring?

Whether Roger and Mary lived happily ever after, I am not sure—though when I last heard about them, a few years after their marriage, they were still going strong and had no regrets. Nor does their success necessarily prove that Mary's premarital tactics will *always* work as well as they did for her. Many other Rogers will not be led into wedlock no matter how well their sweetheart treats them before marriage, nor no matter how beautifully she explains that she just can't go on comfortably in a non-marital relationship. Others will be led to marry, when they are treated as Mary treated Roger, but will only do so with great reluctance, and will never forget the fact that they were forced to wed somewhat against their will. Not all males act alike; and it is foolish to assume that your particular boyfriend will follow Roger's example—when he may well be quite a different kind of Tom, Dick, or Harry.

Nonetheless, being exceptionally nice and unresentful to a man for a period of a few months before you let him know that you cannot carry on a non-marital affair with him forever is one of the very best ways to put him in a pro-marrying mood. The more you carp and wail and hold back on your best efforts because you are unhappy when your man is not proposing, the less he is likely to become maritally inclined. If, as noted above, you insist on trying various jealousy-arousing and other tricks of the trade to get your man to the license bureau, go ahead and try them. But if you will keep in mind that almost any good kind of marriage that you might have is likely to be a decidedly warm, cooperative, permissive relationship, I think

251

you will see the wisdom of getting a head start on *this* kind of togetherness before the wedding bells begin to peal.

It has been remarked by Sigmund Freud and other psychologists that many people remain married because their revenge against each other, particularly for some of the nasty games they have played on each other during the courtship stage, has not yet been exhausted. Let us hope that your marriage never falls into this category.

What to do about a reluctant lover

Is there anything else you can do about a man who presumably loves you but who is reluctant to marry, aside from being exceptionally nice and unresentful while you are carrying on an affair with him? Yes, several things, such as these:

1. Be permissive. It is safe and secure for you when you know that your boyfriend is exclusively devoted to you, never looks at other girls, and would never possibly be sexually unfaithful. But to the degree that you demand such security, you may be unduly restricting him, and making him resentful of you. Perhaps, moreover, he actually should have some time to sow some wild oats before he settles down in marriage. Or perhaps he should have some room for comparisons, to see whether you are really better for him than some of his other potential or actual girlfriends seem to be. Also: it is by no means a bad idea to give a man sufficient rope, before marriage, with which to hang himself, if he is actually set to do so. If he is really a runaround, or insists on spending most of his time at the

office, or keeps refusing to do anything but hang around the house with you, it is far better that you know these propensities of his now, before you get solidly hitched, than that you are shocked to discover them afterward. The more you discover about your potential mate's worst leanings, the better position you are in to decide whether or not it is worth marrying him.

2. Be sexy. Nine out of ten men, at least, marry because they believe that they will have steadier and better sex relations in marriage than they have previously had during their bachelorhood. Most of these men, alas, will eventually be sadly disappointed: since it is almost incredible how *little* sex there is in the average American marriage, particularly during the early years of pregnancy and infant-rearing, which frequently reduce the copulatory urges of the wife (and often of the husband as well) to a minimum. But at the point when they actually marry, males generally do not realize how well off they may be with their generally exciting, if also somewhat sporadic, premarital affairs; and they have the highest hopes (or illusions) about what a great ball they will continually have when their girlfriend becomes their wife.

Don't disillusion your man *before* marriage! Try to be, at this time in particular, the grandest sexpot he has yet encountered. For one thing, you will then be able to keep him from being very interested in your competitors—who, let us face it, are many, and some of whom actually *are* mainly interested in his bed prowess. For another thing, he will almost always construe your violent sex interest as interest in *him* rather than in his genital agility. Tell a woman that she is great in bed, and she will frequently be insulted: since

253

she thinks that you think she is *only* good for one limited purpose. But show a man that you truly appreciate his copulative ardor, and you indicate that you think him a great guy and a scholar.

So be sexually imaginative. Try to devise, in your spare time, a new coital trick or two. Think, specifically, of how to please your man *sexually*, and not merely conversationally, appetitively, or companionably. Almost any woman can adequately sew on his buttons or whip up a soufflé when he is hungry. But how many of your competitors can really *swing?*

3. Be loving. If you sit back cautiously, and wait until your man has cast himself at your feet and promised to love you forever, you may possibly intrigue some self-punishing individual who does not love until he is stepped on, or some big-game—hunting male who is mainly out for difficult conquests and will not love any woman who is fairly easily available. But who needs a masochistic man? And who wants one who, being primarily interested in the conquest side of amour, will most probably become supremely disinterested once he has succeeded in warming up an initially cold lady?

Love, more frequently than not, begets love. If you are consistently warm and outgoing—especially when your man is more than a bit cool and reserved himself —you will tend to present to your partner a side of life that is more intriguing and exciting than his own uninvolvement and neutrality. If he himself is highly affectionate and ardent, he will feel most comfortable with your own warm-heartedness; and if he is somewhat deficient in this respect, he may be most pleasantly surprised to find that, under your thawing rays, he begins to show feeling which he thought he was hardly capable of having before you came along.

Super-romanticism, as we previously pointed out, may defeat its own purposes. But a more moderate degree of romantic passion may call forth a surprising responsiveness in the man of your choice. If you, for example, send a card on the anniversary of the day you met, or write him a poem when he is on a business trip, or tell him how much you would like to see him on a weekday night when you usually do not get together, he may quite unconsciously take similar flights of fancy himself; and, before you know it, you may be sailing away on the same romantic carpet.

No nagging, now! Telling your boyfriend that he never sends you roses, like your previous lover or husband used to do, and that therefore how could he possibly, possibly love you, will usually get you nowhere—except out in the cold, looking for a new boyfriend. He will tend to see you as being obnoxiously demanding, and may well think back on *his* last sweetheart, who (with all her faults) at least didn't keep baldly pressuring him to do what he didn't want to do. If, however, without many overt demands whatever, *you* send the roses, he may soon find himself *wanting* to respond in kind; and may even start devising original romantic approaches to you.

Moreover: just as the male's persistent sexuality frequently wears down female resistance and eventually induces the girl *willingly* to jump into bed, there is no reason why persistent female romanticism cannot encourage the male willingly to jump into romantic courtship and marriage. You are obviously not likely to get very far in this respect if you select a distinctly reluctant partner, and then put on a campaign of telephone calls, telegrams, letters, visits, and other means of intimate contact. Very probably, he will think you a royal pain in the gullet, and resist you more and more.

Toward a man, however, who at least seems half-willing to become involved with you, and who continues to seek your sexual and nonsexual companionship when he very well could go elsewhere, your affectionate, romantic overtures are likely to fall on much more fertile soil. So don't, just because he *is* a male, necessarily wait for him to start the loving preludes. The millennium may arrive sooner.

4. Be understanding. Loving a man is often rather easy, since you are not going to select, in the first place, someone for whom you do not have some spontaneous interest or involvement, and if you do fall in love with this individual you usually will manage to do so unconsciously, unthinkingly, without much concerted effort on your part.

Understanding is much harder to achieve—and I mean *achieve.* For understanding usually involves several acts which are not entirely spontaneous, and which are to some degree self-sacrificing. Thus, in order to understand fully how an individual is behaving and to accept his behavior even when it is not exactly kindly or appropriate or correct, you must first listen carefully to his point of view and forbear jumping to any immediate conclusions.

Whatever your *first* and *spontaneous* reactions to his deeds and misdeeds may be, you have to stop and take a second or third look—literally hold yourself back, in many instances, from making a quick judgment; and patiently continue to get all the facts of his actions, until you have obtained pretty much the whole story behind them.

Secondly, to understand a person's behavior, you must temporarily be objective and withhold *any* judgment about it until you have given him time and opportunity to offer excuses, extenuating circumstances, and special exceptions to many of the usual rules of living. If, for example, your boyfriend tells you that he has double-crossed his business partner, you must not immediately respond: "Oh, that's wrong! How could you have possibly done such a thing?" Instead, you must give him a chance to explain how his partner previously has double-crossed him; what his special reasons for behaving in this manner toward his partner were; why he thinks his "wrong" deed was really necessary in this particular instance; what unusual stresses he was under when he committed the deed; etc.

Thirdly, understanding—as we have been emphasizing throughout this book—consists of acceptance of the other's behavior even *after* you have finally decided that it is mistaken or immoral. Thus, you may never like the fact that your lover has double-crossed his partner or treated his mother very badly—but you can nevertheless understand that he *is* a fallible human, and consequently can only be *expected* at times to do distinctly wrong things. Understanding this, you can still fully accept, though not necessarily approve, his behavior, and can concentrate on trying to help him change it for the better next time instead of blaming him for committing it this time.

Understanding another, then, consists of holding back your immediate responses to his actions, carefully giving him every benefit of the doubt, objectively weighing whether or not he has really done wrong, and accepting him even after it has been clearly proven that he has behaved badly. Understanding is consequently a *highly disciplined* form of responding to another; and, in the short run, it tends to be self-sacrificing, since at the moment of understanding you are considering this other rather than only yourself, and you may even be going along with some of his behavior (such as his nastiness toward you) which is inimical to your own happiness.

In the long run, however, understanding of a lover or husband need not be self-sacrificing, since it is basically to your *own* interest to comprehend and forgive his poor conduct, so that (*a*) you will not unduly upset yourself about it, and (*b*) you will eventually get him to see that you are truly on his side and that he would be wise if he similarly understood and loved you. Understanding of another person, in other words, usually leads to long-run rather than to short-run hedonism. It is difficult; but in the end it is often most rewarding.

By way of illustration, let us take the case of one of my patients who was recently invited to a wekeend with some charming people; and when she delightedly told her boyfriend that he was invited, too, and that she looked forward to their spending the weekend with these people, he suddenly balked and refused to go. She was shocked by his refusal, was certain that he was deliberately punishing her for another occasion when she did not want to meet his boss (who she was afraid would not approve of her affair with her boyfriend), and came close to breaking off their relationship because she felt he was spiting her.

As a result of my talking over this incident with my patient, she began to see things differently and to be more understanding. She realized that her boyfriend did not want to go away for the weekend because he was afraid that the people they would be spending it with were more educated than he, and thought that they would despise him, and also because he was afraid that she would imbibe too much liquor during the visit and might do something to shame him. Instead of condemning him for having these fears, she calmly accepted the fact that he was this fearful, and she tried to help him see that there was nothing to be afraid of. She also indicated that if he still remained fearful and didn't want to go way for the weekend with her, she would be quite willing (though regretful) to go away alone—or, if he wished, to stay at home with him.

Seeing that she had reversed her previous angry stand, and that she was able fully to understand (though not to like) his position, her boyfriend at first agreed that it would be quite all right if she went visiting alone. Then, at the last minute, he thought things over again, decided that there really wasn't that much for him to be afraid of, and went on the weekend visit with her. In the process, he did manage to become considerably less fearful, and their relationship considerably improved.

Understanding, then, must usually be *worked at*. It does not come spontaneously; is not an inborn gift. It involves creative listening and acting; and, especially when it is added to permissiveness, sexiness, and loving, it is hard to resist. Give a man this combination of acceptance, and even if he is a most difficult customer, and comes to the relationship with you with

259

little or no idea of marrying, he is very likely to sacrifice his freedom willingly. If he does so, and if you still continue to give him a similar sex-love relational pattern after you are legally wed, he may even come to enjoy marriage. And so may you!

Chapter 11

Overcoming Your Own Blocks to Marrying

Men are hardly the only refugees from marriage, since many females, too, consciously or unconsciously avoid taking the plunge. If you are one of those females who, even though you tell yourself that you really want to marry and are looking forward to a home and family life, somehow keep winding up in the wrong situations, and never quite achieving double-yoked blessedness, perhaps you have some serious emotional block that prevents you from making the kind of a marital tie that you say that you are eager to enter. Let us therefore examine some of the common emotional blocks that females (and males) set up against marrying, and see what can be done to overcome them.

Perfectionism

There is a wide gap between selectivity and perfectionism. The selective woman asks herself what she really wants in a male, discovers that there are many traits which she definitely does *not* want, and then carefully excludes nine out of ten possible suitors because they have one or more of these traits. Considering that she will only, at most, marry a few times during her lifetime, and that each of her matings is likely to last for a number of years (and one of them, perhaps,

261

for forty or fifty years), she is not so crazy in being selective. In fact, the less choosey she is about picking a mate, the zanier she is likely to be.

The perfectionist girl, while pretending to be selective, is actually impossibly eliminative. She sets up *so many* male traits as being totally undesirable that she leaves herself virtually no one from whom to choose; and, almost by definition, she winds up as a spinster or a wholly disgruntled wife. Like nearly all perfectionists, she is not merely saying to herself, "I dislike a man who smokes or gambles or works long hours or wants to copulate every night in the week." But she is also convincing herself: "*I can't stand* an imperfect male, who will not thoroughly satisfy me in every conceivable way, and who will do things that I may dislike."

The perfectionist, in other words, is only seemingly strong and firm; actually, she is anxious and weak. She refuses to live in a world of probability and chance—where her husband *may* get drunk at times, or be unfaithful to her, or forget their anniversary—and demands an absolutistic, certain world where she *knows* that there will never be any serious marital difficulties for her to overcome. Naturally, she can never know such a world—for the simple reason that it doesn't exist—so she lives, usually with a false security, in another, non-marital part of the universe, where at least she can control her destiny in a somewhat neater and safer manner.

A special kind of perfectionism in our society is super-romanticism. The ultra-romantic woman (or man) feels that marriage must be one continual air-built ball, with all manner of love and esthetic interplay omnipresent, and the crasser aspects of mating—such as financial hassles, housecleaning schedules, and disciplining of the children—magically non-extant. Noting, from their personal affairs as well as their observations of the marriages of others, that such super-fanciful relationships are as rare these days as Moorish castles in Kansas, the devotees of super-romance soon withdraw from the marrying field and confine their amours, if any, to premarital interludes.

How can marriage-destroying perfectionism and ultra-romanticism be overcome? By analyzing and parsing the irrational ideologies that lie behind and create these attitudes. The perfectionist is telling herself: "Because I dislike certain traits in men, I simply cannot live with such traits. Rather than risk living with a man who has a minimum of these traits, or of finding one who has a moderate amount of them and helping him overcome some of his behavior which I do not like, I will, if necessary, wait forever until the perfect male, who has no such traits, comes along. If I marry an imperfect man, I shall be completely destroyed. If I find the perfect one, my underlying slobbishness will be compensated for, and I will be able to get along satisfactorily in this terrible, terrible world."

These self-defeating sentences can be vigorously challenged with several pertinent questions, such as: *Why* can't I live with a man who has some traits that I happen to dislike? *What* is really so risky about marrying someone who has some undesirable characteristics? *Why* *can't* I help a potential mate overcome some of his habits and attitudes that I happen to deplore? *How* would I be completely destroyed if I did happen to marry a man who was imperfect? Where is the *evidence*

263

that I am such an innate slob that I must mate with a perfect male in order to compensate for my utter lousehood?

The more you question your own perfectionism, and the so-called horrors of your being a quite imperfect, fallible wife in this quite imperfect, fallible world, the less perfectionistic and ultra-romantic you will tend to be. The more you unthinkingly assume that you *must* have a perfect man to make up for your own awful deficiencies, the more you will actually need such a paragon of all virtues. Moreover: the more you think you require godliness in a male, the weaker you will keep yourself, the more self-hating you will be—and the less, ironically enough, you are likely to be able to win and keep a reasonably good man if and when he comes your way.

Perfectionism is a self-inflicted vice. Designed to make you feel holier-than-thou, it invariably winds up by making you feel unworthier-than-all. Your one chance of being happily mated when you are perfectionistic is for you to be Mrs. Jehovah; and Jehovah, apparently, was so infallible that he never married at all.

Fears of rejection

Many women who are emotionally blocked against marrying have dire fears of rejection. They are afraid to meet males, in the first place, because they cannot have the guarantee that they will be accepted by these males. Or, sometime later in the dating and mating game, they feel that they will be thrown over by their boyfriends, and that that would be disastrous. Some of these women have actually suffered by a previous rejection, and have no wish to suffer so cruelly again. Others have never let themselves get close enough to a man to be finally spurned by him, but they so graphically imagine the horrors of such a possible occurrence that they continue to stay out of the area of serious courtship.

Claudia V. was a real honey of an avoider when it came to meeting males. At dances, she would stand rigidly on the side lines, glaring malevolently at any boy who happened to look invitingly in her direction. On trains and buses, even if she was most attracted to a male who was sitting next to her, she never looked his way, and ignored his overtures or grunted back a discouraging retort to any proposal he might make. Actually, she was dying to meet eligible males and was miserably lonely as she sat home, night after night, waiting for telephone calls that rarely came.

Claudia insisted, when I first saw her for psychotherapy, that she really liked herself. She was sufficiently good-looking, she thought; she had been bright enough to do very well getting her Master's degree (in, of all things, psychology!); and she kept making rapid advances on the personnel job that she held. Why should she doubt, therefore, that she was a fine enough person and that she had a good estimation of herself?

"Baloney!" I insisted. "You're obviously scared witless to approach a strange male or even to have one approach you. You clearly are telling yourself that if you became intimate with him and he really found out how weak and inept you are socially, he'd quickly leave you, and that that would be catastrophic. Isn't that so?"

"Yes, but I'm just describing what's true. I *am* socially inept; my whole history proves that I am, doesn't it?"

"It proves," I replied, "that you *have been* inept at talking to males: that you *have been* tongue-tied and uncommunicative."

"Well? Isn't that enough?"

"Yes, it's more than enough. But how does *has been* prove *always will be?*"

"But when I keep trying and failing—doesn't that prove that I simply can't? Like the other day, when I wanted, really wanted, to speak nicely to the boy who sat next to me at the lecture I attended, and who tried several times to talk to me. And I just couldn't! I tried, but no matter how hard I tried, I just couldn't. Now doesn't that prove that I *can't?*"

"It proves nothing of the sort. It merely proves that when you *think* you can't do a thing, you can't."

"But why should I think I can't, except that whenever I've tried I haven't been able to? Isn't that why I'm so sure I can't?"

"No, it's really the other way around: you actually haven't tried because you *think* you aren't able to. Then, not trying, but falsely *believing* that you're trying, you conclude: 'I can't!' "

"But how do you know I can? All the evidence points the other way."

"The hell it does! Let me prove to you that it doesn't. Suppose, for example, that the boy who sat next to you at the lecture, and whom you say you could not talk to, suppose that you suddenly noticed that smoke was coming out of his pocket. Could you *then* talk to him?"

"Why—uh—yes. I guess I could."

"You could quickly tell him that his pocket seemed to be on fire, and that he'd better investigate and put it out?"

"Yes, I'm sure I could."

"And after telling him that, you could then go on, could you not, to talk further with him—once the ice was broken like that?"

"Yes. I guess so."

"Well? Under *those* circumstances you could open your mouth and talk quite freely. Then why this bosh about 'I can't'? Obviously, you can."

"Then why do I keep thinking that I can't?"

"Very simply. For two reasons. First, you keep imagining that it would be horrible, if you did talk to this boy, or anyone like him, if he rejected you. *This* is where you are self-hating: for, of course, if you did talk to him and he did thoroughly disapprove of you, it would only mean that he didn't like you, and not that *you* would have to dislike yourself. But clearly, you would dislike yourself if he rejected you—would you not?"

"I—I suppose I would."

"Which proves what I first said: that in spite of the fact that you like yourself in various ways—for your various good points and efficiencies—you still basically dislike yourself whenever anyone else thinks that you are not good enough for them."

"Doesn't everybody?"

"Almost everybody in our silly society, yes. But we're not talking about everybody now, but about you. The fact is that *you* dislike you. Instead of saying to yourself, 'Too bad; so he rejects me; I can still live happily without his acceptance,' you tell yourself, 'How terrible that he rejects me! How low I am because of his rejection.' And those sentences constitute your essential self-hatred, your low estimation of you."

267

"But how does that make me think that I *can't* talk to males?"

"That's the second point. After first thinking, quite irrationally, that you are no good if you do speak up with men and get rejected, you naturally withdraw from such speaking up, and practice silence or evasion. Time after time, when you think of speaking up, and when you even want to do so very much—as you did with the boy at the lecture—you make yourself so uncomfortable by your fear of rejection that you run away from the situation and force yourself to shut your mouth. In fact, whenever you force yourself to keep still, at these times, you immediately feel relieved, comfortable."

"That's right. I do feel very comfortable as soon as I know that I can't say anything."

"*Can't*, hell! As soon as you *don't* say anything. And that, of course, your feeling comfortable temporarily when you don't say anything, gives you a great incentive for convincing yourself 'I can't, I can't!' For the more you are convinced that you *can't* speak up, the quicker you will give up trying, and the more comfortable you will (temporarily!) tend to be."

"Hmm. I see. I reduce my conflict by keeping quiet; and because I know I am reducing my conflict, I have an incentive to quiet myself again and again. So I tell myself that I can't talk."

"Right. Moreover, what may be called 'false verification' soon tends to creep in. You keep telling yourself that you can't talk; consequently you never do talk; consequently you build up a long history of never talking; and finally, observing this history, but not observ-

ing the fear that caused it, you falsely conclude: 'Well,
because I never *have* talked, I obviously can't.' This is
like saying, 'Well, because I never have eaten carrots,
once I became convinced that they would harm my
complexion, I can't eat them.' Can't, crap! Of course
you can eat the carrots, if you tackled your idiotic fear
of eating them; and of course you can talk to males, if
you tackle your idiotic fear of talking to them."

"I never saw it that way before. Though I haven't
seen that it was connected with self-hatred. But I
mean about my fearing to do the talking, and then
getting a history of not doing it, and then using the
history as a false proof of my not being able to do it."

"Oh, yes. That's very common among human beings.
They don't do a thing, for one reason or another—
usually a fear of some sort. Then they see that they've
never done it. Then they falsely conclude that they
can't. But, of course, they can. They just haven't ever
tried. And, by convincing themselves that they can't,
as we said before, they avoid the pain of trying, the
conflict over trying. So they have a kind of double
incentive to believe that they can't."

"And by believing that I can't, I've made myself this
miserably lonely, haven't I?"

"Yes, that's the real irony. You avoid the conflict and
pain of the moment, by not speaking to boys, and by
convincing yourself that you can't. But then you get
the much greater pain of continually being alone at
home and desperately wanting the telephone to ring,
when of course it won't. So you produce, in the end, a
much greater pain than the one you avoid in the beginning."

"That's what I really haven't seen, I guess: that I can't afford to avoid the pain at the beginning, since then I'll bring on this awful loneliness at the end."

"Exactly! You get a very false gain when you avoid the initial pain of making contact with the boys. And you get a very real pain when you sit home alone, night after night, not doing what you'd most like to do —which is to be with boys."

"I never saw that before."

"Are you seeing it very clearly right now? Do you see that there's simply no percentage in avoiding the boys, no matter how frightening it at first might be to talk to them, when you finally only avoid life itself and bring on the loneliness you desperately do not want?"

"Yes, I think I'm beginning to see it clearly."

"Fine! Now let's see how you can work on it, work on what you're seeing: by forcing yourself, if necessary, to talk to the boys whom you now say you *can't* possibly talk to."

Claudia, hesitatingly and slowly, did start to work on her new observations and insights, and within the next several months began to force herself to speak to some of the males who were eager to approach her. At first, she had quite a hard time of it; but, as I predicted, it soon became easier and easier, and in time even enjoyable. And her sitting home alone became a thing of the past, as she made more and more dates.

Fear of rejection, and the false concept of the impossibility of making involving moves toward males to which it so often leads, can similarly be tackled by anyone. The basic philosophy of the woman who fears social disapproval is that she will be downed as a person, proved to be a worthless individual, if she actually makes a social move and is rejected. This philosophy is obviously definitional: since her rejection by *others* hardly means that she *has* to reject *herself*. Nor does her refusal by A, B, and C, if it actually occurs, mean that she must inevitably be refused by X, Y, Z, and everyone else in the wide world.

This does not mean that being rejected is a good thing, nor that you should not feel sorry or sad when you lose out with a male whom you very much would like to win out with. Rejection is a *bad* thing, normally; and it is most appropriate for you to feel sorry about it. But since you still *are* you, no matter how many times you are spurned by others, and since you still can most probably find *someone* to your liking who will ultimately accept you, rejection is not catastrophic—unless you, definitionally, *make* it so. And if you refuse, as you can refuse, to make it so, you will eliminate one of the most serious emotional blocks to dating and marrying that now exists among literally millions of people.

Over-attachment to your own family

Having close ties to your parents, siblings, or other family members can be a rewarding and beautiful thing; but it can also be an interference with marital urges. For one thing, it can be a dependency rather than a mature love relationship. Your parents literally raised you from the time you were a pup, and they frequently would like you to remain a charming, dependent puppy (so that they themselves will not have to face and work through more grown-up relations with each other and other members of the outside world). They consequently may easily forgive you all

271

your nastinesses, encourage you to be financially dependent on them, take special care of you when you are sick or low in spirits, and otherwise baby you when you are long past the chronological time of childhood.

Males, naturally, are *not* very likely to do the same. They expect you to be reasonably able to take care of yourself—and often, in fact, to help care for them as well. They want you to be something of a responsible, self-initiating woman, and not to be eternally demanding of their time and attention. Consequently, they may be harsh and rejecting where your parents or siblings are mollycoddling and lenient; and you may well be tempted, after a boyfriend has asked in no uncertain terms that you toe the line of independency, to run back to Mama and Papa. This is dangerous for several reasons:

1. There is no real safety in being attached to your family members. Your mother and father are inevitably twenty or thirty years older than you are, and will not be around forever. Your brothers and sisters, although closer to you in age, may easily marry themselves, move to distant places, or otherwise desert you. Although you may therefore feel temporarily secure in your family's support, in the long run you may well defeat yourself by relying on it.

2. Even when your family members stay around forever and keep helping you, you cannot avoid being underlyingly anxious. For to be dependent means to be incapable of helping oneself, of relying on one's own abilities; and anxiety, lack of self-confidence, and often acute self-hatred tend to follow from your knowledge that you have not learned to help yourself.

3. No matter how satisfying the love that you receive from your family members may be, it is rarely an adequate substitute for forming a good heterosexual loving relationship. Love that you build between yourself and a man has many important aspects—including, of course, the sexual aspects—that are necessarily going to be missing from interfamily relations. Just because your boyfriend or husband is, at the start, essentially a stranger to you, and because you have to *work* at accepting him, adjusting to him, and remaining happy with him, the intimacy that exists between you will be considerably different from that between you and your parents or you and other family members. Achieving a marital love is the kind of experience that radically differs from attaining most other kinds of love relations; and it is generally a decidedly worthwhile kind of experience—even when it is not entirely successful.

Conjugal love and family love, moreover, are not mutually exclusive. There is no reason why you cannot maintain a good kind of intimacy with your parents and other close relatives and have a satisfactory relationship with your lover or husband *too.* If you are so closely involved with the former that there is just no room for the latter, that is usually a clear-cut loss, and you are depriving yourself of one of life's great potential satisfactions. Similarly, if you have a highly involved, egoism-à-deux involvement with your mate that excludes all kinds of other love relations (including, perhaps, those with your own children) that, also, may become a loss, since there is room in life for *several* different kinds of attachments, and one kind need not completely shut out all others.

For several reasons such as these, your remaining

over-attached to your parents or siblings is a dangerous, albeit somewhat advantageous, state. And this state should be opposed by your continually asking yourself:

Do I really need to be dependent on my family; or can I not enjoy myself better by learning to rely more on my own judgment, my own initiative? *Is* it really awful that I must adjust to a member of the other sex, when my parents will give in to me so easily and make such adjustment unnecessary? *Can* I live fully and happily by withdrawing from heterosexual involvements and remaining only "safely" involved with members of my own family? *Will* I truly be satisfied with a perpetually continued nonsexual love affair with my father or mother, when I can maintain that kind of relationship and work at making a satisfying heterosexual adjustment too?

If you keep questioning and challenging the basic philosophic premises that lie behind your overinvolvement with your family members and your "sour grapes" mechanism of staying away from erotic and conjugal intimacy with members of the other sex, the chances are that you will soon be able to take the risks of courting and marrying a suitable male, and that you will thereby add considerably to your enjoyment of living and loving.

Fear of responsibility

Many men notoriously refrain from marrying because of the responsibilities that they would have to assume, or at least think they would have to assume, if they did head for the altar. By the same token, and to a much greater degree than is usually imagined, many women also shy away from marriage because they do not think that they would be up to its responsibilities and difficulties.

Some women, for example, do not think that they would be able to run a household properly. Some feel that they would make exceptionally poor mothers. Some feel that being a steady companion, or bedmate, or help to their husband's career would place too much onus on them; and that therefore they would be much better off living the relatively carefree and irresponsible life of a bachelor girl.

Some of these women who object to marrying because of its responsibilities are of course correct: for marriage *is* a kind of serious affair, and wives *do* have to accept various hardships and restrictions on their freedom, just as husbands do. But, by the same token, they presumably derive from marriage advantages that are not easily derivable in any other kind of heterosexual relation.

If you, then, really feel that it is going to be too hard for you to buckle down to the responsibilities of wedlock, and that you can live just as happily if not more so in a state of singleness, by all means think seriously of *not* marrying. But you cannot have your cake without baking it; and if you want the benefits of marriage —which most women, for one reason or another, seem to want—then you must gracefully accept its predictable discomforts in order to gain these benefits. If you find yourself unduly emphasizing marital inconveniences, then it may well be that you are either fearful that you will fail in courtship and marriage, and hence be "hurt"; or that you are childishly rebelling against

275

some of the necessary frustrations of any state of to-getherness.

Here again, it is not particularly helpful if you rail against the marital state, nor against those lousy males who make it so terrible. Neither marriage nor men is the real problem: *you* are. For it is you who keep telling yourself sentences like: "If I take a chance on marrying Jim, and it turns out that he expects too much of me, and I just can't live up to his expectations of being a responsible wife, what a nincompoop I'd show myself to be, and how loathsome I would find myself!" And: "I just can't *stand* the difficulties of adjusting to a man and of raising children. Why should marriage *have to be* so hard?"

If you would look, even for an objective moment, at these internalized sentences that you keep feeding yourself in regard to marrying, you might quickly find how silly and self-defeating they are. For if by any chance you couldn't measure up to Jim's expectations of a responsible wife—and the probability is at least ten to one that you could if you stopped believing that it would be so awful if you didn't—you could surely, at worst, divorce Jim and benefit considerably by the honest try that you had made. Or if you actually did find marriage too hard—which, again, you probably wouldn't if you stopped complaining about its difficulty and settled down to making it easier on yourself —you could arrange to have a sex-love affair without marriage, or could live by yourself with a bunch of cats, or could find various other solutions to your problems.

The main point is that yes, marriage is a real responsibility; but that no, responsibility is hardly a horror or an impending catastrophe. At worst, it is a pain in the neck. At best, it is a vital absorbing interest, that gives you something significant to which to commit yourself.

Responsibility, it is true, involves the possibility of failure: since, try as you may, you may not be able to meet your responsibilities perfectly, and may be blamed by others who think that you should be perfect. All right: so you may fail. So did Leonardo, when he tried to invent the airplane. So did Edison, when he got around to making movies a short while after a couple of others had beaten him to it. In point of fact, not only *may* you fail; you damned well, in the long run, *will*. We—at least we who try—all fail. So we fail! But at least, if we keep trying, if we keep making an effort to be responsible, we also are bound to have some successes. And a fair *proportion* of successes is all we can hope for in this life.

So stop your crap! If you fail to be a responsible wife to Jim or a fine mother to Joe's children, that's too bad. But if you fail to *try* to be a responsible wife or mother, that's much worse: for that's not living, not being *you*. In marrying as in most things in life: 'tis better to have tried to be responsible and lost, than never to have tried at all.

Homosexual tendencies

If we are to believe the Freudians, almost all men and women who are blocked in marrying are, whether they are aware of the fact or not, homosexually inclined; and it is their latent homosexuality which panics them when they are faced with marital situations and

277

which induces them to find various rationalizations for not marrying.

True? To a slight degree, yes. A few persons who believe that they are quite heterosexually inclined are actually homoerotically-oriented; and a few of these are even led to their homosexuality by a classic Oedipus or Electra complex: that is, the males are so horrified at their unconsciously lusting after their mothers, and the females by their unwittingly wanting to copulate with their fathers, that having sex relations with any member of the other sex reminds them of their unconscious incest desires, and makes they shy away from heterosexuality.

This kind of latent homosexuality, however, is quite a rarity today. Millions of men and women are more or less homosexual—but most of them tend to be decidedly consciously so. These overt homosexuals either have conscious blocks against marrying; or else, in a surprisingly large number of instances, they marry for non-sexual reasons—e.g., to have children, or to lead a more stable and safer existence than they would be leading in the "gay" world. To believe that the average male who does not want to marry is really a latent homosexual is to be unusually gullible: since it is much more likely that this unmarrying male is highly heterosexual than homosexual, and that he has merely figured out, and with some good reason, that he will have a more uninhibited heterosexual life when he is unmated than when he is legally wed.

The same thing, of course, may go for you. If you are somewhat free of conventional sex shackles, you will soon find that, as a single woman, you are most in demand as a bedmate, and that you can practically write your own ticket when you want to sleep with Tom or Dick or Harry. Marrying one of these males, however, generally coerces you into giving up the others; and this you may not particularly care to do. Your real block against marrying, if you have one, therefore, may not be your "latent homosexuality," but your decidedly overt heterosexuality; and in order to overcome your block, you will have to convince yourself that a ring on your finger is worth half a dozen rings on your doorbell by different men each week.

Suppose, however, you *do* happen to be homosexually inclined, and you find yourself looking at and thinking about other women instead of men; and suppose that, nonetheless, you want to marry and raise a family. What then?

What you should first of all do, in that case, is to determine *why* you are so strongly attracted to women and not to men. The fact that you may like females, and even enjoy them sexually, is not terribly unusual or important: since human beings, as I point out in *The Art and Science of Love* (New York: Lyle Stuart, 1960) and *The American Sexual Tragedy* (New York: Lyle Stuart, 1962), are born to be plurisexual animals, who can easily get sexually excited by men, women, children, animals, inanimate objects, and whatnot. But the fact that you *don't* enjoy sex with men—that *is* significant, and bears detailed further investigation.

Some of the main reasons for lesbian fixations include (*a*) early puritanical upbringing, leading to enormous fear of heterosexuality and guilt in connection with it; (*b*) early sexual traumas, such as seduction or attack by an older man during one's childhood; (*c*) hostility to the father or brother, and consequently

279

to many other males; (*d*) revolt against the antifeminine discriminations which are still so prevalent in our society; (*e*) overwhelming feelings of inadequacy, with the consequent belief that one will never be able to succeed sexually with a male; (*f*) self-blame about one's sexual frigidity, with a consequent withdrawal from the field of heterosexuality; (*g*) hostility against males because they are such poor lovers who mistakenly believe that penile-vaginal intercourse is the one way to satisfy a female; (*h*) fear of having children or of being able to be a competent, responsible wife.

All these main causes of female homosexuality can be subsumed under the usual two main neurosis-creating sets of irrational beliefs: (*a*) I cannot do well in or be approved mightily for my sex-love relations with males; therefore I am a worthless slob and would better withdraw from the field of heterosexuality; and (*b*) I cannot stand the frustrations and difficulties that men place in my way; therefore to hell with the bastards!

Confirmed lesbianism, in other words, is almost always a direct or indirect result of deepseated feelings of anxiety and/or hostility. It is by no means (as many "authorities" erroneously seem to believe that it is) a specifically inherited trait; and it does not always arise from early childhood training. It is almost always a neurotic or psychotic symptom, and it can be tackled and overcome just as many other symptoms of emotional disturbance can be ameliorated or cured.

Can you fight your own lesbian tendencies yourself? You certainly can. If you will discover what nonsense you are telling yourself to make yourself afraid of or hostile to males, and if you will then contradict and challenge this nonsense, you will be well on the way to undercutting any homosexual tendencies that you may have.

At the same time, however, you must of course *practice* what you preach: that is to say, you must keep trying heterosexual relations with males, and give yourself an honest-to-goodness chance to enjoy them.

Is intercourse with a man painful and disgusting? Try it enough times, with the kind of man you really like, and see if it remains so. Do males make love poorly, and usually leave you unsatisfied and frustrated? Get a willing partner, and instruct him carefully exactly what to do in order to satisfy you. Or seek for an experienced lover who is only too willing to try those sex practices which especially send you. Continual practice at *de*indoctrinating yourself from the antimasculine or antisexual irrationalities that you have been consciously or unconsciously indoctrinating yourself with for years, and at forcing yourself to do and keep doing the sexual acts which you have previously avoided with males—this kind of practice will overcome your lesbian tendencies, if you have any, in almost all instances.

And if this kind of practice doesn't work? Then you are obviously not doing it correctly, and need professional help. Go see an experienced psychotherapist—one who is *not* a classical Freudian, but who will actively-directively help you in a reasonable amount of time—and work with him against your lesbian leanings. Not that remaining homosexual is a horrible or wicked thing. But it is, in our society, damned inconvenient, and usually remarkably unrewarding. And it does, in almost all instances, block the achieving of a successful marital relationship.

281

Attachments to ineligible males

In the course of my seeing literally hundreds of females during the last twenty years who say that they definitely want to marry but who have never got very close to doing so, I have found that one of the most common and serious blocks to marrying is the selection by these females of obviously ineligible males, followed by their compulsively remaining attached to these ineligibles.

Gertrude R. was an excellent case in point in this respect. She was thirty-five when she first came to see me; was one of the few truly beautiful (as distinguished from pretty or attractive) women I have ever met; and was well-educated and highly cultured. Yet she had only been proposed to by a few males who patently were not for her, and had never been asked to marry those men to whom she was considerably attracted.

Gertrude's problem was that she insisted on becoming attached to highly dedicated men who were much more interested in their work than they were in her or in marriage. She found their dedication to some project or cause most appealing; and she also thought it a challenge to try to win a man who was so devoted to something outside himself.

At first, Gertrude usually succeeded: since the men she chose would become attracted to her, would willingly enter into a passionate affair, and would even neglect their work—for awhile. But sooner or later they would be back at their central activity in life; and their interest in her, while not waning, would be considerably reduced. This she could not stand, and would make herself very unhappy about. Instead, however, of leaving such a man, and going on to a more suitable lover, Gertrude would prolong the affair for months and months, trying to win back his attention and devotion; and the more she tried, the more her lovers would find her a real bother, and would want to break off the relationship. Eventually, they did; whereupon, she would look for a similar kind of man again, and get herself into the same kind of bind.

Gertrude had two kinds of problems with men: (*a*) picking the wrong kind of man for her own marital requirements; and (*b*) staying with him much too long in a nonmarital situation. The first of these characteristics might not have been so fatal if it had not been combined with the second trait; but both together were poisonous. Similarly with many other women: they pick the wrong men in the first place, and then endlessly stay with them in the second place. To make one of these errors is human; to make both of them is inhumanity to oneself.

There are many wrong kinds of choices that you can make in your love partnerships. Men, for example, who are many years older than you are will tend to be settled in their ways, already tied to previous wives and children, and often afraid to take on a wife who is much younger than they. Men who are several years younger than you will commonly be reluctant to marry you, even though they may find you a delightful companion and bed partner.

Men who are married already will (as we noted in a previous chapter) frequently promise you the earth and the sky—and yet somehow will not be able to break away from their wives. Men who are exceptionally handsome will sometimes be so spoiled by women, and so adept at finding easy sex-love consorts, that they will be loath to marry and thereby cut off their best chances. Men who are unusually wealthy will also have easy access to other girls—and will sometimes be afraid that a woman is marrying them primarily for their money. Men who are outstandingly talented may very well (like Gertrude's lovers) be so devoted to their talents that they have little time and energies for serious involvements.

This does not mean, now, that *none* of these kinds of males would make good husbands. A man who is much older than you may, just because he appreciates your youth and beauty, be a more considerate and more loving mate than someone who is a few years your senior. A man who is five or more years younger than you may, because of some quirk on his part, find you more attractive than he finds girls of his own age; and he may be a devoted and faithful husband forever.

In any given case, therefore, you should by all means at least consider the possibility of marrying someone who, at first blush, looks like he would not make the best possible mate for you. Although mixed marriages, especially those between a devoutly believing member of one religion and an equally devoutly believing member of a different religion, are *generally* inadvisable, since they lead to additional difficulties which may not be present in unmixed marriages, they are not *always* poorly made, and occasionally work out very well. By the same token, you may select a much older, a much younger, a much married, or a much work-preoccupied man and just happen to pick the right one for you, in spite of the obvious dangers of your choice.

Nonetheless: a man who has serious objections to

marrying you, for any reasons whatever, usually is not going to change his mind within a reasonably short length of time; and even if he does, there is an excellent chance that he will not make a good husband. When, therefore, you find that your current lover is non-maritally inclined and that he probably will stay in that class for a long period to come, your best bet is to get the deuce away from him—and quickly! The longer you stay, the more you will tend to become attached, and the more deep-seated will become your habit patterns of being with him. No matter what the *immediate* wrench of leaving him may be, you will almost always be happier in the long run by leaving him to his non-marital state and becoming involved with a more marriageable prospect.

Blocks to getting away from an ineligible male in a decently short period of time usually include: (*a*) convincing yourself that you simply *can't* live without him; (*b*) deluding yourself that he *will* marry you if you simply hang on to him long enough; (*c*) fearing that you just won't be able to get any other worthwhile man if you let this one go out of your life; (*d*) telling yourself that even though you could get another man, it would just be too much of a hassle getting back into the rat race and going to the trouble of meeting and winning him; and (*e*) getting yourself to believe that, with all his faults, there just isn't nor ever will be anyone like the present man, and that therefore any possible substitute for him would be blah and unsatisfactory.

Virtually all these excuses—and many more like them which you may cook up to rationalize your staying with an ineligible male—are variations on the same major theme: namely, that you are really an awful hunk of garbage and that *therefore* you can't live without this man, can't get a better one, and might just as well not go to any trouble to try to get the kind of man who would, as soon as he knew you, find out what garbage you were and refuse, just as this present one is doing, to marry you.

If you believe this kind of rot, then your belief in it —and concomitant lack of belief in yourself—will actualize *what* you believe: will make you act in such a dispirited, self-defeating manner that men actually will see that you hate yourself, and will consequently lower your value to themselves. If you tackle and challenge this rot, then you will be able to see that it is not you who are incapable of winning a worthy companion, but that it is the false and self-depreciated "you" who must inevitably fail yourself.

More concretely: you must convince yourself that you are, just because you are alive and breathing, a potentially valuable person to yourself; and that no possible negative evaluation by others can negate your worth to you. Then, because you are self-worthy, and because you deserve to get a man who will accept and love you (even though many or most of the men you meet may not), you must continue to seek and seek for one who is psychophysically attractive to you, and who likewise finds you lovable.

When you find such a man, you should enter into as full a relationship with him as you can both arrange, to see whether marriage would be practicable for both of you. If, for any reason of yours or his, your chosen partner appears to be unmarriageable, then you should normally leave him, and soon. Then, without self-recrimination or personal devaluation in regard to this breakup, on to the next! and the next! and the next!

Does this concept of manhunting appear to be too crass or scheming? Perhaps, in an ultra-romantic perspective, it is. But good, enduring, career-enhancing jobs are rarely obtained by romantic longings. Nor are good, enduring, life-enhancing marriages.

Devotion to non-marital interests

A great many girls are blocked from marrying, who say that they would be delighted to have a man and a family, because they are so devoted to certain non-marital interests that they let nearly all their marital opportunities pass by. Some are devoted to careers, such as medicine or teaching. Some spend large amounts of time pursuing some sport, such as tennis or swimming. Others are devoted bridge players, or church leaders, or amateur thespians.

Not only do some of these interest-absorbed females take time away from their social-sexual involvements to give to their careers or hobbies, but in many instances they virtually remove themselves from the society of eligible males in pursuing these interests. Thus, a woman who is a pediatrician will spend practically all her time with mothers and their young children. And a woman who is devoted to training horses or raising cats is not likely to find a suitable mate among the four-legged creatures with whom she fondly relates!

Feminine careers and vital absorptions, moreover, sometimes repulse men. Even among the relatively enlightened of today's males, nineteenth century notions of male-female division of labor are sometimes prevalent. The man, consequently, takes a dim view of

287

his wife's not being home to prepare his meals and serve his dinner when he comes home from the office; and the fact that she may be saving patients' lives or winning a bridge championship is small comfort to him when he thinks in these old-fashioned ways.

What, then, is the vitally absorbed contemporary woman to do—give up all thought of having a career or an intense interest? Or stick to jobs and hobbies—such as joining the Woman's Army Corps or playing in chess tournaments—where she is likely to encounter a good many eligible males?

The first of these choices would be distinctly unhealthy, because (as we have previously noted) a woman's being devoted to a career or an avocational interest is usually a sign of emotional health. Such devotion provides her with the very preoccupation that saves her from being over-absorbed with finding and winning a male, and from being frantically concerned with her love life.

Besides, women who do expend much of their time and energy in pursuing some long-range project or goal may well be on the deprived side when it comes to making good marriages; but there is no evidence whatever that they lead less happy lives than do millions of women who do marry well, but who never manage to find a vital absorption outside of their homes and families.

Indeed, since most married women's lives are largely occupied with their children as well as their husbands, and since these children usually grow up and become more or less removed (and often alienated) from their mothers, while at the same time most female careerists continue to work actively at their chosen fields until they are well into their sixties or seventies, a case could easily be made for the hypothesis that marriage-centered women are usually not as happy as career-centered women, and that if a female could have only one of these two central choices to make during her lifetime, she would be wiser to pick an intensely involving career rather than marriage.

Fortunately, however, this kind of either-or choice is not necessarily mandatory for all women. It is quite possible, if a female plans her life intelligently, for her to have the cake of marriage and still eat the other cake of career involvement.

She can manage this in either of two fairly common ways: first, by mapping out a major career or avocational interest for herself and, while she is going about preparing for or working at this field, also managing to find and win a suitable mate who will not too seriously object to and interfere with her life's work; second, by turning her efforts mainly toward marrying a male and raising a family, but then, especially when her children are somewhat grown, devoting herself to some significant field of endeavor and becoming an absorbed worker in this field.

Although the first of these choices is perhaps preferable—since it orients a woman toward her life interest during her youth and better guarantees that she will receive the proper training to follow it adequately—the second choice also has various advantages, and is not to be minimized as a possible solution to this important problem of a woman's finding herself both within and without a marriage and family framework.

The problem that often arises in connection with a woman's marrying and retaining outside interests is that of one-sidedness or of emotional blocking. Thus, she may become so genuinely absorbed, during her late teens and early twenties, with some arduous career or avocation that she may carelessly assume that her dating and marrying will take care of themselves.

Driven to study hard, or to work long hours in some field in which she is trying to make headway, such a woman may unwittingly forego dates, social affairs, dances, and other usual ways of getting to know and to become intimate with eligible males; and before she knows it, she finds that she is in her late twenties or early thirties, and that most of the males whom she would have found suitable had she made more contact with them are now husbands and fathers, while most of those who remain for her to contact are far from being the best marital bets.

On the other side of the fence, a career-bound woman may at first try hard enough, even when she is in the midst of pursuing her chosen vocational goals, to meet suitable males, and may do almost as well with them as her less career-minded sisters. But just as soon as a few affairs go sour—which, statistically speaking, is par for the course of love, rather than being unusual—she may become so hurt and bitter that she *then* begins to use her vocational interests as an excuse for keeping herself from much further courting activity.

If, especially, this would-be career girl is not quite as pretty as some of the other girls are, or if she has relatively low sex drives, she may find that she is genuinely handicapped in finding and keeping the kind of male she would like to mate with. Then, instead of doing everything possible to make up for her handicaps (such as, of course, making sure that she meets *more* men and makes *greater* efforts to charm them than do her more fortunately endowed girlfriends), she may take the "easier" way out, throw herself all the more into her careerist activities, and delude herself that this is the only thing that she really wants.

If you happen to be unusually devoted to a career or to some other outside interest, and find that this devotion is interfering with your marital goals, what can you do? The first thing you can do is to review your basic interests, particularly in terms of timing. Is it, for example, absolutely necessary that you become the greatest physician or physicist who ever lived *right now*? Must you devote practically all of your *present* energies to getting ahead in whatever main field of endeavor you have chosen? Could you not, instead, work at a somewhat slower, though still steady, pace, and manage to get some more social-sexual activity into your life, too? And could you not plan, *after* you had managed to marry and perhaps even to have a child or two, to go full steam ahead in your chosen profession or interest?

Various other aspects of your vital absorption may also be scheduled to fit in better with your love and marital goals. If, for example, you are determined to be a physician, one branch of medicine (such as, say, internal medicine) may be a better field in which you might make social-sexual contacts than another field (say, pediatrics). Or taking a job in a large hospital, where there are many eligible male residents, might be better than taking one in a small hospital or better than practicing in a small community.

If this kind of practical timing and scheduling does not help, because you have more severe emotional blocks concerned with your profession or vital interest, then you will have to uncover and uproot the irrational philosophies of life that lie behind these blocks. Florence B. found that she was avoiding serious involvements with males because she was too occupied with studying to be a clinical psychologist and she felt sure that her work at school suffered whenever she carried on an active dating and courting pattern. Therefore, she preferred to put off almost all social activities until she had obtained her Ph.D. and was occupationally secure in her chosen field.

When Florence's motives for being a psychologist were psychotherapeutically investigated, however, she discovered that a good part of her interest stemmed from the fact that she considered herself an inadequate person who had no good reason for living unless she devoted herself to others. Consequently, she had chosen clinical psychology as a profession, even though she personally preferred experimental work, so that she could have a picture of herself as a helping individual who made herself useful to others, and hence had a legitimate reason for living.

Florence also discovered, as we checked into her love-avoiding behavior, that she placed so little value on herself as a person in her own right that she was sure that no good man would accept her unless she did something outstanding—unless he could proudly introduce her to others as *Doctor* So-and-So, who was absorbed every day with helping others to solve their personality problems. Both as an individual and as a potential wife, then, she believed that it was necessary for her to earn her right to existence and happiness by devoting her life to the service of others. Otherwise, she was sure that she had no good reason for living and loving.

"I'm beginning to see it clearly now," she said to me during her ninth psychotherapy session. "I really think that *in myself* I have no purpose, and that I must make such a purpose by taking care of others and winning their undying appreciation. So why, with this set of beliefs, should I try to win a husband or to have children who would be good for *me* and make *me* happy? I only deserve to be happy when I am good to *others*. No wonder I have never tried to get what *I* want in life or to build the kind of relationship with a man that I would want for myself!"

"Yes, you are beginning to see this quite clearly," I agreed. "You've been doing this sort of thing all your life; but now you *see* what you have been doing; and now you can *stop* doing it. How, precisely, are you going to get around to stopping it?"

"Well, I'll tell you one thing I'm going to do, just as soon as the school term starts again. And that is to change my course immediately, get out of clinical psych—which may be all right for others but which is just not the thing for me—and get into experimental. Fortunately, I haven't gone so far yet that I will have lost very much by starting in clinical. But even if I had, I'd definitely change. After all, I'll probably be working in this field for another thirty or forty years yet. And I'm determined, now, to work at something that *I* definitely want to do during that long period of time.

"My parents, I'm sure, won't like it at all, my changing. They'd much rather see me as a practicing clinician than working with smelly rats. But that's *their* problem, and I don't intend to be unduly influenced by it.

They'll just have to accept me as I am, rats and all!"

"And what will you do about men?"

"There, too, I'm determined to stop my nonsense and at least give myself a decent *chance* to get what I want. Maybe I never will get it, since my standards will probably remain pretty high, and I don't intend to marry *any* male who comes along and wants me. But I do intend to keep looking and looking—and for someone *I* want and who will accept me pretty much as I am.

"If any of my boyfriends, like my parents, want me to be a practicing psychologist, rather than an experimentalist, in order that *they* may boast to their friends what kind of a wife they have, so much the worse for them. There must be someone who will want me the way I am, even without my being of great and noble service to others, and that's the someone I'm going to look for. And, you know, this time, somehow, there's just something new in me that tells me that one of these days I'll find him."

"I think you're right. There *is* something new in you this time: your new and better estimation of yourself. Just because you now *are* beginning to see yourself as a worthy individual in your own right, whether or not you set the world afire by being the greatest and most loved clinician it has ever known, just because of this new outlook you're not only becoming determined to get what you want out of life, but you're beginning to feel that you *can* get it. And I'm sure, if you continue this more confident, less other-directed attitude, that you can."

"I'm sure, too. I don't know exactly when the right man will come along, or how I will get him to appreciate me. But one of these days I am sure it will happen

—or, rather, I will *make* it happen. Just as I'm sure I'll be a good experimental psychologist. If it doesn't happen that way, then it won't, and I'll have to go along on my own. But I really think it will!"

This time Florence was a good prognosticator. Even though she threw herself, with more vigor than ever, into her newly chosen field of experimental psychology, she found more time and energy than ever to keep her eyes peeled for a suitable mate. Within a year, she was engaged to a fellow graduate student, and there is every reason to believe that her relationship with him will work out well. For she now has the main ingredient of a potentially happy life: her own high estimation of herself, independently of whether she devotes herself to the service of others or wins social approval by so doing.

Not all emotional blocks to marriage that are connected with vocational preoccupations are the same as were Florence's. But many are. Behind the drive to get ahead in one's career, even at the cost of sacrificing love and marriage, frequently lurks some unrealistically low estimation of oneself, with the concomitant conviction that one is not worthy of a good man unless and until one "proves" oneself vocationally and thereby wins his and also the world's esteem. Such a self-depreciating philosophy of life has to be incisively uncovered and vigorously uprooted before a girl can untangle the conflictual skeins of her professional and her marital goals.

If you are mixed up in this regard, then, look into your own heart for your personal self-negating views. Do you think that you *must* succeed at work in order to be a worthwhile person? Do you feel that you simply *can't* get what you amatively and maritally want until you have proven yourself, career-wise, to your potential mate and to the rest of the universe? If so, you'd better start forcefully asking yourself *why*. *Why* must you be a great careerist to be a valuable human being or an estimable love partner? Who said so? Why are you not deserving of the kind of sex-love relationship you want merely because you are you? Who said you aren't? And who the hell is he who said it?

Overcoming basic fears and hostilities

It is difficult to say which of the two basic neuroticizing emotions, acute anxiety or strong hostility, most interferes with loving and marrying; but probably it is pointless to try to decide which is the worse of these villainous traits, since they are more commonly than not integrally intertwined. Their interrelationship can perhaps best be exemplified by the case of Marion D., who had more than her fair share of both destructive feelings.

Marion's greatest fear was that she was both stupid and incompetent, that the people with whom she associated were soon going to find this out, and that then they would never want to have anything to do with her. Actually, she was quite bright (though hardly brilliant) and she managed her business and personal affairs unusually well, in spite of the fact that she had been forced (by her father's poverty) to quit school in the tenth grade and had never (largely because of her dire needs to keep socializing) been able to gain any great amount of self-education.

Like most of us, however, Marion made numerous

mistakes and blunders in her everyday life, considered each one as absolute proof of her own idiocy, and blamed herself enormously for being imperfect. Moreover, when any of her attempts to maintain deep friendships with others failed, she never even considered the fact that the people with whom she chose to make these friendships might possibly be amiss, but at first always took all the responsibility for the breakup of the relationship on her own shoulders, and excoriated herself severely for what had happened. Then, when she could no longer stand the beatings which she thereby gave herself, she reviewed the events of the breakup all over again, and usually came to just the opposite conclusion: namely, that the people with whom she had been involved had been one hundred per cent wrong—and that she herself was no damned good for continually becoming attached to such obviously wrong people.

To make matters still worse, Marion became so sensitized, after awhile, to the fact that her relations with others might well end disastrously, that she began to look *in general* for the nasty traits of almost everyone with whom she came in contact, in order to give herself an excuse for any rejection that occurred. Consequently, she would find that this person was too untidy, that one was stupid, the next one was vicious, etc. And not only would she come to believe strongly in her criticisms of others—which, of course, were sometimes justified and sometimes highly exaggerated—but she would voice these criticisms to her new boyfriends and lovers, within a few minutes of meeting them.

She did this so often, moreover, that soon these boyfriends began to say to themselves: "My God! there she goes again. Isn't there *anyone* she likes? When will I be *next* on her hate list?" And, of course, they ceased to think seriously of her as a marital partner, and often stopped seeing her entirely.

Since Marion was basically more frightened than angry, and since she usually went out of her way to be exceptionally nice to each new boyfriend with whom she went for awhile, she couldn't understand why she lost so many of them so quickly. She had a picture of herself as a weak, exploited person; and didn't recognize her defensive hostility even when it was occasionally brought to her attention.

"Me hostile?" she would incredulously ask. "Why, that's ridiculous. I haven't a hostile bone in my body. In fact, I'm much *too* nice—as all my friends will tell you." And she *was* too nice, but was also too hostile as well—as all of her friends would also tell you, but would never dare to tell her.

I had quite a time convincing Marion that she was not altogether sweetness and light; but finally, by showing her how many nasty cracks she had made to me about others, and how many hostile remarks she had also parenthetically passed about me when I contradicted her in any way, I got her to see that perhaps she did have a hostile side, and that if she ever wanted to meet the right man and get him to care for her permanently, she'd better do something about changing her hostile attitudes.

"But how can I stop being hostile if I usually don't even see that I am?" she asked me one day.

"By stopping your self-blaming, so that you can then permit yourself to see how hostile you are."

"You mean that I won't face my anger against others,

298

because if I did I'd then have to see myself as the sort of a person I wouldn't like to be, and that I would blame myself terribly for being this sort of a person?"

"That's exactly what I mean. And I also mean that your self-moralizing tendencies cause you to be defensive in the first place, and to become highly critical of others when you think that you are merely being nice."

"How so?"

"Well, as we've said many times before, you think that you've simply *got* to be approved by almost everyone you meet, especially the men you go out with. And you'll do anything whatever to get this approval—such as helping your first husband in those crooked deals he pulled, and going along with your last boy-friend even though you knew that he was living off you and making no effort to get a job."

"Yes, you're right. And I hated myself for remaining in both those relationships."

"Yes, that's your second-level self-hatred. After you have nauseatingly kowtowed to some man in order to win or to keep his love, you beat yourself savagely for making such a fool of yourself. But there's a first-level self-hatred that even comes before that."

"You mean, that I hate myself right at the start, even before I start to give up my soul to these men to keep their love, or I should say their so-called love, for me?"

"Right. You define yourself, even before you meet a new mate, as a worthless creature who can only achieve some value by being adored by some man. And you look frantically for such a man to adore you. Then, when he seems to do so for awhile, you forget entirely that he may well be the worst possible man for you—as both your husband and your last friend certainly were—and you feel temporarily worthy and are sure that this is it, that now you're fixed up for all time. What you really mean is that a dunce and an incompetent like you has finally been tied up and glued together by some great person, and that as long as he is around to keep adding a little more glue and mending tape from time to time, you won't fall apart at the seams. But it's never *you* who are good in yourself—only his continued presence and acceptance that gives you a miniscule of goodness."

"How right you are! Even when I think I am loved, and am relatively happy for awhile, I still feel that I just about can make it in the world, and that if my friend leaves me and fails, as you put it, to keep adding more glue and mending tape, I can't make it any longer, and must go back to my chronic state of falling apart."

"Yes. So you *start* with a feeling of self-depreciation; and, in fact, you are often goaded into beginning an affair in order to convince yourself, at least for a short while, that you are really not as horrible as you basically think you are—because someone else, at least, finds you partially acceptable. But because you are such a terrible moralist, and look for and exaggerate every flaw you may have, you feel comfortable (especially when a loving man is not, at the moment, around) by moralizing about others, too, and looking for and over-emphasizing their deficiencies. You thereby become angry as well as anxious.

"Finally, as we said before, you temporarily find approval, demean yourself to retain this approval at all costs, and then become more self-hating—and more angry at the man you are demeaning yourself for and

300

at the world in general. A vicious circle of self-blame, blaming others, more self-blame, and then more blaming of others, thus is set up."

"And I must break this entire cycle if I am to get somewhere in ridding myself of my hostility. Is that what you were going to point out?"

"Yes, that's just what I was going to point out. If you are to try to get rid of the hostility, but still keep your self-blame tendencies, you are practically doomed to failure from the start. For you *will* be hostile toward others if you are so extremely self-critical; you *will* use against them precisely the same overly-moralistic, perfectionistic attitudes that you take toward yourself. What is more, as long as you demean yourself so severely, you will lose one lover after another—for why should any man respect a woman who has so little respect for herself?—and then you will tend to be angry toward these men, who leave you after you have been so masochistically nice to them."

"I *must* then attack my self-blaming tendencies first. Without changing them, I'm not likely to get anywhere with becoming less hostile."

"Correct. First things first: and your overweening self-depreciation must go before you start to get anywhere with either your enormous feelings of anxiety or hostility. This is the cornerstone with which you set up and indefinitely prolong your neurotic symptoms. Until it falls, the main structure of your emotional disturbance is not likely to be demolished."

Marion, like so many of my other highly disturbed patients, had quite a time tackling her deeply fixed self-immolating tendencies. Before she even recognized what she was doing, she would find that she was blaming herself for her appearance, her talk, her manner of approach to people, her work methods, and almost everything else she did. Then, when she discovered that she was doing this blaming, she would blame herself for that—for the blaming. Then, when she found that she was still beating herself, and was consequently still neurotic, she would severely castigate herself for that—for still being neurotic.

Whenever Marion narrated a simple event in her life, and one that even had a fairly fortunate outcome, I could usually pick up the self-criticism in her tone or her gestures; and I had to watch my step in bringing this to her attention, since she would almost immediately agree with my interpretation, but then excoriate herself for still being a blamer. After several more weeks of getting her to review her perfectionistic philosophies and getting her calmly—rather than blamefully!—to challenge and contradict them, she finally began to become more self-accepting and less self-hating. She came to me one day and said:

"Boy, what an experience I had last night. Everything possible went wrong. I knew that I shouldn't have gone out with this particular man, Ed, in the first place, since I could see at the start that he wasn't for me. But I liked his looks, closed my eyes to his negativistic ways, and went out with him anyway. Then I pulled every mistake in the books. I stayed up with him too late, though I knew I had to get up early in the morning, and kept reminding myself that I must bid him goodnight. I went to bed with him, even though I didn't want to do so; but I let him talk me into it, and knew as I was giving in that I was just selling myself short, because I was afraid that he would be hurt, instead of thinking of myself first. And I even found myself having sex, at first, without using any contraceptive, since I let myself be sold on his line that he was sterile and that nothing could happen—though I've heard *that* line before, and know damned well that it's usually the bull. Anyway, I soon stopped that nonsense, and got up to put in my diaphragm.

"Aside from that, I can't think of a thing that I did right the whole evening. Some foolishness! Anyway, what I really want to say—and to thank you for, incidentally—is that after he left, I was able very calmly to review everything that had happened, to agree that I had been almost one hundred per cent wrong, and then *not* to give myself a hard time about having been wrong. I don't know *when* I was able to do that sort of thing before! But I just said to myself, 'Look! No more of this kind of crap. None of that stuff again.' And I turned on my side and went to sleep. And here, after working all day and thinking about it from time to time, I'm still not blaming myself for anything I did. I was wrong, all right: there's no escaping that. O.K.: so I was wrong! But for once I'm thinking of the *next time*—and how I'll manage to be less wrong then. And that sort of thinking is certainly revolutionary in *my* life!"

That was the real beginning of Marion's "conversion" from rampant self-blaming to fairly consistent self-acceptance. Since then, she has continued to make progress in this direction; and, without consciously ever knowing what her problems were or how she was tackling them, the men in her life have somehow noted a distinct change in her attitudes and behavior. She still hasn't met or married the one man she wants, but she is getting along infinitely better with those she does go out with, and for the first time in her life has had several successive proposals of marriage from men whom she did not quite want. Better yet, where her relations with males used to be a continuous series of hassles, with consequent hurt and bitterness on her part and theirs, she is now fully enjoying the heterosexual relations in which she does engage and gaining fine experiences through having them.

So may you, too, if basic anxiety or hostility is plaguing you in your social-sexual affairs. For such negative, self-defeating emotions invariably stem from the internalized sentences that you tell yourself in connection with the life situations that you face. These sentences, deeply rooted in your unconsciously or consciously held philosophies of living, can always be looked at, logically parsed, and forcefully and repetitively challenged.

What are some of the fundamental irrational ideas that you may hold that will inevitably lead you to be anxious, guilty, or depressed? As I explain in more detail in my recent book, *Reason and Emotion in Psychotherapy* (New York: Lyle Stuart, 1962), these include:

1. The idea that it is a dire necessity for an adult human being to be loved or approved by virtually every other significant person in his community.

2. The idea that one should be thoroughly competent, adequate, and achieving in all possible respects if one is to consider oneself worthwhile.

3. The idea that it is awful and catastrophic when things are not the way one would very much like them to be.

4. The idea that human unhappiness is externally caused and that one has little or no ability to control his sorrows and disturbances.

5. The idea that if something is or may be dangerous or fearsome one should be terribly concerned about it and should keep dwelling on the possibility of its occurring.

6. The idea that one should be dependent on others and needs someone stronger than oneself on whom to rely.

7. The idea that one's past history is an all-important determiner of one's present behavior and that because something once strongly affected one's life, it should indefinitely have a similar effect.

8. The idea that there is invariably a right, precise, and perfect solution to human problems and that it is catastrophic if this perfect solution is not found.

All these ideas, unfortunately, are an integral part of our culture, and are continually propounded to us, from early childhood onward, by our parents, teachers, clergymen, fairy tales, books, TV shows, films, stage dramas, etc. If we are foolish enough unthinkingly to accept them and uncritically to *assume* that they are true and realistic notions, we will inevitably become, to one degree or another, anxious, self-hating, and emotionally disturbed.

At the same time, there are several other powerful irrational ideas which commonly induce us to be hostile, rebellious, irresponsible, and grandiose. These include:

1. The idea that certain people are bad, wicked, or villainous and that they should be severely blamed and punished for their villainy.

2. The idea that it is easier to avoid than to face certain life difficulties and self-responsibilities; that the world owes one a living and eventually it should come across with that living.

3. The idea that one should become quite upset over other people's problems and disturbances.

Here again, all you have to do is to stick closely and pigheadedly to these kind of notions, and you will definitely, assuredly, and inevitably be angry and embittered, and keep ranting against the failings of others rather than trying to correct and lessen your own fallibilities.

Can there be, then, especially in this highly insane world, a reasonably sane philosophy of life that you can acquire that will help you live with a minimum of anxiety and hostility, and keep you from seriously blocking yourself emotionally and thereby interfering with your fondest heterosexual ideals? Yes, there definitely is such a philosophy; and many of our wisest thinkers—such as Epictetus and Marcus Aurelius in ancient times, Spinoza in the seventeenth century, and Bertrand Russell and Robert S. Hartman in modern times—have outlined some of its main tenets. After many years of studying the views of these sages and of doing intensive psychotherapy with hundreds of individuals who obviously had a poor and unworkable view of themselves and the world, I would tend to summarize a good working philosophy of living in these terms:

1. Do not try to eradicate all or even most of your desires for approval and love by others, since man is an animal who naturally and normally thrives on warmth

and good fellowship; but do try to eradicate any inordinate, all-consuming love *needs* that you may have. Realize that true self-respect does not come from the plaudits of others but from liking yourself and following most of your own fundamental interests *whether or not* others approve of your doings.

2. When you are not appreciated or approved by those you would very much like to have care for you, fully admit that this is annoying and frustrating but refrain from convincing yourself that it is horrible and catastrophic. To the extent that it is desirable and practical for you to win the love of others, try to do so in a calm, intelligent, planful way rather than in a frantic, hit-and-miss manner. To this end, you should realize that one of the best methods of winning love is unstintingly to give it.

3. Try to *do* various things that you enjoy in life, rather than kill yourself endeavoring always to *do well*. Focus on flavoring the *process* rather than only the result of what you do. When you do try to do well—which is often permissible, since there are real advantages (such as monetary rewards or increased pleasure in participation) from succeeding at certain events—do not insist on always doing *perfectly* well. Try, on most occasions, for *your* best rather than *the* best; and try to do well for your *own* sake rather than to please or to best *others*.

4. Learn to welcome your mistakes and errors— rather than to become horrified at them—and thereby to put them to good account. Accept the necessity of your practicing, practicing, practicing the things you want to succeed at; often force yourself to do what you

307

are afraid to fail at doing; and fully accept the fact that humans are limited animals and that you, in particular, have necessary and distinct fallibilities.

5. Do not criticize or blame others for their misdeeds (although you may calmly point out to them their mistakes), but realize that they invariably commit wrong acts out of stupidity, ignorance, or emotional disturbance. Try to accept people when they are stupid and to help them when they are ignorant or disturbed.

6. When people blame you, first ask yourself whether you have really done anything wrong; and if you have, try to improve your behavior in the future. If you haven't, in your own eyes, made the mistakes of which you are accused, try to realize that other people's criticism is often *their* problem and stems from defensiveness or disturbance on their part.

7. Try to understand *why* people act the way they do. Try to see things from *their* frame of reference when you think they are behaving badly. If there is no way of changing them (as is all too frequently true!) convince yourself that it is too bad that people are the way they are, but that's all it is—too bad. It is *not* terrible, horrible, or catastrophic.

8. When frustrating or painful circumstances arise, determine whether they are truly annoying or whether you are imagining or highly exaggerating their irritating qualities. If certain circumstances are distinctly unpleasant, do your best to face them calmly and to work at improving them. If you cannot, for the present, improve conditions, philosophically accept them or resign yourself to their existence. Instead of convincing yourself that you *can't stand* these conditions, show

yourself that it's too bad that they exist, but that you *can* gracefully lump them.

9. Whenever you believe that something or someone is bothering or upsetting you, ask yourself whether it is truly that person or thing that is disturbing, or whether it is not your *own* attitude toward him or it. Track down your anxieties and hostilities to the simple exclamatory sentences that *you* are telling yourself *about* various irritating persons and things; think about these sentences; and logically parse and forcefully question and challenge them until you become convinced that they are definitional, contradictory, and untenable.

Thus, if you think that your boyfriend may be unfaithful to you and that he or his infidelity is upsetting you, find your *own* upsetting sentences *about* his behavior—such as, "If he is unfaithful, I simply can't stand it, because that would prove that he doesn't really love me, and it would be utterly catastrophic for me to live in a world where he doesn't love me." Then examine these internalized sentences, instead of ruminating endlessly about whether or not he is unfaithful.

10. Realize that practically all your worries are caused not by external dangers that may occur but by your telling yourself "Wouldn't it be awful *if* this danger occurred?" Instead of continuing to worry endlessly about something, force yourself to examine your catastrophizing sentences and to change them for the saner and more realistic philosophy: "It would be a distinct nuisance or a bad thing if this danger occurred; but it would *not* be awful, and I *could* cope with it if I had to do so."

11. Recognize that most of your fears are disguised forms of the fear of what others think of you; and continually question and challenge this fear and make yourself see how silly it is. Realize that it certainly may be inconvenient if So-and-So does not like you or thinks you are wrong; but that that's *all* it normally is: inconvenient.

12. As often as possible, actually *do* the things you are most afraid to do—such as speaking in public, telling your boyfriend what you really think about something, or standing up for your own rights—in order to prove to yourself that there *is* nothing frightful about doing these things. Force yourself, as much as you can, to be *yourself*, rather than some pale reflection of what you think *others* would like you to be.

13. Uncomplainingly do the things that are necessary for you to do in life, no matter how much you dislike doing them, while at the same time figuring out intelligent methods of avoiding the *un*necessary painful aspects of living. If, at present, you have to work at an unpleasant job in order to earn a living, that's tough: you'd better do it. But there's no reason why you can't plot and scheme so that in the future you *won't* have to work at this kind of job in order to provide for yourself.

14. If you find that you are goofing on various life problems and responsibilities, don't cavalierly assume that you are just naturally "lazy," but realize that behind such goofing there usually exists a chain of your own anxious or rebellious sentences. If you are not, for example, going out to meet the men you would like to meet, it is not because you are "just too lazy," but almost invariably because you are anxiously telling

yourself: "If I did go out to meet men, I'd be rejected, and that would be terrible!" Or because you are rebelliously and childishly telling yourself: "Why should I *have* to go out to meet those lousy bastards, when they're not doing anything to meet me, and when society is making it so difficult for me to meet the men I want?" Go after *these* internalized—and crummy—philosophies, rather than giving yourself excuses for your inert behavior.

15. Accept the fact that your past is important and that you are bound to be influenced by your early experiences in many ways. But also acknowledge that *your present is your past of tomorrow* and that, by working at and changing this present, you can make your future significantly different from, and in many ways more satisfactory than, today.

This, in simple outline, is a rational way of living—and one that will, if you follow it, not only prevent you from being emotionally blocked in regard to dating and marrying, but will help you to rid yourself of innumerable other needless anxieties and hostilities. Outlines, of course, are easy to make, and sometimes most difficult to fill in with detailed, confirmatory activity. This particular one will take you, conservatively speaking, an entire lifetime to follow—a lifetime, moreover, of steady self-discipline and work.

So, ironically enough, will an outline of a bad philosophy of living. If you program for yourself, as most of us do, a working philosophy of catastrophizing about unpleasant events, of severely blaming yourself and others whenever you or they behave in an all-too-human fallible manner, of insisting that you have no real control over your feelings and emotions, of believing that

311

the world owes you a living and that you are too weak and dependent to get for yourself what you truly want out of life—if this is the view of yourself and the world that (consciously or unconsciously) motivates (or *un*-motivates!) you, you will work your foolish head off, literally day and night, to worry, fret, ruminate, plot, and scheme to defeat yourself. Then, having marvelously succeeded at the self-sabotaging at which you were endlessly working overtime, you will continue to labor at blaming, and blaming, and still further blaming yourself for being so hard-workingly inept.

Being neurotic, in other words, is exceptionally difficult, and requires immense amounts of time and effort. It *seems* easy to be continually anxious and hostile; but it's really quite a job—and one that pays worse than any other known form of occupation. If, therefore, you must work so hard at destroying yourself, and blocking your own fondest sex-love desires, don't you think that it might well be worth at least a little effort to *stop* the nonsense you keep telling yourself to create and maintain your neurotic blocks?

Why not try it and see?

Selected Readings

Although knowledge is power, the "knowledge" that is contained in most contemporary articles and books on sex, marriage, and human personality is as much prejudice and speculation as it is truth and fact. The intelligent woman will tend to be well-read; but she will also be *selectively* and *thinkingly* informed.

The list of books that follows includes works that you should know about and at least have skimmed. None of them, including my own books, is perfect, nor should be accepted as gospel. All of them contain some truths—and some fiction that you will largely have to weed out for yourself, on the basis of your own judgment and experience. By all means dip into these books—skeptically, questioningly, taking them with the usual grain and a half of salt.

Adler, Alfred. *What life should mean to you.* New York: Blue Ribbon Books, 1931.

Anderson, Camilla M. *Saints, sinners and psychiatry.* Portland, Oregon: Durham Press, 1962.

Ansbacher, Heinz, and Ansbacher, Rowena. *The individual psychology of Alfred Adler.* New York: Basic Books, 1956.

Anthony, Rey (pseud). *The housewife's handbook on selective promiscuity.* Sun Building, Tucson, Ariz.: Seymour Press, 1960.

Berg, Louis, and Street, Robert. *Sex: methods and manners.* New York: McBride, 1953.

Brown, Helen Gurley. *Sex and the single girl.* New York: Bernard Geis Associates, 1962.

Ehrmann, Winston W. *Premarital dating behavior.* New York: Holt, 1960.

313

Ellis, Albert. *How to live with a neurotic.* New York: Crown Publishers, 1957.

Ellis, Albert. *Sex without guilt.* New York: Lyle Stuart, 1958. New York: Macfadden Books, 1960.

Ellis, Albert. *The art and science of love.* New York: Lyle Stuart, 1960.

Ellis, Albert. *The American sexual tragedy.* New York: Lyle Stuart, 1962. New York: Grove Press, 1963.

Ellis, Albert. *Reason and emotion in psychotherapy.* New York: Lyle Stuart, 1962.

Ellis, Albert. *If this be sexual heresy . . .* New York: Lyle Stuart, 1963.

Ellis, Albert. *Sex and the single man.* New York: Lyle Stuart, 1963.

Ellis, Albert, and Abarbanel, Albert (eds.). *The encyclopedia of sexual behavior.* New York: Hawthorn Books, 1961.

Ellis, Albert, and Harper, Robert A. *Creative marriage.* New York: Lyle Stuart, 1961.

Ellis, Albert, and Harper, Robert A. *A guide to rational living.* Englewood Cliffs, N. J.: Prentice-Hall, 1961.

Ellis, Albert, and Sagarin, Edward. *Nymphomania: a study of the oversexed woman.* New York: Julian Messner, 1964.

Epictetus. *The works of Epictetus.* Boston: Little Brown, 1899.

Freeman, Lucy. *Fight against fears.* New York: Crown, 1951.

Freud, Sigmund. *Basic writings.* New York: Modern Library, 1938.

Freud, Sigmund. *Letters.* New York: Basic Books, 1960.

Fromm, Erich. *The sane society.* New York: Rinehart, 1950.

Fromm, Erich. *The art of loving.* New York: Harper, 1956.

Guttmacher, Alan F., Best, Winfield, and Jaffe, Frederick S. *The complete book of birth control.* New York: Ballantine Books, 1961.

Guyon, René. *The ethics of sexual acts.* New York: Knopf, 1934.

Guyon, René. *Sexual freedom.* New York: Knopf, 1950.

Harper, Robert A. *Psychoanalysis and psychotherapy: 36 systems.* Englewood Cliffs, N. J.: Prentice-Hall, 1959.

Hartman, Robert S. "Science of value." In Maslow, A. H. (ed.), *New knowledge in human values.* New York: Harper, 1959.

Hartman, Robert S. *The measurement of value.* Crotonville, New York: General Electric Co., 1959.

Horney, Karen. *Neurotic personality of our time.* New York: Norton, 1937.

Horney, Karen. *New ways in psychoanalysis.* New York: Norton, 1939.

Johnson, Wendell. *People in quandaries.* New York: Harper, 1946.

Kelly, George. *The psychology of personal constructs.* New York: Norton, 1955.

Kinsey, Alfred C., Pomeroy, Wardell B., Martin, Clyde E., and Gebhard, Paul H. *Sexual behavior in the human female.* Philadelphia: Saunders, 1953.

Klemer, Richard H. *A man for every woman.* New York: Macmillan, 1959.

Kraines, S. H., and Thetford, E. S. *Managing your mind.* New York: Macmillan, 1947.

Munroe, Ruth L. *Schools of psychoanalytic thought.* New York: Dryden, 1955.

Marcus Aurelius. *Meditations.* Boston: Little, Brown, 1890.

Phillips, E. L. *Psychotherapy.* Englewood Cliffs, N. J.: Prentice-Hall, 1956.

Rank, Otto. *Will therapy and truth and reality.* New York: Knopf, 1945.

Reich, Wilhelm. *The sexual revolution.* New York: Orgone Institute Press, 1945.

Reiss, Ira L. *Premarital sexual standards in America.* Glencoe, Ill.: Free Press, 1960.

Rogers, Carl R. *Client-centered therapy.* Boston: Houghton Mifflin, 1951.

Russell, Bertrand. *The conquest of happiness.* New York: Pocket Books, 1950.

Stokes, Walter. *Married love in today's world.* New York: Citadel, 1962.

Sullivan, Harry Stack. *The interpersonal theory of psychiatry.* New York: Norton, 1953.

Thorne, Frederick C. *Personality: a clinical eclectic view.* Brandon, Vermont. Journal of Clinical Psychology, 1961.

Tillich, Paul. *The courage to be.* New York: Oxford University Press, 1953.

Watts, Alan W. *Nature, man and sex.* New York: New American Library, 1959.

Acknowledgments

Grateful acknowledgment is made to Bernard Geis, for collaboration on the original idea for this book; to Fiddle Viracola and Rhoda Winter Russell, who read the work when it was still in manuscript and made valuable suggestions; to Eileen Brand and Edward Sagarin for helpful editing; and to myself, myself, and myself, for invaluable assistance in typing the manuscript and editing the goddam galley and page proofs.

About the Author

Albert Ellis was born in Pittsburgh and grew up in New York City. He holds a bachelor's degree from the City University of New York; and M.A. and Ph.D. degrees in Clinical Psychology from Columbia University. He has taught at Rutgers University and New York University; has been Chief Psychologist of the New Jersey State Diagnostic Center and then Chief Psychologist of the New Jersey Department of Institutions and Agencies; is a Consultant in Clinical Psychology to the Veterans Administration; is Executive Director of the Institute for Rational Living, Inc.; and for the last twelve years has been in the private practice of psychotherapy and marriage and family counseling in New York City.

Dr. Ellis is a Fellow of the American Psychological Association (and Past-President of its Division of Consulting Psychology), as well as a Fellow (and Past-President) of the Society for the Scientific Study of Sex. He is also a Fellow of the American Association of Marriage Counselors, the American Sociological Association, and the American Association for the Advancement of Science. He is Vice-President of the American Academy of Psychotherapists; and has been a member of the Executive Committee of the American Association of Marriage Counselors, Psychologists in Private Practice, Psychologists Interested in the Advancement of Psychotherapy, and the New York Society of Clinical Psychologists. He is a Diplomate in Clinical Psychology of the American Board of Examiners in Professional Psychology. He has been Chairman of the Marriage Counseling Section of the National Council on Family Relations and an Associate Editor of *Marriage and Family Living*, the *International Journal of Sexology*, and *Advances in Sex Research*.

Dr. Ellis has published over two hundred papers in psychological, psychiatric, and sociological journals and anthologies; and has authored or edited the following books and monographs: AN INTRODUCTION TO THE PRINCIPLES OF SCIENTIFIC PSYCHOANALYSIS (1950); THE FOLKLORE OF SEX (1951; rev. ed., 1961); SEX, SOCIETY AND THE INDIVIDUAL (with A. P. Pillay, 1953); SEX LIFE OF THE AMERICAN WOMAN AND THE KINSEY REPORT (1954); THE AMERICAN SEXUAL TRAGEDY (1954; rev. ed., 1962; paperback ed., 1963); NEW APPROACHES TO PSYCHOTHERAPY TECHNIQUES (1955); THE PSYCHOLOGY OF SEX OFFENDERS (with Ralph Brancale, 1956); HOW TO LIVE WITH A NEUROTIC (1957); SEX WITHOUT GUILT (1958; paperback ed., 1959); WHAT IS PSYCHOTHERAPY? (1959); THE PLACE OF VALUES IN THE PRACTICE OF PSYCHOTHERAPY (1959); THE ART AND SCIENCE OF LOVE (1960); THE ENCYCLOPEDIA OF SEXUAL BEHAVIOR (with Albert Abarbanel, 1961); CREATIVE MARRIAGE (with Robert A. Harper, 1961); A GUIDE TO RATIONAL LIVING (with Robert A. Harper, 1961); REASON AND EMOTION IN PSYCHOTHERAPY (1962); IF THIS BE SEXUAL HERESY ... (1963); SEX AND THE SINGLE MAN (1963); THE INTELLIGENT WOMAN'S GUIDE TO MAN-HUNTING (1963); NYMPHOMANIA: A STUDY OF THE OVERSEXED WOMAN (with Edward Sagarin, 1964); THE CASE FOR SEXUAL LIBERTY (1964); THE THEORY AND PRACTICE OF RATIONAL-EMOTIVE PSYCHOTHERAPY (1964).